BIBLE GUIDELINES

By the same author

QUESTIONS ON THE CHRISTIAN FAITH ANSWERED FROM THE BIBLE

BIBLE GUIDELINES

Derek Prime

HODDER AND STOUGHTON

LONDON SYDNEY AUCKLAND TORONTO

British Library Cataloguing in Publication Data
  Prime, Derek
    Bible Guidelines
    1. Christian life
    1. Title
    248   BV4501.2

BIBLE GUIDELINES

Number   *Page*

The Ten Commandments

1. Loyalty to God   11
2. Worship of God   14
3. Reverence   17
4. Rest   20
5. Respect for, and submission to, proper authority   26
6. Respect for life   32
7. The sanctity of marriage   35
8. Respect for property   39
9. Truthfulness   41
10. Contentment   45

Subjects arising, directly or indirectly, from the Ten Commandments

11. Temptation   49
12. Worldliness   51
13. Spiritual decline   56
14. Spiritual restoration   59
15. Christian worship   62
16. Prayer   68
17. The state   72
18. Social responsibility   76
19. Work   79
20. Leisure   85
21. Guidance   89
22. The family   95
23. Education   100
24. Sex   106
25. Giving   111

Desires and works of man's sinful flesh
("The seven deadly sins")

26. Pride   115
27. Wrath   120
28. Envy   123
29. Lust   125
30. Gluttony   129
31. Avarice   134
32. Sloth   140

Christian character
("The fruit of the Spirit")

33. Love   144
34. Joy   147
35. Peace   152
36. Patience   157
37. Kindness   160
38. Goodness   163
39. Faithfulness   167
40. Meekness   174
41. Self-control   179

Commitment to Christ and the gospel

42. Christian discipleship   183
43. Obedience   188
44. Christian witness   192
45. Personal evangelism   198
46. The missionary task and missionary motives   204
47. Missionary work   209
48. Missionary strategy   212
49. Hidden factors in missionary enterprise   218
50. Supporting missions   221

USING THE BOOK

This book should be studied or referred to *with the Bible at hand*. The concern throughout has been to state what the Bible has to say in answer to each question. Where possible every statement has a Bible reference which should substantiate or illustrate it in some way.

The material has been set out in sections and sub-sections, both numerically and alphabetically, to make it easy for the book to be studied by sections, rather than read through hurriedly.

Read without the Bible this book will appear heavy and solid. Read with the Bible it should become alive through the power of Bible-truth.

This book, with its emphasis on the practical and ethical aspects of the Christian life, is meant to be complementary to *Questions on the Christian Faith answered from the Bible* which deals with Christian doctrine and the fundamentals of the Christian faith.

BIBLE REFERENCES

(Alphabetical list of the books of the Bible and the abbreviations used)

Acts	Acts	*I Kings*	I Kings
Amos	Amos	*II Kings*	II Kings
I Chron.	I Chronicles	*Lam.*	Lamentations
II Chron.	II Chronicles	*Lev.*	Leviticus
Col.	Colossians	*Luke*	Luke
I Cor.	I Corinthians	*Mal.*	Malachi
II Cor.	II Corinthians	*Mark*	Mark
Dan.	Daniel	*Matt.*	Matthew
Deut.	Deuteronomy	*Micah*	Micah
Eccl.	Ecclesiastes	*Nahum*	Nahum
Eph.	Ephesians	*Neh.*	Nehemiah
Esth.	Esther	*Num.*	Numbers
Ex.	Exodus	*Obad.*	Obadiah
Ezek.	Ezekiel	*I Pet.*	I Peter
Ezra	Ezra	*II Pet.*	II Peter
Gal.	Galatians	*Philem.*	Philemon
Gen.	Genesis	*Phil.*	Philippians
Hab.	Habakkuk	*Prov.*	Proverbs
Hag.	Haggai	*Ps.*	Psalms
Heb.	Hebrews	*Rev.*	Revelation
Hos.	Hosea	*Rom.*	Romans
Isa.	Isaiah	*Ruth*	Ruth
Jas.	James	*I Sam.*	I Samuel
Jer.	Jeremiah	*II Sam.*	II Samuel
Job	Job	*S. of Songs*	Song of Solomon (Song of Songs)
Joel	Joel		
John	John	*I Thess.*	I Thessalonians
I John	I John	*II Thess.*	II Thessalonians
II John	II John	*I Tim.*	I Timothy
III John	III John	*II Tim.*	II Timothy
Jonah	Jonah	*Tit.*	Titus
Josh.	Joshua		
Jude	Jude	*Zech.*	Zechariah
Judg.	Judges	*Zeph.*	Zephaniah

Finding References

A few hints may be helpful for those not used to finding references in the Bible.

An example: I Thessalonians 2: 13

The name "Thessalonians" refers to the book in the Bible. All Bibles have a list of books in the front and some have an alphabetical list as well. Look up "Thessalonians" in this list and you will find the page number. The "I" before the name indicates that there is more than one book of this name. "Thessalonians" has books "I" and "II"

The figure immediately after the name is the number of the chapter in that book and the last figure is the number of the verse.

In the Authorised or King James' Version the verses are all separated, but in some modern translations the chapters are in paragraphs but the equivalent verse number is placed in the margin. A little practice will soon make you familiar with the lay-out of the Bible. Where the Bible is directly quoted in this book, quotations are from the New International Version (NIV).

I. LOYALTY TO GOD

Exodus 20: 3: "You shall have no other gods before me."

Question: What does the first commandment teach?

Answer: The first commandment teaches that our first loyalty is to be to the Lord Himself, and idolatry of any sort is forbidden. The loyalty that is acceptable to God is sincere, unreserved, and carefully maintained.

1. Loyalty to God is His proper due for two principal reasons: God's uniqueness, and the redemption He has provided.

God's uniqueness.

(a) There is only one God (*Deut.* 4: 39; *II Sam.* 22: 32; *I Cor.* 8: 4): He is God in heaven above and on the earth beneath (*Deut.* 4: 39).

(b) God made us (*Ps.* 100: 3): He is the almighty Creator who spreads the canopy of the sky over chaos and suspends the earth in the void (*Job* 26: 7); He alone has power over creation (*Jer.* 14: 22).

(c) None can be compared with God: He is altogether different and unique in His majesty and glory (*Ps.* 98: 6–8; *Isa.* 44: 6).

(d) While to some people, there are a great many gods, both in heaven and on earth (*I Cor.* 8: 5, 6), these have no existence in the real world (*I Cor.* 8: 4), and are impotent (*Jer.* 14: 22).

(e) When other so-called gods are confronted with the Lord, men and women are compelled to acknowledge that "the Lord is God" (*I Kings* 18: 39); He has every right to our exclusive loyalty and the false gods of men's creation are not worthy to be mentioned in the same breath (*Isa.* 45: 5, 21–23; *Jer.* 10: 1–10).

(f) We are to understand the Lord's uniqueness and take it to heart (*Deut.* 4: 39), the only proper conclusion being that we should obey His laws (*Deut.* 4: 40).

God's provision of redemption.

(g) The Lord liberated His people from their slavery in Egypt (*Ex.* 20: 2), and Christians know a similar and even greater deliverance and redemption (*I Pet.* 1: 18, 19).

(h) The supreme loyalty of the Christian is to the Lord Jesus

Christ (*Eph.* 5: 21), who loved him and gave Himself for him (*Gal.* 2: 20).

(i) Even as the passover feast served to keep fresh in the Israelites' memory the deliverance God had given them (*Ex.* 12: 14), so the Lord's Supper keeps fresh in Christians' memories the redemption God has achieved for them through the death of His Son, our Lord Jesus Christ (*I Cor.* 11: 20–26).

2. Loyalty to God forbids idolatry in any form.

(a) The heathen worship idols of gold, silver, bronze, iron, wood and stone, made by their own hands (*Ps.* 135: 15–17; *Dan.* 5: 4, 23).

(b) By such idolatry men exchange the glory of the immortal God for images representing mortal man or birds or animals or reptiles (*Rom.* 1: 23), and then trust in them (*Hab.* 2: 18).

(c) The error of idolatry is that it worships the created thing rather than the Creator (*Judg.* 8: 24–28; *Rom.* 1: 25; *Eph.* 5: 5).

(d) But idolatry is not limited to the worship of material idols of man's manufacture, for anything or any person claiming our primary loyalty becomes "another god" (cf. *Col.* 3: 5).

(e) Idolatry begins in the heart (*Deut.* 11: 16), and that which has most of our heart and thoughts is our god (*Luke* 12: 34).

(f) Whatever men boast of tends to be a god to them: for example, wisdom (*Jer.* 9: 23, 24), human strength or resourcefulness (*Jer.* 17: 5), good works (*Isa.* 64: 6), respectability and reputation (*Luke* 18: 11).

(g) Wealth is a most common idol (*Mark* 10: 22; *Job* 31: 24; *Matt.* 13: 22), and covetousness is identified as idolatry (*Eph.* 5: 5; *Col.* 3: 5).

(h) Men make a god of pleasure (*II Tim.* 3: 4), especially of their appetites (*Phil.* 3: 19), insofar as they are proud of what they should be ashamed of and this world is the limit of their horizons.

(i) Having the heart set on the good things of this life is a form of idolatry (*II Tim.* 4:10; *I John* 2: 15, 16).

(j) Even Christian leaders can become idols, having the place

12

in people's affections and loyalty which belongs to God (*I Cor.* 1: 11, 12).

(k) Idolatry dishonours God (*Dan.* 5: 23): it represents man's rejection of God (*Rom.* 1: 18–23), his forsaking of God (*Jer.* 1: 16), his refusal to hear God's words (*Jer.* 13: 10, 11) and his breaking faith with God (*Judg.* 2: 17).

(l) Idolatry is spiritual harlotry (*Hos.* 12: 12–14) or adultery (*Judg.* 2: 17; cf. *Jas.* 4: 4).

(m) Idolatry brings forth God's judgment (*Hos.* 8: 4; *Amos* 5: 25–27; *Micah* 1: 7): those who fall into idolatry find many sorrows, in marked contrast to those who serve the Lord (*Ps.* 16: 4, 8–11).

(n) Idolatry must be rooted out (*Micah* 5: 14), utterly destroyed and the Lord's rightful place re-established (*Judg.* 6: 25–27), for He can be served only as other gods are put away (*Josh.* 24: 14).

3. Loyalty to God must be sincere, unreserved and carefully maintained.
Sincere loyalty
(a) The Lord is to be served with sincerity (*Josh.* 24: 14).

(b) Professions of loyalty which are insincere serve only to increase sin (*Hos.* 8: 11); our motives must be right as well as our actions (*Amos* 5: 18–27).

(c) Loyalty to God is a spiritual matter, and includes, in the light of God's uniqueness and redemption, the presenting of our bodies as a living sacrifice, holy – the kind He can accept (*Rom.* 12: 1).

(d) God looks for loyalty which springs from a willing mind (*I Chron.* 28: 9).

Unreserved loyalty.
(e) God demands our first loyalty (*Josh.* 24: 14); He will countenance no rival, for He is a jealous God (*Ex.* 20: 5; 14: 14), in that He will not share His praise – which includes our loyalty – with anyone else (*Isa.* 42: 8).

(f) We have to choose whom we will worship: the one true God, the Lord, or the so-called gods which abound around us (*Josh.* 24: 14, 15; *I Thess.* 1: 9).

(g) Love for God must be absolute: He is to be loved with all our heart, soul, and mind (*Matt.* 22: 37).

13

(h) "I belong to the Lord" should be our glad testimony (*Isa.* 44: 4).

Carefully maintained loyalty.

(k) We are to cleave to the Lord our God (*Josh.* 23: 8), which means being very careful to keep on loving the Lord our God (*Josh.* 23: 11).

(l) To avoid idolatry we have to watch our heart (*Deut.* 11: 16), deliberately shunning the worship of idols of any sort (*I Cor.* 10: 14), and keeping ourselves away from anything that might take God's place in our hearts (*I John* 5:21).

(m) This carefully maintained watchfulness is necessary because behind idolatry of every kind there is the activity of Satan (*I Cor.* 8: 5; 10: 19; cf. Acts 5: 3), and he is unceasing in his wiles and deceits (*I Pet.* 5: 8).

(n) We are to be always thinking of the Lord (*Ps.* 16: 8), having our eyes ever looking to Him (*Ps.* 25: 15).

5. Loyalty to God is rewarded by God.

(a) There is no limit to the benefits which come when we are faithful in our loyalty to the Lord (*Deut.* 28: 1ff).

(b) Loyalty to the Lord—the supreme wisdom—brings a long, good life, riches, honour, pleasures and peace (*Prov.* 3: 17).

(c) Those committed to the Lord have the secret of joy (*Isa.* 56: 7).

(d) When the Lord is our God, we may be sure of His blessing (*Ps.* 67: 6), knowing that the whole of our life is under His control, with everything fitting into His good purposes (*Rom.* 8: 28).

(e) The rewards of loyalty extend beyond this life with the promise of the gift of the kingdom of God (*Luke* 12: 32), and a never-ending share in God's glory and honour (*I Pet.* 5: 4).

2. WORSHIP OF GOD

Exodus 20: 4–6: "You shall not make for yourself an idol in the form of anything in heaven above or on the earth beneath or in the waters below. You shall not bow down to them or worship them; for I, the Lord your God, am a jealous God, punishing the children for the sin of the fathers to the third and fourth generation of those who hate me, but showing love to thousands who love me and keep my commandments."

Question: What does the second commandment teach?

Answer: The second commandment teaches that God alone is to be worshipped, without any visual symbols of Himself, and in strict accordance with the manner in which He has revealed Himself to us.

1. God is to be worshipped.

(a) Worship is God's due as our Creator (*Ps.* 100; *Rom.* 1: 25): it is the natural expression of our obedience to the first commandment (*Ex.* 20: 3).

(b) Worship is the giving of glory, honour, and thanks to God (*Rev.* 4: 9); and in our worship of the Lord we acknowledge that He alone is worthy to receive such (*Rev.* 4: 11).

2. God alone is to be worshipped.

(a) The Lord Himself is the proper object of all worship (*Ex.* 20: 2, 3).

(b) He is jealous of His honour as the one Lord (*Ex.* 20:

5); He will not give His glory to anyone else (*Isa.* 42: 8).

(c) He will share neither our affection nor our obedience with any other (*Ex.* 20: 5, 6).

3. God is to be worshipped without any visual symbols of Himself.

(a) We are forbidden by this commandment both to worship images of other so-called gods and to use images of the one true God (*Ex.* 20: 4).

(b) God is against any representation of Himself (*Lev.* 26: 1): we are not to make for ourselves "an idol in the form of anything in heaven above or on the earth beneath or in the waters below" (*Ex.* 20: 4).

(c) Men act corruptly when they make an image of God, in the form of any figure whatsoever (*Deut.* 4: 15–19), so that we may conclude that idolatry is not only the worship of false gods, but even the worship of the one true God by images.

(d) This demand that the Lord should be worshipped without visual images is reinforced in the Old Testament by the reminder that the Israelites saw no form of God on the day

15

that the Lord spoke to them at Horeb. Since the Lord did not give a visible form of Himself, but instead spoke to them, so now we are not to seek visual symbols of Him but simply to obey His Word (*Deut.* 4: 15–19).

Reasons for the prohibition of visual symbols of God.

(e) God's glory is jeopardised when images are used in worship (*Isa.* 40: 18–31): wherever we go in creation, all things were created by the Lord, and are subject to Him, thus making it ridiculous to seek a likeness of Him in the created order (*Ex.* 20: 4; *Deut.* 5: 8).

(f) When men picture their god in human form they soon reckon to him their own human weaknesses (*I Kings* 18: 26–29).

(g) Furthermore, it is impossible for man to make an image of God because God is spirit (*John* 4: 24): He cannot be made static or controlled as the manufactured images would suggest.

(h) The Lord requires us to guard against unworthy conceptions of Him, and of creating false images of Him in our hearts (*Ex.* 20: 4, 5).

4. God is to be worshipped in the manner He has laid down.

(a) The second commandment insists that worship must be in accord with divine revelation; we are warned against ways of worship that lead us to dishonour God and to put aside His truth (*Ex.* 20: 4, 5).

(b) We are to receive nothing, practise nothing, and own nothing in the worship of God but what is of His appointment (*Rev.* 22: 8, 9).

(c) We are summoned to recognise that God is so great that we may worship Him acceptably only when we do so in the manner He chooses to lay down (*Isa.* 55: 8, 9; *Rom.* 11: 33, 34).

(d) There is a wrong as well as a right way to worship God (*John* 4: 23, 24): God is spirit and those who worship Him must worship in spirit and in truth—i.e. spiritually and truly.

(e) The New Testament reveals that there is only one image of God that is wholly true and worthy, and that is the Lord Jesus Christ Him-

16

self who is the image of the invisible God (*Col.* 1: 15ff): thus all Christian worship centres around God's Son because in His face we see the glory of God as nowhere else (*II Cor.* 4: 6; *John* 1: 14, 18).

5. God desires worship springing from love, and expressed in obedience (Ex. 20: 6).

(a) Worship is in vain if the feelings of the heart do not correspond with the expression of the lips (*Isa.* 1: 11–17; *Amos* 4: 4; 5: 18–27; *Matt.* 15: 8, 9).

(b) Acceptable worship is a response to the mercies of God (*Rom.* 12: 1ff): we love Him because He first loved us (*I John* 4: 19).

(c) Our worship is expressed in obedience to His Word rather than any respect for visual images of God (*Deut.* 4: 15–19).

(d) True worship presupposes the willingness to obey the Lord (*Josh.* 5: 14, 15; *Isa.* 6).

(e) At conversion we turn away from idols to worship and serve the true and living God with joy (*I Thess.* 1: 6–9).

3. REVERENCE

Exodus 20: 7: "**You shall not misuse the name of the Lord your God, for the Lord will not hold anyone guiltless who misuses his name.**"

Question: What does the third commandment teach?

Answer: The third commandment teaches us to avoid all wrong use of God's Name, to treat His Name with the greatest respect, and to make it our deliberate purpose to honour and reverence Him.

1. The Special Use of the word "Name" in the Bible.

(a) Names have meanings, and this particularly applies to the Name of God (*Ex.* 3: 13–15).

(b) God's Name proclaims and reveals His character (*Ex.* 33: 19), all that He is and all that He does (*Ex.* 34: 5, 6).

(c) God's Name is linked, therefore, with His attributes and characteristics, and the Psalms provide many illustrations:

righteousness (*Ps.* 89: 15, 16);
faithfulness (*Ps.* 89: 24);
salvation (*Ps.* 96: 2);
holiness (*Ps.* 99: 3, 4);

goodness (*Ps.* 100: 4, 5);
mercy (*Ps.* 109: 21);
love (*Ps.* 138: 2);
truth (*Ps.* 138: 2);
glory (*Ps.* 148: 13).

(d) The adjective most commonly associated with God's Name is "holy" (*Ps.* 33: 21; 103:1;106:47;111:9;145:21).

(e) So close is the identification of the Lord with His Name that He may be spoken of as The Name (*Prov.* 18: 10; *Isa.* 30: 27).

2. Ways in which God's Name is used wrongly.

(a) **Perjury.** Perjury is the sin of taking an oath in the Name of God and then uttering falsehood (*Lev.* 19: 12; *Num.* 30: 2; *Deut.* 6: 13; *Ps.* 15: 4; *Zech.* 5: 4).

(b) God's Name is defiled or polluted when men shrug aside promises and oaths made in His Name, holding them of little account (*Jer.* 34: 16) and when they make a vow they never intend to keep (*Deut.* 5: 11).

(c) Solemn and legal oaths are not prohibited; it is the abuse of them that is wrong (*Lev.* 19: 12; cf. *Rom.* 9: 1; *II Cor.* 1: 23).

(d) **Rash and unnecessary swearing.** When men introduce the Name of God into their conversation by an oath simply to strengthen what they are saying, they use His Name wrongly (*II Kings*, 5: 20).

(e) Even swearing by heaven is swearing by God's throne, and swearing by the earth swearing by God's footstool (*Matt.* 5: 34, 35; cf. *Matt.* 23: 21, 22).

(f) Jephthah, for example, rashly swore an oath in God's Name which was entirely out of keeping with God's character (*Judg.* 11: 31).

(g) **Blasphemy.** Blasphemy is to treat irreverently the Majesty of God, to utter His Name, and then to curse Him (cf. *Lev.* 24: 11).

(h) Blasphemy occurs when men deliberately defy God by mentioning His Name and casting doubt upon His character (*II Kings* 19: 4, 10, 22).

(i) **Unnecessary and irreverent use of God's Name in ordinary conversation** (*Matt.* 7: 21–23).

(j) Sarah, for example, wrongly put the whole weight of blame upon Abraham for their shared mistake concerning Hagar, and unnecessarily brought God's Name into her conversation for emphasis (*Gen.* 16: 5).

(k) **Offering religious worship while living a godless life** (*Mal.* 2: 13–16).

(l) To say we are the Lord's by the performance of religious worship but not to obey Him, so that our worship is mere words, reeled off by heart, is to use God's Name wrongly (*Isa.* 29: 13).

(m) God's Name is brought into disrepute by bad conduct on the part of those who profess loyalty to Him (*Prov.* 30: 9).

(n) Absalom, for example, expressed the desire to worship the Lord, and went through the forms of doing so, only to further a political conspiracy (*II Sam.* 15: 7, 8, 12); he used God's Name for a completely unworthy purpose.

3. Ways by which we honour and reverence God's Name.

(a) **Praise and Thanksgiving.** We honour God's Name by praising Him for the wonders of His grace towards us (*Joel* 2: 26), and for the glorious truth that everything about Him is good (*Ps.* 54: 6).

(b) **Meditation and study.** We reverence the Lord by thinking about His Name, and pondering all He has revealed to us of Himself (*Mal.* 3: 16).

(c) **Love.** We show our reverence for God by loving His Name (*Ps.* 5: 11), and being jealous for His interest (*Ps.* 69: 9; *John* 2: 17).

(d) **Carefulness.** We reverence God's Name by keeping before us His holiness, and speaking about Him with care, encouraging one another to serve and worship Him with holy fear and awe (*Ps.* 89:7; *Heb.* 12: 28, 29).

(e) **Obedience.** We show our respect for God's Name by living in conformity to the will and character that Name reveals (*Micah* 4: 5).

(f) **Prayer.** We honour God by calling upon Him in prayer for help because it is His Name, His unchanging character, which gives us the assurance that He hears and answers prayer (*Ps.* 99: 6).

(g) **Confidence.** We reverence God by showing publicly that our confidence is in the Lord, and that, having committed ourselves to Him, we can wait with assurance and without impatience for His answer (*Ps.* 52: 9).

(h) **Evangelism.** We reverence God's Name by taking seriously the fact that He alone is the supreme Lord, whose saving deeds need to be known in all the world around (*Isa.* 12: 4).

(i) **Truthfulness.** We honour and reverence God's Name by being committed to complete truthfulness in every sphere for one of the main purposes of the third commandment is to prevent us ever calling upon God to confirm a lie (*Ex.* 20: 7). God is truth (*John* 1: 14; 14: 6) and He calls us to commitment to truth (*Eph.* 4: 25; 5: 9; 6: 14).

4. REST

Exodus 20: 8–11: "Remember the sabbath day by keeping it holy. Six days you shall labour and do all your work, but the seventh day is a sabbath to the Lord your God. On it you shall not do any work, neither you, nor your son or daughter, nor your manservant or maidservant, nor your animals, nor the alien within your gates. For in six days the Lord made the heavens and the earth, the sea, and all that is in them, but he rested on the seventh day. Therefore the Lord blessed the sabbath day and made it holy."

Question: What does the fourth commandment teach?

Answer: The fourth commandment teaches that the keeping of one day in seven as a sabbath is a special means of honouring God our Creator and Redeemer and of renewing our minds, bodies, and souls in the manner their constitution and well-being require.

It encourages us, upon a weekly basis, to lay aside material considerations, so that the worth of God, the worth of our soul, and spiritual issues and concerns, may occupy our thoughts and more effectively influence our living.

1. The change from Saturday, i.e. the original sabbath, to Sunday.

(a) The vital element in the commandment is that there should be six days of work and a day of rest—the particular day set apart is not the essence of the commandment (*Ex*. 20: 9, 10).

(b) The first Christians soon recognised that the Old Testament regulations for the Sabbath are part of the ceremonial law which has been fulfilled in our Lord Jesus Christ, so that they are no longer binding on God's people (*Rom*. 14: 5–6; *Col*. 2: 16, 17).

(c) In principle, every day is the Lord's Day, and is equally suitable for worship (*Acts* 2: 46).

(d) Yet it was also appreciated that if the purposes of the day are to be fulfilled it should, as far as possible, be the same day for all (*Acts* 20: 7; notice in *I Cor*. 11: 17–20 the emphasis on "coming together as a church").

(e) It soon became the practice to meet on Sunday in honour of our Lord's resurrection from the dead "on the first day of the week" (*John* 20: 1ff).

(f) The Lord Jesus appeared to His disciples on the first Easter Sunday, and again on the following Sunday.

(g) There are references to Christians meeting on "the first day of the week" (*Acts* 20: 7; *I Cor*. 16: 2), and it would seem to have been the recognised day for Christians to assemble together.

(h) The change not only bore witness to the fact of the Resurrection, but it emphasised the difference between the Christian Sunday and the Jewish Sabbath; the Jewish Sabbath came at the end of six days and spoke of a rest to come, the Christian Sunday comes at the beginning of the week symbolising "the rest" which Jesus Christ has won for those who trust in Him.

2. **The reasons for the appointment of the sabbath.**
First, God's own glory.

(a) It is His sabbath (*Ezek*. 20: 16, 21, 24).

(b) God's glory is His own Person: when we observe the sabbath we display the likeness of God in a pattern of work and rest for He made us in His own image (*Gen*. 1: 26, 27).

(c) The sabbath provides us with a special opportunity for remembering and meditating upon His work of creation and redemption. We cannot do this without wanting to praise Him, and thus to glorify Him (*Ps.* 50: 23).

(d) By our proper use of the sabbath we honour God by acknowledging His claim upon our time and service (*Ex.* 23: 25).

Secondly, man's own good.

(e) God blessed the sabbath, i.e. made it for man's blessing (*Gen.* 2: 3).

(f) The sabbath was made for man, not man for the sabbath (*Mark* 2: 27): that is to say, it was made for man's own true well-being in body, mind and soul. The need for one day's rest in seven is built into man's physical and mental constitution. It is not something that was peculiar to the Jews as part of their religious heritage, but something which is a necessity for all. As man needs daily rest, so he needs a weekly rest.

Thirdly, a covenant sign.

(g) It is a reminder of the covenant between God and His people for ever (*Ex.* 31: 13, 17; *Ezek.* 20: 12).

(h) It helps God's people to remember that they have a special and unique relationship to the Lord who sets them apart for Himself, for His own possession (*Ex.* 31: 13).

3. Our duties regarding the sabbath or Sunday.

(a) **To remember it.**

(i) The word "remember" (*Ex.* 20:8) bears the meaning of **imprint** or **mark** so as to be recognised. We are to imprint its importance upon our minds, and by our speech and actions mark it out as recognisably different from other days.

(ii) To remember it is to hold it as a delight (*Isa.* 58: 13).

(iii) To remember it is to count the keeping of it as an honour and privilege (*Isa.* 58: 13).

(b) **To keep it holy** (*Ex.* 20: 8).

(i) The idea behind the word "holy" is that of being cut off, separated, or set apart.

(ii) God calls upon us to set one day in seven apart, and to view it, and use it differently from the rest.

(iii) We keep it holy by using it in such a way that we show that the Lord has our first loyalty.

(c) **To lay aside our daily work** (*Ex.* 20: 9, 10).

(i) Work is an essential element in God's plan for human life (*Gen.* 2: 15) but man needs rest from work (*Ex.* 23: 12).

(ii) We are, therefore, commanded, to rest (*Ex.* 31: 15): "You shall not do any work" (*Ex.* 20: 10).

(iii) We are to put aside our ordinary callings on this one day (*Neh.* 13: 15–18).

(iv) The Hebrew word **shabbâth** translated "Sabbath" means **cessation, intermission or rest.**

(d) **To allow others the same opportunity of rest (Ex. 20: 10).**

(i) We are to do our utmost to ensure that in so far as our own conduct is concerned, others may enjoy rest too.

(ii) We have a measure of responsibility for others to see that they have the opportunity of rest: "You shall not do any work, neither you, nor your son, or daughter, nor your manservant or maid servant, nor your animals, nor the alien within your gates."

(e) **To remember God's mighty acts of creation and redemption.**

(i) We are to remember God's rest from His great work of creation (*Ex.* 20: 11): God Himself "worked" for the first six days and "rested" on the seventh day (*Gen.* 1: 31; 2: 1–3).

(ii) We are to remember God's redemption: the Jews were instructed to remember on the sabbath how they were servants in the land of Egypt, and the Lord their God brought them out of Egypt with a mighty hand and an outstretched arm (*Deut.* 5: 15).

(iii) Christians remember on the Lord's Day a far greater deliverance in which they were ransomed from the empty folly of their lives lived without God by the precious blood of Jesus Christ, in whom they have come to trust knowing that He was raised from the dead on the first day of the week for their justification (*I Pet.* 1: 18, 19; *Rom.* 4: 25).

(iv) The particular focus of Christian worship, therefore, will be the glory of the Risen Lord (*Rev.* 1: 10ff).

(v) We delight ourselves in

23

the Lord, calling the sabbath a delight for it gives us the opportunity of occupying ourselves with the Lord (*Isa*. 58: 13, 14).

(f) To engage in humanitarian action.

(i) It is lawful to do good on the sabbath (*Matt*. 12: 12).

(ii) It is imperative to do good on the sabbath (*Luke* 13: 10–17 notice the word "ought" in verse 16).

(iii) We are to seize the special opportunities it affords of doing good to others (e.g. *Mark* 2: 1–5; *Luke* 13: 10–17; 14: 1–6; *John* 9), and that probably includes activities such as visiting a hospital, opening our homes to the lonely, and calling in to see the elderly.

(iv) The Lord's Day is never to be an excuse for avoiding rightful duties to our fellow men (*Mark* 3: 1–6).

(g) To remember that it is God's institution.

(i) The choice of one day in seven was not man's, but God's: God hallowed it (*Gen*. 2: 3).

(ii) "In six days the Lord made the heavens and the earth, the sea, and all that is in them, but he rested on the seventh day. Therefore the Lord blessed the sabbath day and made it holy" (*Ex*. 20: 11).

4. Benefits of observing the sabbath principle.

(The reason for using the term "the sabbath principle" is that contemporary life with its complex machinery and shift systems frequently involves some working on the recognised "sabbath", i.e. Sunday. Where this is the case, both employers and employees should be strongly encouraged to observe the **principle** still by giving another day that week in lieu, and insisting that it should be taken as a day of rest.)

(a) Blessing from God.

(i) We shall find joy in God (*Isa*. 58: 14).

(ii) We shall have God-given success in our endeavours (*Isa*. 58: 14).

(iii) We shall obtain our full share of the blessings promised us (*Isa*. 58: 14).

(b) Rest and renewal.

(i) By rest both we and all

24

associated with us, including animals, are refreshed (*Ex.* 23: 12).

(ii) We shall renew our strength, according to His promise to those who wait upon Him (*Isa.* 40: 31).

(c) **A necessary corrective is imposed upon our proneness to self-seeking** (*Amos* 8: 5).

(i) We deliberately turn aside from our own business, from seeking our own interests or attending to our own affairs and honour the Lord (*Isa.* 58: 13).

(ii) By putting aside "getting" for a day at least, we symbolically reject covetousness as a motive for living (*Col.* 3: 5–8).

(iii) We remember on the "sabbath" that this world is not everything and that there is another world and kingdom to be put first (*Matt.* 6: 33; *Col.* 3: 1, 2).

(iv) We deliberately turn aside for a brief while from the natural preoccupations of our daily work so that the well-being of our soul, and spiritual issues and concerns occupy our thoughts and more effectively influence our living

(*Ps.* 73: 17; 77: 13; *II Cor.* 4: 18; *Heb.* 10: 10, 13–16).

(d) **The proper exercise of our soul in the worship of God.**

(i) We delight ourselves in the Lord (*Isa.* 58: 13, 14), making the sabbath a day of joy as we do so.

(ii) We esteem a day in His courts better than a thousand elsewhere (*Ps.* 84: 10).

(iii) We are provided with the opportunity to cultivate our spiritual life to which we are continually exhorted (*Ps.* 27: 4, 8; *II Pet.* 3: 18).

(e) **The strengthening of family life and unity.**

(i) All the members of a family are instructed and encouraged to rest together (*Ex.* 20: 10).

(ii) It is a day for being at home—being "in one's place" (*Ex.* 16: 29).

(f) **The encouragement and profit of Christian fellowship.**

(i) We are able to enter into the worship and fellowship of God's people (*Ps.* 55: 14; 122: 1; 132: 7).

(ii) We are able to benefit from the teaching of God's Word (*Luke* 4: 31; 6: 6; *Acts*

13: 13, 14, 15, 44; *Acts* 17: 2; 18: 4).

(iii) Assembling ourselves together, we may stir up one another to love and to good works (*Heb*. 10: 24).

(g) A helpful anticipation and reminder of the everlasting rest God prepares for His believing people.

(i) God's rest on the seventh day is a type of the messianic rest which God will yet give to His people (*Heb*. 4: 4, 9).

(ii) Our Lord Jesus Christ, having completed His work for us by His death and resurrection, has entered into His rest, and one day we are going to share in that eternal heavenly rest (*John* 14: 2, 3).

5. RESPECT FOR, AND SUBMISSION TO, PROPER AUTHORITY

Exodus 20: 12: "Honour your father and your mother, so that you may live long in the land the Lord your God is giving you."

Question: What does the fifth commandment teach?

Answer: The fifth commandment teaches us the general principle of paying respect to whom respect is due, and honour to whom honour is due by underlining the fundamental and specific responsibility children have to honour their parents, a responsibility which is at the very heart of a nation's well-being.

1. The meaning of the word "honour".

(a) The Hebrew word for "honour" is "kabed" with the basic meaning of "to be heavy" from which comes the sense of making weighty, and of lading respect upon a person. Thus, to honour our parents is to regard them as eminently worthy of respect— to recognise that they deserve a "weight" of respect.

(b) The Greek equivalent of the Hebrew word, used in the New Testament, "timaō", conveys the thought of fixing a valuation, and, by implication, to revere.

(c) Thus, to honour our parents is to fix a right valuation upon their worth, causing us to revere them.

(d) The honour we give to

26

parents is to be a reflection of the honour we know we ought to give to God our heavenly Father (*Mal.* 1: 6).

(e) The honouring of parents is part of practical holiness (*Lev.* 19: 2, 3).

2. The duties of children to their parents.

Reverence and respect.

(a) Children are to revere their parents (*Lev.* 19: 3).

(b) Negatively, this means never to despise or mock them (*Prov.* 30: 17), curse them (*Ex.* 21: 17; *Prov.* 20: 20), strike them (*Ex.* 21: 15) or speak evil of them (*Matt.* 15: 4).

(c) Positively, it means to deliberately honour them by speaking well of them, respecting their persons, and showing them courtesy (cf. *Gen.* 47: 7, 11, 12; *I Kings* 2: 19, 20).

Demonstrated and genuine love.

(d) The love of children for their parents is always assumed in the Bible: such love is a first, and entirely natural, love (*Matt.* 10: 37).

(e) Love, to be acceptable to God, must be genuine and without hypocrisy (*Rom.* 12: 9).

(f) Children should be unashamed of showing their affection for their parents (*Gen.* 46: 29).

Obedience to their commands.

(g) Both parents are to be obeyed (*Deut.* 21: 18), and they are to be obeyed in everything (*Eph.* 6: 1; *Col.* 3: 20).

(h) To honour parents, therefore, is the opposite of stubbornness and rebelliousness towards them (*Deut.* 21: 18).

(i) We honour our parents by giving deference or regard to their requests (*I Kings* 2: 20), neither despising their instruction nor their direction (*Prov.* 1: 8; 15: 5).

Submission to their discipline.

(j) The rightful submission of children to parents is to respect them for the discipline they exercise (*Heb.* 12: 9).

(k) Proper discipline, rightly appreciated, is not a disadvantage to a son or daughter but a privilege (*Prov.* 3: 11–12; *Heb.* 12: 5–8).

Faithfulness to their interests.

(l) Children can fall into the

peril of regarding lightly their parents' property: a man who, in effect, robs his father or mother and says, "It's not wrong" is no better than a murderer (*Prov.* 28: 24).

(m) To honour our parents is to give them joy by living wisely, and we do the right thing when we aim at giving them this joy (*Prov.* 23:24,25).

Repaying the love, care and trouble they have given.

(n) To honour our parents is to care for them, and to provide for them when they are in need, in other words, to make some return to them, not least financially, if that is the help required (*I Tim.* 5: 4).

(o) Children are not to conceive excuses—least of all religious excuses—for not fulfilling their obligations to their parents (see the "Corban" argument in *Matt.* 15: 1–6; *Mark* 7: 1–13).

The limitations of the rightful submission of children to parents.

(a) The obedience and subjection God commands are neither absolute nor universal—they are "in the Lord" (*Eph.* 6: 1), i.e. in such things as

parents require us to do with the Lord's authority.

(b) If anyone, including parents, commands that which is contrary to the law and will of God, then we ought to obey God rather than men (*Acts* 5: 29).

(c) Furthermore, the day must come when children recognise their independence of their parents, and, for the majority, this comes through marriage in particular (*Matt.* 19: 5, 6; *Mark* 10: 7, 8).

(d) Prior to marriage a man or woman has his or her closest bond with parents, and owes to them the greatest obligation; the new bond and obligation which marriage involves transcends the old (*Eph.* 5: 31).

(e) A man's duty to his wife, and a woman's duty to her husband, and their united duty to their children, clearly bring a change of priorities so far as their relationship and duties to their parents are concerned, although no lessening of their respect and sense of responsibility for them (*Eph.* 5: 21–33).

(f) If at any stage parents seek to make loyalty to themselves a priority over their children's loyalty to the Lord, they demand that which is unlawful: love for the Lord ought to be so great that the best of human loves is hatred by comparison (*Luke* 14: 26).

(g) Nevertheless, all commands about loyalty to Jesus Christ must be seen in the context of genuine filial piety as a Christian duty (*Mark* 7: 13).

(h) We may be quite sure that the priority of loyalty to God will never be detrimental to the wellbeing of those we love most, much as we may not see how it can be so at the time (see Abraham and Isaac in *Genesis* 22).

4. The responsibilities rightful submission of children to parents places upon the parents.

(a) Parents must realise their responsibilities for their children for they are the first and foremost educators of their children (*Prov.* 4: 1–4).

(b) Parents must manage their own households well, keeping their children submissive and respectful in every way (*I Tim.* 3: 4).

(c) Parents should be clear as to the kind of children to be proud of, so that they don't place false objectives before their children (*Prov.* 23: 22–25).

(d) Children are gifts from the Lord (*Gen.* 4: 1; 25: 21; *Ruth* 4: 12, 13; *I Sam.* 1: 5, 6, 11), given to parents for a while, and parents do well to give their children back to the Lord, as it were, lending them to Him for as long as they live (*I Sam.* 1: 11, 27, 28).

(e) Children are given to parents to rear and to train up in the way they should go (*Prov.* 22: 6): they are to be nurtured like tender plants with a view to their future fruitfulness in character (*Ps.* 128: 3).

(f) God desires godly offspring from the marriage union (*Mal.* 2: 15).

(g) Parents' **actions** and **words** in relation to their children are all to be with their spiritual good in view—what the New Testament calls "the discipline and instruction of the Lord" (*Eph.* 6: 4).

(h) Parents' **actions** must be right towards their children, particularly in regard to the discipline they exercise because, first, foolishness is bound up in the heart of a child and it takes more than words to dislodge it (*Prov.* 22: 15), and, secondly, character is a plant which grows more sturdily for some cutting back (*Prov.* 15: 32, 33; 5: 11, 12; *Heb.* 12: 11), and from early days (*Prov.* 13: 24b; 22: 6; 29: 15).

(i) The motive of love is to be behind all exercise of discipline (*Prov.* 13: 24), and love demands that a restraint should be placed upon children by their parents when they do wrong (*I Sam.* 3: 13).

(j) Parents' words must be right towards their children, for they are to be instructed from their earliest days in the law of God (*Eph.* 6: 4; *Josh.* 8: 35) with loving persistence (*Prov.* 1: 8; 3: 21; 4: 8, 9, 12).

(k) Parents need to be in that tender relationship to their children in which their children expect to receive instruction from them (*Prov.* 4: 1–4).

(l) Parents are not to make it difficult for their children to obey the commandment, "Honour your father and your mother" by making unreasonable demands (*Col.* 3: 21), needlessly provoking them to anger (*Eph.* 6: 4), perhaps by favouritism (*Gen.* 25: 29) or by neglect (*II Sam.* 14: 13, 28).

(m) The important factor in a child's upbringing is not the money parents have with which to supply their children's needs but rather the example they set (*Prov.* 20: 7): parents pass on a heritage for good or ill according to their fear of God (*Ps.* 25: 12, 13; *Hos.* 4: 6).

(n) Parents themselves are to be an example of loyalty to God, never allowing their children to take precedence over their own discipleship of our Lord Jesus Christ (*Mark* 10: 29; *Luke* 18: 29; *Matt.* 19: 29).

(o) Parents are to be an example themselves too of dutiful children in relation to their own parents (*Luke* 6: 31).

5. **Examples of obedience to this commandment.**

(a) Joseph is a conspicuous example of obedience to this commandment in his concern for his father (*Gen.* 45: 3), his provision for him (*Gen.* 45:

30

9–13), his demonstrated affection (*Gen.* 46: 28–34), his filial pride (*Gen.* 47: 7, 27–31), and his obedience (*Gen.* 50: 1–14).

(b) Our Lord Jesus Christ is the supreme example of obedience to this commandment, as to all others, in His earthly submission and obedience (*Luke* 2: 51), and His concern and provision for His widowed mother (*John* 19: 26, 27).

6. Examples of disobedience to this commandment.

(a) The two sons of Eli, Hophni and Phinehas, are sad examples of disobedience to this commandment in that they refused to listen to the voice of their father (*I Sam.* 2: 25), and had no regard for the Lord or His commandments, with disastrous consequences (*I Sam.* 2: 12; 4: 11, 17).

(b) A second example of disobedience is the manner in which the Jews evaded obedience to the implications of this commandment to maintain needy parents by instead vowing their property insincerely to the Temple (*Mark* 7: 1–13; *Matt.* 15: 1–6).

7. The fundamental importance of this principle of respect for, and submission to, parents.

(a) This commandment is the application of a general Christian principle: we are to pay respect to whom respect is due, and honour to whom honour is due (*Rom.* 13: 7 cf. *Mark* 12: 17).

(b) Parents are the first authority we learn to respect and the pattern of submission we learn towards them influences our submission to all men, for we are taught to honour all men (*I Pet.* 2: 17), so that, for example, we rise up before the hoary head (*Lev.* 19: 32), and honour widows and such like by caring for them financially and in other ways open to us (*I Tim.* 5: 3).

(c) Inevitably the pattern of submission we learn from our earliest years influences our submission in other spheres, whether towards our teachers, our rulers or our employers: those who show proper respect and submission to parents are unlikely to find difficulty in honouring the civil authorities (*I Pet.* 2: 17) or treating earthly masters or employers with all respect (*I*

Pet. 2: 18): in other words, the well-being of a people or a nation begins in the home.

6. RESPECT FOR LIFE

Exodus 20: 13: "You shall not murder."

Question: What does the sixth commandment teach?

Answer: The sixth commandment condemns murder, which is the deliberate, malicious and unlawful taking of life, and teaches us the sanctity of human life which, as a gift from God, is to be neither violated nor threatened, whether by actions, threats, motives or words.

1. Life is a gift from God and is sacred.

(a) Man's breath is God's prerogative (*Gen.* 2: 7; *Isa.* 42: 5; *Dan.* 5: 23).

(b) Man's life is sacred (*Gen.* 9: 6), so sacred that even the life of a murderer is not to be carelessly taken away (*Gen.* 4: 15).

(c) Man's life is sacred because man was made in the image of God (*Gen.* 1: 27; 9: 6).

(d) Man's life is his dearest possession (*Matt.* 16: 26; *Mark* 8: 37; *John* 15: 13; cf. *Acts* 27: 18, 19, 22).

(e) Man's redemption in and through our Lord Jesus Christ emphasises the sanctity of human life (*John* 10: 10, 28; *Rom.* 5: 21).

2. Murder violates God's commandment.

(a) It despises God's sixth commandment and is evil in God's sight (*II Sam.* 12: 9).

(b) It offends, more than any other sin, the commandment "Love your neighbour as yourself" (*Rom.* 13: 9).

(c) It offends the special value given to the life of man because of the awareness that all men are brethren (*Acts* 17:26).

(d) God hates murder (*Prov.* 6: 16, 17).

(e) Murder cannot be concealed from God (*Isa.* 26: 21; *Jer.* 2: 34) and it cries out for God's vengeance (*Gen.* 4: 10).

3. Human attitudes and emotions which can give rise to murder are forbidden by this commandment.

(a) At first sight the sixth

commandment appears to be concerned with nothing more than the murderous act (*Ex.* 20: 13), but the Lord Jesus gave the commandment a further and deeper meaning: all sins which lead to murder and are the occasions of it are forbidden (*Matt.* 5: 21–26). Anger and hatred are perhaps the two most obvious examples.

Anger

(b) Anger, like a fire can be kindled and do great damage (*Ps.* 124: 3).

(c) Anger is a work of the flesh (*Gal.* 5: 20).

(d) Anger can be foolishly harboured and kept alive (*Amos* 1: 11; *Eccl.* 7: 9).

(e) Anger and insult can constitute both the spirit of murder (*Matt.* 5: 22), and cause murder (*Gen.* 49: 6).

(f) A distinction is recognised between anger and malice, in that the former under control is sometimes allowable (*Eph.* 4: 26, 27), but malice—mental murder—is always evil (*I John* 3: 15).

Hatred

(g) Hatred is synonymous with darkness, and walking in darkness (*I John* 2: 9).

(h) Hatred distorts our perspective (*I John* 2: 11).

(i) Murder is the fruit of hatred (*I John* 3: 15).

(j) Murder is first committed in the heart and then completed by actions: e.g. Cain and Abel (*Gen.* 4: 5, 8), Saul (later known as Paul) who breathed out threats of murder against the disciples of the Lord (*Acts* 9: 1) and was a "man-slayer" before his conversion (*Acts* 9: 1, 4, 5; 22: 4, 7; 26: 10).

4. **There are important exceptions in the taking of human life which are not infringements of this commandment.**

The civil authority and capital punishment.

(a) The just punishment of crime by magistrates is not murder: the powers that be are ordained of God to bear the sword and execute wrath (*Rom.* 13: 1–7; *I Pet.* 2: 13–17).

(b) The assumption is always present that there are crimes worthy of death (*Gen.* 9: 6; *Acts* 25: 11).

(c) Under the Mosaic law the

death penalty was prescribed for certain offences (*Ex.* 2: 12, 14, 23–25; *Lev.* 24: 17; *Num.* 35: 21; *Deut.* 19: 11–13), and the institution of capital punishment for murder would seem to be of permanent obligation (*Gen.* 9: 5, 6).

War

(d) The lawfulness of defensive war is distinctly recognised in the Bible, and the taking of life in time of war is not murder (*Judg.* 5: 23; *I Sam.* 15: 2, 3).

(e) When consulted through the Urim and Thummin, or by the prophets, as to the rightness of military enterprises, God answered (*Judg.* 20: 27; *I Sam.* 14: 37; 23: 2, 4; *I Kings* 22: 6).

(f) Since magistrates are given power of life and death over their citizens, they plainly have the right to declare war in self-defence (*Rom.* 13: 1–7; *I Pet.* 2: 13–17).

Manslaughter

(g) The life of a person taken away by accident is not murder (*Deut.* 19: 5).

(h) The cities of refuge were intended to provide refuge for those guilty of manslaughter so that their case could be properly judged (*Num.* 35: 9–28).

(i) The life of a person taken in self-defence is not murder (*Ex.* 22: 2).

5. The implications of this commandment are many.

(a) Love for our neighbour means the protection and preservation of his life (*Luke* 10: 25–37).

(b) The opposite of murder is self-sacrificing love (*I John* 3: 11–18), which should be the Christian norm (*Phil.* 2: 5–8; *I Pet.* 2: 21–25).

(c) We need to guard our hearts if we would avoid breaking this commandment (*Prov.* 4: 23; *Matt.* 5: 21–26).

(d) We should never let the sun go down on our anger (*Eph.* 4: 26), or any other harmful and wrongful attitude of heart.

(e) Human relationships matter to God (*I John* 4: 21; 5: 1).

(f) Attitudes and works recognised as incitements to murder are to be recognised by the Christian as belonging to his old life, and are to be put away, e.g. bitterness, anger, clamour, slander, and malice (*Eph.* 4: 31; *Col.* 3: 5; cf. *I Pet.* 2: 1).

7. THE SANCTITY OF MARRIAGE

Exodus 20: 14: "You shall not commit adultery."

Question: What does the seventh commandment teach?

Answer: The seventh commandment teaches the sanctity of marriage and, by implication, forbids all impurity of thought, speech and behaviour.

1. God's institution of marriage.

(a) Marriage is a divine institution (*Gen.* 2: 24).

(b) It was founded before the existence of civil society, and it is, therefore, not simply a civil institution but a creation ordinance (*Gen.* 2: 18–24).

(c) It was founded on the nature of man as constituted by God: He made male and female and ordained marriage as an indispensable condition for the continuance of the human race (*Gen.* 1: 27, 28; 2: 18–24).

(d) One of God's purposes in marriage, therefore, is procreation and fruitfulness (*Gen.* 1: 28; *Ps.* 127: 3, 5).

(e) Children are to be brought up within the marriage relationship (*Prov.* 5: 16, 17), and God desires godly offspring from the marriage union (*Mal.* 2: 15).

(f) The other equally important purpose of marriage is the support and help that marriage partners are able to give one another (*Gen.* 2: 20–22).

(g) For the welfare of the human race marriage is not to be within certain close family relationships (*Lev.* 18: 6ff; 20: 11–21; *Deut.* 22: 30; 27: 20–23).

(h) Beneficial as marriage is, the marriage relationship is not to be coveted (*I Cor.* 7: 1ff; *Ex.* 20: 7).

(i) Marriage brings its own cares and distractions, and can in some measure bring divided loyalties in that God is not served with the same freedom from entanglements

as before marriage (*I Cor.* 7:
32–34).

(j) Considerations arising from
the kingdom of God and its
best interests may cause some
men and women to forego
the privileges and joys of the
marriage state (*Matt.* 19: 11,
12; *I Cor.* 7: 7).

(k) Marriage is a relationship
limited to this life, for at the
resurrection men and women
do not marry but are like the
angels in heaven (*Matt.* 22:
30; *Mark* 12: 25; *Luke* 20: 35).

2. The proper pattern of behaviour in marriage.

(a) The natural aim of marriage partners is to please one
another (*I Cor.* 7: 32–34).

(b) The passion of lust is not
to characterise the sexual relationship within marriage but
rather holiness and honour (*I
Thess.* 4: 4, 5), with a proper
recognition of the other partner's conjugal rights (*I Cor.* 7:
3).

(c) The marriage relationship
is to be modelled upon that
between the Lord Jesus Christ
and His Church: the husband
is to love, protect and cherish
his wife as himself; and the

wife is to love, honour and
obey her husband (*Eph.* 5:
21–30).

(d) The secret of happy marriage is that neither party
should demand his or her
rights but each should give to
the other appropriate love and
service willingly and freely
(*Eph.* 5: 22, 25).

(e) Marriage partners need to
appreciate the real nature of
their oneness, and its mystery,
which means understanding
that to hurt one's partner is to
hurt oneself (*Eph.* 5: 28–33).

(f) The marriage couple are to
find joy in one another, and
to keep strictly to one another;
they are each other's cistern
from which alone they are to
drink (*Prov.* 5: 15, 18, 19).

3. The sanctity of marriage.

(a) At marriage two people become one (*Matt.* 19: 5, 6;
Mark 10: 7, 8).

(b) Marriage is for life, and
this is the Lord's ruling (*Matt.*
19: 9; *Mark* 10: 11, 12; *Luke*
16: 18; *I Cor.* 7: 10, 11, 39).

(c) Marriage is a compact between a man and a woman to
live together, as husband and
wife, until separated by death

(*Gen.* 2: 23, 24; *Rom.* 7: 2, 3), and God is witness to that covenant (*Mal.* 2: 14).

(d) It is the most intimate and sacred relationship which can exist between human beings, and all other human relationships must be reckoned as secondary to it if necessary (*Gen.* 2: 24; *Eph.* 5: 31).

(e) It is the point at which adult children rightly recognise their independence of their parents, and enter into a oneness with a marriage partner which is deeper than that known with their respective parents (*Matt.* 19: 5, 6; *Mark* 10: 7, 8).

(f) The marriage compact is permanent, and cannot be dissolved at the will of either of the parties (*Matt.* 5: 31, 32; 19: 3–9; *Mark* 10: 2–12; *Luke* 16: 18).

(g) The union is properly dissolved only by the death of one of the parties (*Matt.* 19: 6; *Mark* 10: 6).

(h) Marriage is to be held in honour among all, and the marriage bed is to be undefiled—that is to say, the sexual act is a sanctuary sacred to the husband and his wife (*Heb.* 13: 4).

(i) The sanctity of marriage is underlined by the fact that it is made the symbol of the relationship between God and His people (*Isa.* 62: 5; cf. *Hos.* 2: 14–23).

(j) It is used to illustrate the union between the Lord Jesus Christ and His Church (*Eph.* 5: 22–33; *Rev.* 19: 7, 9; 21: 9).

(k) The uncompromising nature of our Lord Jesus Christ's teaching on marriage surprised even His disciples (*Matt.* 19: 10).

4. Adultery.

(a) To commit adultery is to sin against God as well as against another human being (*Gen.* 20: 6), for it offends God's law (*Ex.* 20: 14).

(b) We cannot break the seventh commandment without in some way cheating our fellow men (*I Thess.* 4: 6).

(c) Adultery offends the commandment, "Love your neighbour as yourself" (*Rom.* 13: 9).

(d) Adultery is the final expression of thoughts given place to in the heart and expressed in the eyes (*Matt.* 5: 28, 29).

37

(e) Adultery is the putting asunder of those whom God has joined together (*Matt.* 19: 6; *Mark* 10: 9).

(f) If a man arbitrarily puts away his wife and marries another, he commits adultery (*Matt.* 19: 9; *Mark* 10: 11, 12); similarly, a wife is an adulteress if she lives with another man while her husband is alive (*Rom.* 7: 3).

(g) Marriage can be dissolved through the unchastity on the part of one partner, the implication being that the mysterious sense in which the Bible declares a husband and wife to be one has been dreadfully abused and marred (*Matt.* 19: 9).

(h) If a man repudiates his wife on the above grounds, however, and marries another, he commits no offence, and likewise with the wife if she is the offended party (*Matt.* 19: 9; *Mark* 10: 11, 12).

(i) Adultery displays an absence of the fear of God (*Mal.* 3: 5).

(j) To fail to recognise the sanctity of marriage is to bring God's judgment upon the individual (*Heb.* 13: 4),

and His judgment is sure (*I Cor.* 6: 9, 10).

(k) Divorce is contrary to the whole purpose of God in marriage (*Mark* 10: 1–12; cf. *Gen.* 12: 17–20), and its sinfulness should remind men and women of the seriousness of marriage before they embark upon it (*Matt.* 19: 10).

5. **The implications of this commandment in regard to personal purity.**

(a) The commandment forbids all impurity of thought, speech and behaviour (*Matt.* 5: 27–30; *Eph.* 5: 4).

(b) In other words, it extends to the heart, mind and imagination as well as to the body and external actions (*Matt.* 5: 28).

(c) To fix our eyes upon a person of the other sex with lascivious desire is adultery of the heart (*Matt.* 5: 27–28).

(d) We need to keep a strict watch, therefore, over our heart for from it flow the springs of life (*Prov.* 4: 23; *Matt.* 15: 19; *Mark* 7: 21).

(e) The will of God is our sanctification which means abstaining from all forms of sexual immorality (*I Thess.* 4: 3).

(f) Every one of us is to learn to control his or her body, keeping it pure and treating it with respect, and never regarding it as an instrument for self-gratification (*I Thess.* 4: 4, 5).

(g) The calling of God is not to impurity but to the most thorough purity, and anyone who makes light of the matter is not making light of a man's ruling but of God's commandment (*I Thess.* 4: 8).

(h) Christian believers in particular must preserve their chastity because their bodies have become the temples of the Holy Spirit (*I Cor.* 6: 15, 19).

8. RESPECT FOR PROPERTY

Exodus 20: 15: "You shall not steal."

Question: What does the eighth commandment teach?

Answer: The eighth commandment teaches us to have a proper respect for other people's property, and forbids all forms
of theft. By implication, it teaches the right of private property, and the honourableness of lawfully acquired wealth.

1. The right of private property.

(a) The earth is the Lord's (*Ps.* 24: 1; 50: 10–12), so that although man has been granted use of the property and wealth of the world his right remains a derived and temporary right (*Gen.* 1: 28–30).

(b) God has so constituted man that he desires and needs this right of exclusive possession, and the foundation of the right of property, therefore, is the will of God (*Ex.* 20: 15).

(c) In the Old Testament every man held his piece of land as an inheritance from the Lord, and the removal of the landmark indicating that inheritance was an offence against the Lord Himself (*Deut.* 19: 14).

(d) The prophets looked forward to the coming days of universal peace which included private property as one of the great blessings yet to be (*Micah* 4: 3, 4).

(e) Personal property is to be respected (*Deut.* 23: 25), and throughout the Scriptures the individual's right to his property is maintained (*I Kings* 21: 1–16).

(f) Even the community of goods which the early Church chose to practice for a period did not involve the denial of the rights of property (*Acts* 5: 4).

(g) The eighth commandment, therefore, forbids all violations of the rights of property (*Ex*. 20: 15).

2. Examples of the many different forms of theft.

(a) Borrowing, and then failing to return what has been borrowed (*Ps*. 37: 21).

(b) Failure to clear oneself of debt when able to do so (*II Kings* 4: 7).

(c) False weights and measures (*Amos* 8: 5; *Micah* 6: 10, 11).

(d) General dishonesty in buying and selling (*Lev*. 25: 14).

(e) Misuse of one's employer's property or time (*Tit*. 2: 10).

(f) Wasting someone else's possessions (*Luke* 16: 1).

(g) Failure to seek the owner of something we have found (*Lev*. 6: 4).

(h) Taking unfair advantage of

either the ignorance or the needs of our fellow men (*Prov*. 11: 26).

(i) Paying bad wages, or withholding or delaying the payment of wages (*Lev*. 19: 13; *Mal*. 3: 5; *Jas*. 5: 4).

(j) Indifference of children in their use of their parents' property (*Prov*. 28: 24).

(k) Failing as adult sons or daughters to make some return to our parents when they need help (*Prov*. 28: 24; *Mark* 7: 11; *I Tim*. 5: 4, 8).

3. The importance of honesty and trustworthiness in regard to other people's possessions.

(a) We are to seek the good of our neighbour rather than just seeking our own good (*I Cor*. 10: 24).

(b) As employees we are to show complete faithfulness to our employer's interests (*Tit*. 2: 10).

(c) Honesty is to characterise the work we do (*Eph*. 4: 28).

(d) We are to strive after honesty in little things for that sets the pattern for larger things (*Luke* 16: 10).

(e) We are not to give any

encouragement to others in defrauding those who have committed some trust to them (*Ps.* 50: 18; *Prov.* 29: 24).

(f) In regard to other people's property and possessions, justice and only justice is what we are to follow (*Deut.* 16: 20).

(g) Theft offends the commandment, "Love your neighbour as yourself" (*Rom.* 13: 9).

(h) At the root of all forms of stealing is selfishness (*Eph.* 4: 28).

(i) Theft is an abomination to God (*Jer.* 7: 9, 10), and brings God's judgment upon the thief (*Zech.* 5: 3, 4).

4. Wealth is not in and of itself wrong, but it must be obtained lawfully and honourably.

(a) The eighth commandment requires that whatever wealth we possess should be lawfully obtained (*Ex.* 20: 15).

(b) Property is not evil in itself but like all material possessions it can present dangers to our spiritual well-being (*Deut.* 6; 10–12; *Luke* 12: 15).

(c) The more easily we obtain our wealth, the sooner we shall probably lose it (*Prov.* 13: 11); whereas the harder it is to earn, the more we shall possess most likely in the long-term (*Prov.* 13: 11).

(d) The most lawful and honourable means of obtaining wealth is to work for it (*Eph.* 4: 28).

(e) In fulfilling our daily work we are to think not only of ourselves but also of those who are in any kind of material need whom we can help (*Isa.* 58: 10; *Eph.* 4: 28; *I John* 3: 17)—the implication being that possessions are a trust from God.

(f) The clear implication of the eighth commandment, therefore, is that we are to restore anything that we have unjustly obtained or taken from others (*Lev.* 6: 4; *Luke* 19: 8; *Eph.* 4: 28).

9. TRUTHFULNESS

Exodus 20: 16: "You shall not give false testimony against your neighbour."

Question: What does the ninth commandment teach?

Answer: The ninth commandment forbids in principle all

untruth and falsehood, and in particular perjury, and proclaims the necessity of truthfulness of speech.

1. Implicit in the ninth commandment is the importance of the tongue.

(a) Truthfulness has special reference to our speech (*Eph.* 4: 25; *Col.* 3: 9).

(b) The abuse of the gift of speech and the wrong use to which words are put are sins to which the Scriptures draw considerable attention (e.g. *Ps.* 120: 1–3; cf. *Ps.* 5: 9; 12: 2–4; 36: 1–4; 52: 1–4; 64: 1–4.)

(c) We sin most easily in our speech (*Eccl.* 5: 1, 2; *Isa.* 6: 5).

(d) If anyone makes no mistake in what he says, he is a perfect man, able to keep his whole body in check (*Jas.* 3: 2).

(e) The tongue can be deceitful in the mouth (*Micah* 6: 12), full of venom (*Rom.* 3: 13), and a dreadful scourge (*Job* 5: 21).

(f) The tongue can be used to deceive (*Rom.* 3: 13), to express malice (*Dan.* 3: 8), and

to bring about mischief (*Ps.* 36: 3).

(g) The tongue has a terrifying power, comparable to that of poison and of fire (*Jas.* 3: 1–12).

(h) In the light of the tongue's potential for good or evil, we are instructed to be extremely careful in the manner in which we speak of others (*Lev.* 19: 16).

2. God's own character is necessarily reflected in this commandment as in all others.

(a) The Lord is revealed to us as the true God (*II Chron.* 15: 3; *Jer.* 10: 10; *John* 17: 3; *I Thess.* 1: 9f; cf. *I John* 5: 20).

(b) Our Lord Jesus Christ is the truth (*John* 14: 6): everyone who loves truth recognises His voice (*John* 18: 37).

(c) The Holy Spirit is the Spirit of truth (*I John* 5: 6; *John* 15: 26): He guides those whom He indwells into everything that is true (*John* 16: 13).

(d) God is the God of truth and all truth derives its sanctity from Him (*John* 17: 3; *I John* 5: 20).

(e) God cannot lie (*Tit.* 1: 2; *Heb.* 6: 18; cf. *Rom.* 3: 4);

to lie would be to contradict Himself, and God cannot deny Himself (*II Tim.* 2: 13).

(f) It is God's perfection to be consistent with Himself, and all His ways are truth (*Ps.* 111: 7, 8; cf. *Deut.* 32: 4; *Isa.* 25: 1).

(g) God requires truth in our inward being (*Ps.* 51: 6).

(h) The Lord has a controversy with us when we choose to put aside truth (*Hos.* 4: 1, 2).

3. In particular, the ninth commandment forbids perjury.

(a) The ninth commandment exemplifies what is the worst form of lying: taking a solemn oath in court and then by failure to tell the truth, or by deliberately misrepresenting the truth, to put someone's reputation or very life in danger (*Ex.* 20: 16).

(b) The commandment forbids the uttering of a false report, or conspiring with others to misrepresent the truth (*Ex.* 23: 1).

(c) False witness takes place when an individual states what is untrue in order to safeguard the interests of someone else, perhaps for personal gain (*Isa.* 5: 23).

(d) The commandment, therefore, forbids us to have anything to do with a false charge, and to have no involvement in the harming of the innocent and the righteous (*Ex.* 23: 7).

(e) The commandment forbids the taking of a bribe, for a bribe blinds men's eyes to justice, and injures the cause of those who are in the right (*Ex.* 23: 6–8).

(f) A man who bears false witness against his neighbour always does him harm (*Prov.* 25: 18).

(g) By bearing false witness we may even put a man's life in jeopardy (*I Kings* 21: 13; *Ps.* 35: 11).

(h) The false witness is a betrayer (*Prov.* 14: 25).

(i) False witness, like other sins, arises from the evil corruption of men's hearts (*Matt.* 15: 19).

(j) The bearing of false witness shows an absence of the fear of God (*Mal.* 3: 5).

(k) God hates false oaths (*Zech.* 8: 17), and He sees to it that a false witness will not go unpunished (*Prov.* 19: 5).

4. In principle, the commandment forbids all untruth and falsehood.

(a) **Slander,** for example, consists of making false statements about a person in order to defame or injure him, and is, in effect, fighting and injuring people with the tongue (*Jer*. 18: 18).

(b) We are not to injure others by initiating or accepting lies or false reports which are harmful to people's good names (*Col*. 3: 9).

(c) Hatred is frequently at the back of slander (*Ps*. 41: 7; 109: 3).

(d) Slander comes from an evil heart (*Luke* 6: 45), and is an abomination to the Lord (*Prov*. 6: 16, 19).

(e) **Deceit** (*Ps*. 120: 2; *Rom*. 3: 13), **lying** (*Eph*. 4: 25), and **flattery** (*Ps*. 5: 9; 78: 36) are likewise forbidden.

(f) **False judgments** and wrong forms of **criticism** are also snares into which we may fall, which constitute sin in the light of this commandment. The command forbids all rash and unwarrantable judging of other men's hearts and destinies which is usually accompanied by ignorance of our own (*Matt*. 7: 1, 3); we are all in danger of rising too quickly to criticise others (*Mark* 9: 38–41; *Luke* 9: 49, 50).

(g) **Tale-bearing** and **backbiting** are both aspects of slander (*Lev*. 19: 16; *Prov*. 17: 9; *Rom*. 1: 30; *II Cor*. 12: 20; *I Tim*. 5: 13).

(h) All these and similar departures from truth bring strife (*Prov*. 26: 20), separate friends (*Prov*. 16: 28; 17: 9), and are utterly destructive (*Prov*. 11: 9).

(i) Everyone who loves and practises falsehood is excluded from the kingdom of God (*I Cor*. 6: 10; *Rev*. 22: 15).

(j) Untruth and falsehood are Satan's habitat (*John* 8: 44), and both lying (*Acts* 5: 3) and slander (*Rev*. 12: 10) are identified with him.

(k) We shall be judged for every careless word we utter (*Matt*. 12: 36, 37).

(l) The Christian, therefore, is to put away from him every form of untruth and falsehood (*Eph*. 4: 25, 31; *I Pet*. 2: 1; 3: 10; cf. *Ps*. 34: 13).

5. The ninth commandment proclaims the necessity of truthfulness of speech.

(a) The commandment aims at the preservation and promoting of truthfulness among men: men should speak the truth to one another (*Zech.* 8: 16; *Eph.* 4: 29).

(b) The Lord Jesus Christ, our example in everything, demonstrated this necessity: no deceit was in His mouth (*I Pet.* 2: 22).

(c) Truth is that to which we are to cling (*I Tim.* 1: 19).

(d) Truth is to be spoken from the heart (*Ps.* 15: 2).

(e) We should mean what we say, ensuring that our speech is both direct and clear (*Matt.* 5: 37; *Jas.* 5: 12).

(f) Truthful speech may be expected to be accompanied by the power of God (*II Cor.* 6: 7).

(g) The necessity of truthfulness in us rests upon God's truthfulness (*I Pet.* 1: 15, 16; cf. *John* 18: 37); upon our exercise of truthfulness depends our experience of fellowship with God (*I John* 1: 5–10).

10. CONTENTMENT

Exodus 20: 17: "You shall not covet your neighbour's house. You shall not covet your neighbour's wife, or his manservant or maidservant, his ox or donkey, or anything that belongs to your neighbour."

Question: What does the tenth commandment teach?

Answer: The tenth commandment forbids wrong attitudes to the possessions and position of others, especially the attitudes of uncontrolled desire, envy and jealousy. It teaches rather that we should be content with what God has given to us, and covet those things He desires us to have and which will never harm anyone.

1. Defining covetousness.

(a) Covetousness, like all other sins, comes from within, out of our hearts (*Mark* 7: 21–23).

(b) It relates particularly to our desires, and our desires find their source in our hearts (*Ps.* 37: 4; *Rom.* 1: 24).

(c) Desires characterise both the body and mind, and prior to the experience of new birth they dominate our lives (*Rom.* 6: 12; *Eph.* 2: 3): we are tempted when we are lured and enticed by our desires (*Jas.* 1: 14, 15).

(d) Covetousness is essentially selfish desire (*Prov.* 21: 26; *Luke* 12: 1), indicating a basic discontent with what we already possess (*Heb.* 13: 5).

(e) The desires of our hearts and minds are prompted usually by what our eyes see and choose to focus upon (*Gen.* 3: 6; *Josh.* 7: 21; *Prov.* 27: 20).

(f) Covetousness, then, establishes a place in our thoughts (*Luke* 12: 17), usually in the form of secret thoughts about the possessions of others (*Micah* 2: 1, 2).

(g) Covetousness is an aspect of loving the world, and the things in the world, with the sad consequence that love for God is absent (*I John* 2: 15).

(h) It is God's law which brings home to us a real awareness of what covetousness is (*Rom.* 7: 7).

2. Some of the objects of covetousness.

(a) Objects of covetousness are mentioned in the commandment itself—for example, our neighbour's home, wife, employees and possessions (*Ex.* 20: 17)—and there are many forms of covetousness (*Luke* 12: 15; *Rom.* 7: 8).

(b) Covetousness finds its preoccupation with all that is in the world (*I John* 2: 16).

(c) Covetousness may have material possessions as its principal object, such as clothes (*Josh.* 7: 20, 21; *Acts* 20: 33) or property (*I Kings* 21: 2).

(d) Covetousness may have its focus upon money (*Acts* 20: 33; *I Tim.* 3: 3; 6: 9)—see, for example, Gehazi (*II Kings* 5: 20–24); Judas (*Matt.* 26: 14, 15; *John* 12: 6); and Ananias and Sapphira (*Acts* 5: 1–10).

(e) Covetousness may have as its wrongful object a physical or sexual relationship (*Eph.* 4: 19; 5: 3, 5, 6)—covetousness can lead a man into adultery (*Matt.* 5: 28).

(f) Covetousness may have as its object position and prestige (*I John* 2: 16—"the pride of life") or power (*Acts* 8: 18, 19).

3. Some of the snares of covetousness.

(a) It leads to deceit in that

the lips will try to cover up often the desires that are in the heart (*Ezek.* 33: 31; *I Thess.* 2: 5).

(b) It makes us slaves to our inward passions and desires (*Tit.* 3: 3; *II Pet.* 2: 19).

(c) It makes us blind to the fact that life is more than food, and the body more than clothing (*Luke* 12: 23).

(d) It makes us essentially selfish in that we think principally of ourselves (*Luke* 12: 19, 21).

(e) It leads us to store and hoard rather than to use our possessions to profit others (*Matt.* 6: 19).

(f) It causes us to store up for a future that may never be (*Luke* 12: 20), as well as neglecting the final accounting with God we must all make (*Luke* 12: 30).

(g) It shuts our life to the helpful influence and transforming power of God's Word (*Mark* 4: 19).

(h) It encourages us to put aside and ultimately destroy all other moral values (*II Tim.* 3: 2ff).

(i) It brings problems to others who are connected with us (*Josh.* 7: 20, 21), especially to our own family (*Prov.* 15: 27).

(j) It always brings antagonisms and conflicts in human relationships (*Jas.* 4: 1, 2) because by it malice, envy and hatred enter into our lives (*Tit.* 3: 3).

(k) It brings no true satisfaction (*Eccl.* 5: 10; *Hab.* 2: 5), but misery (*I Tim.* 6: 10) and ultimate poverty (*Prov.* 28: 22).

4. **The sinfulness of covetousness.**

(a) It is disobedience to the tenth commandment (*Ex.* 20: 17).

(b) It is idolatry, in that the covetous worship a false god (*Eph.* 5: 5): the original desire may be after something lawful in itself, but it grows to such a selfish intensity that it gains the place which God alone should have in our soul (*Col.* 3: 5).

(c) It lies behind many disagreements and disputes which spoil human relationships (*Luke* 12: 13, 14; *Jas.* 4: 1ff).

(d) It breaks one of the great

summaries of the commandments, "Love your neighbour as yourself" (*Rom.* 13: 9).

(e) It is on account of covetousness that we break often the other commandments of God: e.g. covetousness leads to not providing for and honouring our parents (*Mark* 7: 11), murder (*Prov.* 1: 18, 19; *Jer.* 22: 17; *Ezek.* 22: 12, 27), adultery (*II Sam.* 11: 2ff), theft (*Josh.* 7: 21), lying (*II Kings* 5: 22–25), and false accusation (*Acts* 16: 19–21).

5. The commandment teaches us to be content with what God has given to us—the opposite of covetousness.

(a) The willingness to work honestly for our living is put in opposition to covetousness (*Acts* 20: 33, 34).

(b) The awareness that our heavenly Father knows our needs and supplies them as is best for us leads us to appreciate how inappropriate regrets or complaints are in regard to what we possess (*Matt.* 6: 31, 32; *Rom.* 8: 28).

(c) Contentment for Christian believers is based upon the certainty of our Lord Jesus Christ's promises, and His presence (*Heb.* 13: 5), and the glorious assurance that He gives us all we need (*Ps.* 16: 5).

(d) Our contentment needs to be not in what we expect others to give, or what we may strive after, but in what God unfailingly provides for us by one means or another (*Phil* 4: 10–13).

(e) Contentment does not come easily to the majority of us, but it is a virtue that can be learned (*Phil.* 4: 11), as the Lord Jesus becomes the strength of our life (*Phil.* 4: 13).

(f) Those who follow the example of the Lord Jesus Christ remember and act upon His words, "It is more blessed to give than to receive" (*Acts* 20: 35).

6. There is a right kind of coveting.

(a) We usually associate the word "coveting" with unlawful desires but it can be used in a good sense as, for example, of the men and women of faith throughout the centuries who have coveted a better country, that is, a heavenly one, so that God is not ashamed to be called their God (*Heb.* 11: 16).

48

(b) There is a place for coveting spiritual leadership if God has given the necessary potential, and the honest desire is for the well-being of God's people and the glory of Jesus Christ (*I Tim.* 3: 1; *I Pet.* 5: 2–4).

(c) It is right to covet the best for others (*II Cor.* 11: 2; cf. *Rom.* 10: 1).

(d) Christians are to covet earnestly the best gifts, and most of all love (*I Cor.* 12: 31; 13: 1)—coveting like this does harm to no one · but only good!

II. TEMPTATION

Question: What is temptation? and how is it to be viewed and overcome?

Answer: Temptation is seduction into disobedience to God. It is to be viewed as a constant peril, and is overcome only by daily watchfulness and dependence upon God.

1. Defining and describing temptation.

(a) To be tempted is to be faced with the seeming attractiveness of sin so as to be in danger of being drawn into it—an experience common to all (*I Cor.* 10: 12).

(b) Temptation forces us to decide for or against God, and Satan tries by means of it to separate us from God (*Gen.* 3: 1–19).

(c) God is never the author of temptation (*Jas.* 1: 13), so that He can never be charged with being responsible for our sins.

(d) Satan, the ruler of this world (*John* 12: 31; 14: 30; 16: 11), is the tempter, who endeavours to take advantage of our desires (*I Cor.* 7: 5; *I Thess.* 3: 5; *Jas.* 1: 14).

(e) Some distinction must be made between temptations and trials, especially as the New Testament usually employs the identical Greek word for both, the right translation into English being determined by the context—when God's involvement is clear, testing is in view rather than temptation (*Gen.* 22:1–19; cf. *Heb.* 11:17–19; *Job* 1: 6–22; 2: 1–7).

(f) Temptation may come in various ways, but most obviously through our senses (*II*

Sam. 11: 2; *Job* 31: 1; *Matt.* 5: 27, 28), our desires (*I Cor.* 7: 5) and the weakness of our flesh (*Mark* 14: 38).

(g) Temptation may come through pride of position or status which inflates us and makes us forget our place before God (*Acts* 12: 21–23).

(h) Temptation may come through striving to help someone else, as we find ourselves tempted by the sins into which they have fallen (*Gal.* 6: 1).

(i) Temptation may come through the most unlikely instrumentality, like a best friend who misinterprets God's will for us, and wants us to choose an easy way rather than God's way (*Matt.* 16: 22, 23).

2. The encouragement of our Lord's temptation to the Christian.

(a) The temptations He experienced immediately after His baptism and again in the Garden of Gethsemane placed Him in a situation of open choice between surrender to God's will and revolt against it (*Matt.* 4: 1–11; 26: 36–46; *Mark* 1: 12, 13; 14: 32–42; *Luke* 4: 1–13; 22: 40–46).

(b) The three temptations were attempts to reduce the Lord Jesus to disobedience: first, to use His power for purposes out of keeping with His mission (*Matt.* 4: 3; *Luke* 4: 3); second, to invoke God's help on His own behalf (*Matt.* 4: 5; *Luke* 4: 9–11); third, to give up His obedience to God, and to follow Satan (*Matt.* 4: 8, 9; *Luke* 4: 5–7).

(c) It is because He Himself has been tempted by such suffering that He is able to help so adequately those who are now being tempted in the same way (*Heb.* 2: 18)—although He Himself did not sin (*Heb.* 4: 15).

(d) His perfect understanding encourages us to approach the throne of grace in His Name with perfect confidence, that we may receive mercy and find help in time of need (*Heb.* 4: 16).

(e) When we do fall before temptation, He acts as our High Priest, and we receive forgiveness in Him (*Col.* 1: 12, 13; *Heb.* 4: 14–16), as we honestly and contritely confess our sins (*I John* 1: 9).

3. Overcoming temptation.

(a) As a fruit of self-knowledge we must recognise our weakness (*Matt.* 26: 41; *Mark* 14: 38).

(b) We must recognise our essential dependence, therefore, upon our Lord Jesus Christ (*John* 15: 5; *Phil.* 4: 13).

(c) We must practice spiritual watchfulness (*Mark* 14: 38; *I Cor.* 10: 12; *Gal.* 6: 1; *I Pet.* 5: 8), sometimes taking preventative actions (*I Cor.* 7: 5).

(d) We must learn lessons from our past mistakes (*Job* 31: 1) and our previous experience of God's faithfulness (*I Cor.* 10: 13).

(e) We must deliberately put on the full armour of God (*Eph.* 6: 10–17), and then use our two principal weapons—the Scriptures (*Eph.* 6: 17; cf. *Matt.* 4: 4, 7, 10; *Luke* 4: 4, 8, 12) and prayer (*Mark* 14: 38; *Eph.* 6: 18).

(f) We must pray for discernment to know when to flee temptation (*II Tim.* 2: 22) and when it is God's will to withstand Satan and his temptations (*Jas.* 4: 7; *I Pet.* 5: 9), by the exercise of faith in the Lord Jesus (*Eph.* 6: 16).

(g) We must be in no doubt that God's purpose is that by the power of His Son, we may be able to stand our ground, and after we have done everything, to stand (*Eph.* 6: 10, 13).

12. WORLDLINESS

Question: What is worldliness? and why is it so serious?

Answer: Worldliness is essentially love of the world as it manifests itself in the lust of the flesh, the lust of the eyes, and the pride of life. It is so serious because it is in complete opposition to love of God.

1. Worldliness needs to be seen against the background of the Christian's position in the world.

(a) As God made the world, it was good (*Gen.* 1: 31; *I Tim.* 4: 4).

(b) The course of this world, however, has been tragically affected by man, through whose fall, on account of disobedience, death came into the world and rules over it (*Rom.* 5: 12 ff).

(c) The whole world lies in the

51

power of the prince of this world, the devil (*John* 12: 31; 16: 11; *Eph.* 2: 2; *I John* 5: 19).

(d) The whole world of mankind has become guilty before God (*Rom.* 3: 19); and even the created world has been subjected to frustration and longs for liberation (*Rom.* 8: 20–22).

(e) But it is into this world as it is, a world which has fallen into the power of sin and destruction, that God has sent His Son in order to reconcile it to Himself (*II Cor.* 5: 19 ff).

(f) Christians are those who have been delivered from this present evil world (or age) through the giving of the Lord Jesus Christ of Himself for their sins (*Gal.* 1: 3), and they appreciate now that they live in a world which in its present form is passing away (*I Cor.* 7: 31).

(g) Because Christians live in the world, they must have dealings with the world (*I Cor.* 5: 10; *Phil.* 2: 15), but they must resist the world's pressures to squeeze them into its mould (*Rom.* 12: 2), and they must endeavour to live as those who are dead to it (*Gal.* 6: 14).

(h) Christians are assured that everything belongs to them—including the world—but they themselves do not belong to the world any more (*John* 15: 19; 17: 14, 16; *Col.* 2: 20) but to the Lord Jesus Christ (*I Cor.* 3: 21 ff).

(i) Christians are to see the world as the sphere of their obedience to Christ (*Matt.* 28: 19, 20): it is God's harvest field (*Matt.* 9: 38; *Luke* 10: 2), in which they are harvesters, and also sowers by functioning as salt and light (*Matt.* 5: 13, 14), always holding out the word of life, the gospel (*Phil.* 2: 16).

(j) Because Christians are not taken out of the world at their new birth, the important thing is for them not to be conditioned any longer by the world (*Jas.* 1: 27).

2. Defining worldliness.

(a) Worldliness is the expression of the state of a man's heart (*Mark* 7: 21 ff), by his love of the world as a matter of deliberate choice (*Jas.* 4: 4; cf. *II Tim.* 4: 10), by which he lives according to worldly wisdom rather than the wisdom God gives (*Jas.* 3: 13; cf. 1: 5).

(b) Worldliness revolves, first, around the lust of the flesh, our human desires (*I John* 2: 16).

(c) Without a right relationship to God, man's life is dominated by the lusts and desires of this world, for there is little else for which he can live (*Tit.* 2: 12; *I Pet.* 4: 2–4; *II Pet.* 1: 4), and before their new birth Christians lived their lives obeying the promptings of their instincts and notions (*Eph.* 2: 3).

(d) Selfish desires within are always fighting for their own satisfaction, wanting us to indulge them, often leading us into personal conflicts and quarrels (*Jas.* 4: 1, 3, 4).

(e) Our lower nature's desires would constantly set themselves against the guidance and direction of the Holy Spirit (*Gal.* 5: 16); and Satan would fill our lives with wrong desires (*John* 8: 44).

(f) This aspect of worldliness with its emphasis on natural desires constituted the first temptation to which our Lord was subjected in the challenge to command a stone to be made bread (*Luke* 4: 1).

(g) Worldliness revolves, secondly, around the lust of the eyes (*I John* 2: 16), one manifestation of which is covetousness.

(h) Eyes are the organ of desire (*Josh.* 7: 21): the eye is the lamp of the whole body—when our eyes are good, our whole body is full of light, but sadly the converse is also true (*Luke* 11: 34 f),

(i) The desires of our eyes may often act on the philosophy that stolen water is sweet and bread eaten in secret is pleasant (*Prov.* 9: 17).

(j) Sometimes the lust of the eyes has a sexual connotation (*Job* 31: 1; *Matt.* 5: 29).

(k) Covetousness can lead to other sins, such as dishonesty (*II Kings* 5: 19–27) and murder (*I Kings* 19: 1–19; *Jas.* 4: 3).

(l) This aspect of worldliness was the second temptation Satan placed before our Lord when in a flash he showed Him all the kingdoms of this world, and offered them to Him at a price (*Luke* 4: 5, 6).

(m) Worldliness revolves, thirdly, around the pride of life, the empty pride we so often have in possessions and position (*I John* 2: 16).

(n) It is lust for advantage (*Matt.* 20: 21 ff).

(o) It is lust for status (*Acts* 12: 21–23).

(p) It is lust for self-importance, revealed often in boasting (*Luke* 18: 11, 12; *Jas.* 4: 16).

(q) It is lust for possessions (*Gen.* 13: 11; *Josh.* 7: 21; *Luke* 12: 13–21).

(r) The wrongful preoccupation with possessions is the cause of much of human anxiety (*Matt.* 6: 34).

(s) This aspect of worldliness was the third temptation Satan placed before the Lord Jesus as he encouraged Him to claim an open manifestation of God's protecting power, purely for personal prestige and pride of position (*Luke* 4: 9–11).

(t) Worldliness, in essence, therefore, is love of the world or the things in the world (*I John* 2: 15).

3. The seriousness of worldliness.

(a) It finds its roots in a man's heart rather than in the things he does or the places he frequents (*I John* 2: 15, 16), and God looks on the heart (*I Sam.* 16: 7).

(b) In direct opposition to God's will for man (*I John* 2: 17), it is in total opposition to love for the Father (*I John* 2: 15), and constitutes unfaithfulness to God or spiritual adultery (*Ps.* 73: 27; *Jas.* 4: 4), a direct opposite of godliness (*Tit.* 2: 14).

(c) It indicates a failure to appreciate the passing nature of this world (*Heb.* 12: 27; *I John* 2: 17), and the neglect of the all-important question: What shall it profit a man if he gain the whole world and lose his own soul? (*Mark* 8: 36; *Matt.* 16: 26; *Luke* 9: 25).

(d) It demonstrates where a man's heart is (*Luke* 12: 33 f), and where his treasures are to be found (*Matt.* 6: 19 ff), for it is impossible to serve God and mammon (*Matt.* 6: 24; *Luke* 16: 13).

(e) It boasts of itself rather than of God and treats life as if God does not exist (*Jas.* 4: 13–17).

(f) Worldliness is serious because it grows: it begins in the mind, shows itself in conduct, and becomes established in attitude (*Ps.* 1: 1).

(g) It chokes spiritual growth and fruitfulness (*Luke* 8: 14), and it may indicate that an individual is without the Spirit (*Jude* 13).

(h) When a Christian is worldly in spirit and attitude he grieves the Spirit (*Jas.* 4: 5).

(i) Worldliness will take away the Christian's appreciation of the means of grace (*Ps.* 84: 10; cf. *Heb.* 10: 25).

(j) Worldliness may make a man turn aside from that to which he has set his hand, a task which he has known to be God's will (*II Tim.* 4: 10).

(k) It may even reach a point at which his last state becomes worse than his first, in that his entanglement with the world's defilements is worse at the end than at the beginning (*II Pet.* 2: 20, 21).

4. The antidote to worldliness is the constant practice and pursuit of a number of objectives.

(a) An understanding that the purpose of our redemption by the death of Christ is that we, having been set free, purified from all wickedness, made God's chosen people, and inspired to do good (*Tit.* 2: 14; cf. *Gal.* 1: 4; *I Pet.* 1: 18 f; *II Pet.* 2: 20), should give up ungodliness and worldly desires, and, here and now, live lives that are disciplined, righteous and godly, while we await our Saviour's return (*Tit.* 2: 12, 13; cf. *II Pet.* 1: 3, 4).

(b) The realisation of our true character now in the world as strangers and passing travellers (*Heb.* 11: 13), and our essential foreignness (*I Pet.* 1: 17; 2: 11) because of our heavenly citizenship (*Eph.* 2: 19; *Phil.* 3: 20) and our commitment to seek first God's kingdom and His righteousness, leaving it to God to add to us what He knows we need of this world's possessions (*Matt.* 6: 33).

(c) The understanding that we are called upon to enter into the privilege of being friends of God (*Gen.* 2: 23; *John* 15: 14; *Jas.* 4: 4; *Rev.* 3: 20), a privilege which demands wholehearted obedience to Him as a condition of our enjoyment of this unspeakable privilege (*John* 14: 21, 23).

(d) The daily renewed offering of ourselves to God without reserve, in the light of His mercies towards us, so that instead of being conformed to this world we are instead transformed by the renewal of our mind, so that we prove in daily experience what is good and acceptable and perfect (*Rom.* 12: 1, 2), resolving to discover and to do God's will in everything (*I Thess.* 4: 3; *I Cor.* 10: 31).

(e) Honesty with ourselves both to examine ourselves (*I Cor.* 10: 12; 11: 28; *II Cor.* 13: 5), and to exercise self-control over our desires where they war against the best interests of our soul (*I Pet.* 2: 11); and if ever we are uncertain as to the rightness of our desires to present them to God in prayer for His judgment and guidance (*Jas.* 4: 2, 3).

(f) The key antidote to worldliness is the frank recognition of its seriousness and the active pursuit of sanctification, guided by the Word of God (*John* 17: 17).

Question: What is spiritual decline or backsliding?

Answer: Spiritual decline, or what the Bible calls "backsliding", is turning back from following the Lord. It takes a variety of forms, but it always begins with the thoughts, and eventually it shows itself in a life which is no longer wholehearted in its devotion to the Lord Jesus Christ.

1. Spiritual decline describes what the Bible calls "backsliding".

(a) It is the Christian ceasing to make every effort to progress in holiness and obedience (*II Pet.* 1: 5 ff).

(b) It is to turn back by degrees from following the Lord (*Zeph.* 1: 6).

(c) It is the turning of the heart away from God (*I Kings* 11: 9), so that the heart is not wholly true to God (*I Kings* 11: 4).

(d) It is to gradually forget God and the indebtedness the individual should feel to God (*Hos.* 2: 13).

(e) It is to deal faithlessly with the Lord (*Hos.* 5: 7), for inevitably the attempt is made to serve two masters (*Matt.* 6: 24).

(f) It is the abandonment of the love for Christ which the Christian knew at first (*Rev.* 2: 4).

(g) It is the pushing of Christ outside of the life (*Rev.* 3: 20).

(h) It is spiritual adultery (*Hos.* 1: 2; *Jas.* 4: 3).

2. **The form which spiritual decline or "backsliding" takes varies a great deal but certain stages, not always in the order outlined, may be discerned.**

(a) It all begins with the thoughts: the thoughts are led astray from a sincere and pure devotion to Christ (*II Cor.* 11: 3).

(b) Little by little the private aspects of the Christian life—such as private prayer—are neglected (*Jas.* 4: 2; *Luke* 18: 1).

(c) Slackness in service soon follows (*Heb.* 6: 10, 11).

(d) Appreciation of the opportunities for fellowship, public worship, and the ministry of God's Word lessens, and this lessening of appreciation leads to neglect of them (*Ps.* 84: 10; *Heb.* 5: 11, 12; 10: 25).

(e) In spite of this obvious decline, there may be complete complacency about the situation in the individual's mind, a spiritual short-sightedness (*Amos* 6: 1, 4–7; *II Pet.* 1: 9; *Rev.* 3: 17).

(f) It is more than likely that the individual will be inclined to criticise his more spiritual fellow-Christians (*Phil.* 1: 15, 16).

(g) He begins to forget and lose the wonder of the Cross —the manner in which he was first cleansed from his sins (*II Pet.* 1: 9).

(h) Whereas he ought to be able to teach others the Christian faith, he needs, in fact, someone to teach him again the ABC of God's Word (*Heb.* 5: 12).

(i) He loses his appreciation of the deeper truths of the faith and of the Bible (*Heb.* 5: 12; *I Cor.* 3: 2).

(j) He becomes unskilled in using the Bible, whereas once he had facility in doing so (*Heb.* 5: 13).

(k) He loses his ability to discern good from evil in the

everyday situations of life (*Heb*. 5: 14).

(l) The promises of God no longer seem very great and precious, and they cease to influence the course of his life (*II Pet*. 1: 4; *Heb*. 6: 12).

(m) Guidance in daily life is no longer sought (*Zeph*. 1: 6).

(n) Compromise, in situation after situation, makes the individual's spiritual life—and life in general—more and more unstable (*Jas*. 1: 6–8), and the process accelerates (*Gal*. 5: 9).

(o) In the end he becomes completely ineffective and unfruitful in the knowledge of our Lord Jesus Christ (*II Pet*. 1: 8).

3. The causes of spiritual decline or "backsliding" are many and it may be caused by just one such cause or the combination of several.

(a) The neglect of prayer; or, on the other hand, the offering of prayer but from the wrong motives, with conduct completely contrary to God's revealed will (*Jas*. 4: 2, 3).

(b) Giving in to sin, with the sin unrepented of and uncon-fessed (*Ps*. 51: 3, 4; *Gal*. 6: 1).

(c) Disobedience to the obvious and known will of God for the individual's life (*Jonah* 1: 2–3; *Jer*. 8: 5–7; *Neh*. 9: 26; *I Cor*. 10: 23).

(d) Love of the world (*Luke* 8: 14; *Rom*. 12: 2; *II Tim*, 4: 10; *I John* 2: 15–17; *Jas*. 4: 1–3; *Rev*. 3: 4).

(e) A human relationship—especially with someone of the other sex—taking the place which God alone should have (*I Kings* 11: 4; *II Cor*. 6: 14).

(f) Discouragement, through the power of unbelief—this was the case apparently with the Hebrew Christians addressed in the Epistle to the Hebrews (*Heb*. 6: 9–20).

(g) Never having been properly established in the Christian life, as was the case with some of the Corinthian believers (*I Cor*. 3: 1–3).

(h) Self-assurance—instead of self-distrust and trust in Christ—is a cause of spiritual decline (*Prov*. 16: 18; *Mark* 14: 29, 31; *I Cor*. 10: 12).

(i) The pursuit of false and unworthy ambitions (*Jas*. 4: 3).

(j) A lack of self-examination (*I Cor.* 11: 31).

4. The consequences of spiritual decline or "backsliding".

(a) It grieves the Holy Spirit (*Eph.* 4: 30).

(b) It makes the Christian good-for-nothing or useless in fulfilling God's purposes in the world (*Matt.* 5: 13).

(c) It removes the joy of God's salvation (*Ps.* 51: 12).

(d) The sense of God's presence is lost (*Num.* 14: 43; *Isa.* 59: 2, 9–11).

(e) The ability to teach others the way of God is lost (*Ps.* 51: 13).

(f) Some form of idolatry is soon practised (*Zeph* 1: 4–6).

(g) All kinds of sins may follow (*Prov.* 14: 14; *Isa.* 1: 5–6; *Hos.* 4): not least those which arise from unlawful associations (*Hos.* 5: 7).

(h) The backslider may find himself so carried away that he discovers himself to be contending for the world against God (*Judg.* 6: 28–32).

(i) Backsliding leads to a complacency which is full of danger (*Rev.* 3: 17; *I Cor.* 10: 12).

(j) It makes the Christians concerned nauseating to Christ (*Rev.* 3: 16).

(k) Unchecked, it is liable to increase (*Jer.* 8: 5; 14: 7).

(l) It brings the believer under the displeasure of God (*Ps.* 78: 57, 59).

(m) It brings the discipline and judgment of God (*Hos.* 11: 5–7); it brings reproof and chastisement from Christ (*Rev.* 3: 19).

14. SPIRITUAL RESTORATION

Question: How may the Christian in spiritual decline, i.e. the backslider, be restored?

Answer: The Christian in spiritual decline, i.e. the backslider, may be restored when he comes to himself, realises the seriousness of his position and fulfils carefully the conditions given in the Scriptures. As the conditions are fulfilled, God's promises come into operation to accomplish full and glorious restoration.

1. The restoration of the backslider or the Christian whose

spiritual life is in decline is clearly taught in the Bible.

(a) The backslider's state is not hopeless (*Ps.* 37: 24; *Prov.* 24: 16).

(b) Nothing, however, can be done for the backsliding Christian until he feels restless and miserable (*Mark* 14: 72)—his conscience needs to be probed and stirred (*John* 21: 15–17).

(c) Restoration is achieved only by the help of God (*Hos.* 12: 6).

(d) Backsliders are exhorted to return to the Lord (*II Chron.* 30: 6; *Isa.* 31: 6; *Jer.* 3: 12, 14, 22; *Hos.* 14: 1–3).

(e) The Lord uses chastisement to bring the backslider back to Himself (*Hos.* 2: 6; 5: 15; 6: 1).

(f) A spiritual Christian may be used by the Lord to restore a backsliding Christian (*Gal.* 6: 1; *Jas.* 5: 19)—perhaps by a pointed question (*Gal.* 4: 15) or by direct accusation (*II Sam.* 12: 1–13).

(g) Restoration can take place only when the backslider has come to himself (*Luke* 15: 17), perhaps through seeing the chastising hand of God in his circumstances (*Jonah* 2: 2–4).

2. The Lord promises the pardon of the backslider and the reviving of the Christian whose spiritual life is in decline on certain conditions (II Chron. 7: 14).

(a) The recognition that deliverance belongs to the Lord —it is not in the power of the Christian on his own to effect (*Jonah* 2: 9).

(b) The remembrance of the rightful jealousy God has for His people (*Deut.* 32: 16, 21; *Ex.* 20: 5; 34: 14; *Zech.* 8: 2; *Jas.* 4: 5).

(c) All arrogance must be removed—self-assurance must be put aside (*Jas.* 4: 6).

(d) Submission to God—the backslider's return must be accompanied by the humbling of his pride, or else his profession of seeking God is of no avail (*Jas.* 4: 6; cf. *Hos.* 5: 5–7).

(e) Resistance to the devil, for he will surely contest the move to return to the Lord (*Jas.* 4: 7; *I Pet.* 5: 8, 9; *Eph.* 6: 16).

(f) Drawing near to God (*II Chron.* 7: 14; *Jas.* 4: 8)—prayers for restoration are provided in the Bible for our help and guidance (*Ps.* 80: 3; 85: 4; *Lam.* 5: 21).

(g) The sin of backsliding is to be confessed (*Jer.* 3: 13, 14; 14: 7–9) and the merits of Christ's atoning death depended upon, even as when the Christian was first converted (*I John* 1: 9, 7).

(h) The things which have turned the individual aside are to be resolutely abandoned (*Isa.* 1: 16–20; *II Chron.* 7: 14; *Ps.* 24: 4; *Jas.* 4: 8)—backsliding is soon renewed if repentance is not real (*II Cor.* 7: 10); remorse, therefore, is not to be mistaken for repentance (*Judg.* 2: 4, 5, 11–23). (i) Self-humbling before God (*Prov.* 3: 34; *Jas.* 4: 6; *I Pet.* 5: 5).

3. As the conditions God lays down are fulfilled, so His promises come into operation to accomplish restoration.

(a) Praying now out of the right motives, the individual will receive that for which he asks (*Jas.* 4: 2, 3).

(b) The Holy Spirit, who has been grieved, will immediately assist the Christian in his efforts to return to the Lord (*Jas.* 4: 5).

(c) As the Christian seeks to humble himself before God in submission, he will be given grace from God (*Jas.* 4: 6); this grace will include help in resisting the devil to the end that the devil may flee from him (*Jas.* 4: 7).

(d) As he draws near to God, so God will come closer to him (*Jas.* 4: 8).

(e) As he confesses his sin, God is just, and may be trusted to forgive him his sins and to cleanse him from every kind of sin (*I John* 1: 9).

(f) As he continues to humble himself before the Lord, so the Lord will lift him up anew into the joys of new life in Christ (*Jas.* 4: 10).

(g) His desire and ability to teach transgressors God's ways will be regained (*Ps.* 51: 13).

(h) There is no doubt whatsoever about the Lord's healing, love and reviving, if the conditions are fulfilled (*Hos.* 14: 4–7; *Jer.* 3: 22)—the love that first pardoned the Christian's sins heals backsliding (*Micah* 7: 18).

4. From what has been deduced from the Bible about spiritual

decline or "backsliding", certain results obviously follow upon restoration after such an experience.

(a) The regaining of the joy of God's salvation (*Ps.* 51: 12).

(b) A greater appreciation of Jesus Christ—the Saviour and Restorer of the soul.

(c) An increased hatred of sin.

(d) A more sensitive awareness to the first approaches of sin and temptation.

(e) A new appreciation of the means of grace, and a more diligent use of them.

(f) A renewed and deepened dedication to the service of Christ (*Jonah* 3: 1; *John* 21: 15–17).

15. CHRISTIAN WORSHIP

Question: What does the Bible teach about worship?

Answer: Worship is our acknowledgement of God in a manner acceptable to Him which means a wholehearted dependence upon Jesus Christ and the way He has opened up for us into God's presence; a recognition of the inwardness and spiritual nature of true worship; and an obedient awareness that the worship of God cannot be separated from conduct which glorifies Him.

1. Worship is the acknowledging of God in a manner worthy and pleasing to Him.

(a) The English word "worship" means simply "worthship", and denotes the worthiness of the person receiving the special honour due to his worth. Worship and service are presented to us as being virtually the same—the identical Hebrew word can be used for either "worship" or "service" and the same holds true in the New Testament in the use of the Greek word for "worship".

(b) Worship is rejoicing in all that God is, and giving Him the glory, i.e. ascribing to Him the things which rightly belong to Him, such as glory, honour, power, salvation, and thanksgiving (*Rev.* 4: 9, 11; 19: 1, 7).

(c) Worship can be simply that of the individual (*Gen.* 24: 26), but the emphasis is more generally upon corporate worship (*Ps.* 42: 4).

2. God alone is to be worshipped.

(a) The primary reference of worship is Godward—it is "to God" (*Col.* 3: 16).

(b) Worship presupposes that God is, that He rewards those who seek Him (*Heb.* 11: 6).

(c) God does not live in temples made by man. He is in fact not far from each one of us: "In Him we live and move and have our being" (*Acts* 17: 24, 27, 28).

(d) God wants men to seek Him, in the hope that they might feel after Him and find Him (*Acts* 17: 27).

(e) God alone is to be worshipped, and the revelation God has given forbids us to worship anyone besides God (*Ex.* 20: 3; *Matt.* 4: 10; *Rev.* 19: 10).

(f) We must beware of worshipping either the gifts or the messengers of God (*Rom.* 1: 25; *Rev.* 19 :10; 22: 9).

(g) Worship is God's due as our Creator (*Ps.* 100: 1, 2; *Rom.* 1: 25; *Rev.* 4: 11)—He is the Maker of the world and everything in it, the Lord of heaven and earth (*Acts* 17: 24).

(h) Worship is God's due as our Redeemer (*John* 3: 16); God the Father is the source of all blessing, and is thus to be Himself blessed (*Eph.* 1:3).

(i) God in Christ is the definite, special object of Christian worship (*Eph.* 5: 19): spiritual worship of God is synonymous with joy in Christ, and a renunciation of all confidence in the flesh (*Phil.* 3: 3).

(j) In worshipping Christ we worship the Father (*Eph.* 5: 19, 20; *Col.* 3: 16), for He is the Son of God (*Matt.* 14: 33), the visible image of the invisible God (*Heb.* 1: 3; *Col.* 1: 15).

(k) Our praise and thanksgiving go to the Father through the Lord Jesus Christ and in His Name (*Eph.* 5: 20).

(l) The Lord Jesus, as the Lamb who was slain, is rightly the centre of our worship (*Rev.* 5: 8–14), to the glory of God the Father (*Phil.* 2: 11).

(m) Christians are to meet together for worship (*I Cor.* 14: 26; *Heb.* 10: 24), and such worship is appropriate as often as God's people have the opportunity of meeting together (*Acts* 2: 46, 47).

(n) The particular day for worship, however, is the first day of the week, the Lord's Day (Acts 20: 7; *Rev*. 1: 10).

3. The basis of worship.

(a) Whenever men would worship God, they are confronted with the great and glorious, but awesome truth, that God is holy (*Ps*. 24: 3, 4; *Isa*. 6; *I John* 1: 5–7).

(b) Worship rests upon revelation from God as to how worship is possible for sinful men; and Christian worship rests upon the revelation of Jesus Christ and the way He has opened up for us into God's presence (*Eph*. 2: 13–18; *Rev*. 1: 12–17).

(c) Worship depends upon God's grace: He is graciously willing to be approached (*Ps*. 5: 7; 138: 2).

(d) We can approach God solely on the grounds of what the Lord Jesus Christ has done for us: by virtue of His blood shed for us, we may have confidence to come before God (*Heb*. 10: 19).

(e) The Lord Jesus Christ has opened up for us a new and living way into God's presence (*Heb*. 10: 20).

(f) We may draw near to God with a true heart and with fullest confidence, knowing that our guilty consciences have been purified by the sprinkling of Christ's blood, just as our bodies are cleansed by the washing of clean water (*Heb*. 10: 22).

(g) In view of such a provision, worship is indeed part of our gratitude to God (*Heb*. 12: 28): the soul, the heart, and the flesh of the believer long to express worship to God (*Ps*. 84: 2).

(h) Every new experience of God's grace in Christ increases our desire to worship the Lord (*Ps*. 27: 6; *Luke* 5: 8; *Rev*. 1: 12–17).

(i) Worship should be our instinctive reaction to the discovery of some token of God's working on our behalf (*Judg*. 7: 15).

4. Characteristics of true worship.

(a) The place of worship is not important, but the manner of worship is (*John* 4: 20–24).

(b) Worship of God must be on the basis of a knowledge of God that is true (*Acts*. 17: 23) —a fact which underlines the importance of the understanding given to us in the Scriptures (*John* 4: 22); worship must be according to God's Word, and not according to the ideas and precepts of men (*Isa.* 29: 13; *Mark* 7: 6–8).

(c) Expressed another way, worship requires some glimpse of God's glory (*Josh.* 5: 13–15; *Isa.* 6; *II Cor.* 4: 6).

(d) Awe and reverence are to characterise our worship of God (*Ps.* 5: 7; *Heb.* 12: 28).

(e) We should never enter into worship carelessly, allowing our lips to be rash and slick in expression of worship (*Eccl.* 5: 1, 2).

(f) The worship we offer to God is to be spiritual, that is to say, inspired and aided by God's Holy Spirit (*John* 4: 23, 24; *Phil.* 3: 3), for God delights not in outward acts but in the spiritual worship of the heart (*Ps.* 40:6; 50: 7–15).

(g) The worship we offer to God is to be sincere (*Isa.* 1: 11–15): it is acceptable to Him only as our motives are right (*Amos* 5: 18–27).

(h) Worship is in vain if the feelings of the heart do not correspond with the expression of the lips (*Mark* 7: 6, 7); God has regard to our worship when it is sincere and the best we can offer; but He has no regard to that which is formal and less than our best (*Gen.* 4: 3, 5).

(i) Worship is to combine fervour with the use of the mind (*I Cor.* 14: 14, 15); the mind and understanding are to be active in our worship of God (*I Cor.* 14: 14).

(j) Worship should always include the spirit of submission to God (*Josh.* 5: 14), for it cannot be separated from obedience (*Josh.* 5: 14, 15; *I Sam.* 15: 22; cf. *Gen.* 22: 5).

(k) Worship should cost us something (*II Sam.* 24: 22–24; *Mal.* 1: 6–11; cf. *Gen.* 4: 1–7): it is better not to worship God at all than to offer that which is knowingly and deliberately inferior.

(l) Worship is to be conducted decently and in order (*I Cor.* 14: 40), for God is not a God of confusion, but of peace (*I Cor.* 14: 33).

(m) Worship is also to be edifying, for although its primary reference is Godward, it has, at the same time, an edifying influence upon believers (*Col.* 3: 16); nothing is to find a place in the worship of God which is unedifying (*I Cor.* 14: 26).

(n) In our meeting together, we are to think of one another and how we can encourage one another to love and to good deeds (*Heb.* 10: 24, 25): by our hymns, psalms and spiritual songs we should be addressing one another in our worship of God (*Eph.* 5: 19).

(o) It perhaps needs to be pointed out that the evidence of the Bible indicates that worship may influence the posture of the body, even though God's concern is with the inward attitude of the heart rather than the outward activity (*John* 4: 24).

(p) Worship is expressed by posture (*Rev.* 5: 14; 7: 11; 19: 4; cf. *Phil.* 2: 10); the outward attitude of the body is not a matter of indifference (*Gen.* 24: 26; *Ex.* 33: 10; *I Chron.* 29: 20).

5. Worship and morality.

(a) It is important to notice that the major definitions of worship in the New Testament are all inward and ethical (*Rom.* 12: 1 ff; *Heb.* 13: 15, 16; *Jas.* 1: 27).

(b) Worship has no value apart from the person who offers it (*Gen.* 4: 4, 5); Abel's faith in God as he worshipped was decisive for his acceptance (*Heb.* 11: 4); Cain's life, unlike Abel's, gave the lie to his offering (*I John* 3: 12).

(c) Worship of God must be accompanied by righteousness of life (*Ps.* 40: 6–8; *Isa.* 1: 10–17; *Amos* 5: 21–24; *Micah* 6: 6–8): the worship which the Lord requires is a matter not of sacrifices, but rather of justice, kindness, and a humble walk with Himself (*Micah* 6: 6–8).

(d) God is as concerned with the morality of His people as with their worship (*Jer.* 7: 2 ff; *Mal.* 3: 4, 5): worship is not acceptable to God if we are knowingly in a wrong relationship to someone, without having sought to rectify the situation (*Matt.* 5: 23 f).

(e) Worship is linked with the service of our fellowmen (*Heb.* 13: 15, 16; *Jas.* 1: 27); worship must certainly never be an excuse for passing over need

Luke 10: 25–37; *Acts* 3: 1–10, noting verse 1).

5. Parts of worship.

(a) Our worship should always contain praise to God for the understanding we have of His activity on our behalf. (*Ps.* 27: 6); through Christ we continually offer up a sacrifice of praise to God, that is, the fruit of lips that acknowledge His name (*Heb.* 13: 15).

(b) Thanksgiving too should have a regular place in all worship (*Ps.* 136; *Jonah* 2: 9; *Eph.* 5: 20).

(c) Prayer is part of worship (*Luke* 2: 37; *I Cor.* 14: 14–16).

(d) By reason of particular circumstances, perhaps the need for guidance from God, or the necessity of making a decision, fasting alongside prayer is part of worship at times (*Luke* 2: 37; *Acts* 13: 2).

(e) Songs have a place in Christian worship (*Acts* 16:25; *I Cor.* 14: 26; *Eph.* 5: 19; *Col.* 3: 16; *Jas.* 5: 13) for the Holy Spirit inspires a joy which expresses itself in psalms, hymns and spiritual songs (*Eph.* 5: 18, 19).

(f) We may have fragments of early Christian hymns in the New Testament (e.g. *Eph.* 4: 4–6; 5: 14; *Phil.* 2: 5–11; *I Tim.* 1:17; 2:5f; 6:15f; *II Tim.* 2: 11–13; *Rev.* 4: 11).

(g) Singing must be rooted in the word of Christ, for it has as one of its purposes the indwelling of that word in us (*Col.* 3: 16).

(h) The Lord's Supper is part of Christian worship (*Acts* 20: 7; *I Cor.* 11: 23–34).

(i) Worship consists of almsgiving (*I Cor.* 16: 1, 2): our gifts can represent a fragrant offering, a sacrifice acceptable and pleasing to God (*Phil.* 4: 18).

(j) Worship includes the reading of the Scriptures (*Col.* 3: 16; *Jas.* 1: 22), and the preaching of the Word (*Acts* 20: 7; *I Cor.* 14: 19); it is to include instruction and encouragement for believers (*I Cor.* 14: 31).

(k) Christians are to seek to contribute to worship (*I Cor.* 14: 26), which means that we should always be participators rather than spectators.

7. The experience of worship.

(a) As we worship God, by means of all the different parts and aspects of worship, we desire to be in God's presence, to behold His beauty, and to have fellowship with Him (*Ps.* 27: 4; 63:2).

(b) Worship will sometimes be a timely way of escape for us (*I Cor.* 10: 13): living in the world and making our witness there, we shall often be oppressed by the spirit of the world, and the evil prevalent in it, but our means of relief and temporary escape will be the worship of God (*Ps.* 120).

(c) Worship should be a humbling experience (*Gen.* 18: 27; *Job* 42: 5, 6; *Isa.* 6: 1–5).

(d) In worship we should draw near to God to listen (*Eccl.* 5: 1), for it may be a time when God's voice is heard in guidance (*Acts* 13: 1–3).

(e) As we worship the Lord and regain our spiritual balance, we see things more clearly and in a better light (*Ps.* 73: 17).

(f) We should not forget that worship is part of our witness to God in the world (*I Pet.* 2: 9, 10; cf. *I Cor.* 11: 26).

(g) Indeed there will be occasions when God will use the worship of His people as a powerful instrument of conviction in the lives of unbelievers who may be present (*I Cor.* 14: 24, 25).

16. PRAYER

Question: What is prayer? and how should it be exercised?

Answer: Prayer is the communion we know with God as our Father through our Lord Jesus Christ, in which we express our dependence upon Him, and ask Him for the good things He wants us to ask Him for, both for ourselves and others.

1. Defining prayer.

(a) Prayer is asking God for the good things He wants to give to His children (*Matt.* 7: 7, 11; *Luke* 11: 9, 10; *Col.* 1: 9; *Jas.* 1: 5. 6); it is sharing with Him what we or others lack (*John* 2: 3; *Jas.* 1: 5).

(b) Prayer is the offering up of our desires to God (*Ps.* 62: 8).

(c) If we know that a desire is right, we may with confidence and assurance ask for its fulfilment (*Rom.* 10: 1); if, however, we are not sure, we may bring our desire to God, in the form of a request, to which His answer may be "No" (*Rom.* 1: 10; *II Cor.* 12: 8, 9; *I Thess.* 3: 10).

(d) Prayer is the surrendering of our wills of God (*Matt.* 6: 10)—our Lord is our example here as in the Garden of Gethsemane He three times prayed the same prayer (*Matt.* 26: 39, 42, 44).

(e) Prayer is being with God, since it is not always asking but sometimes simply an expression of fellowship with God, with the desire on our part to be in His presence (*Ps.* 27: 4)—we try to be still before Him, recognising that He alone is God (*Ps.* 46: 10, 11), and we share our life with Him (*Rev.* 3: 20).

(f) Prayer is conversation with God (*Gen.* 18: 23 ff; *Ex.* 5: 22; 6: 1, 10, 12, 28–30; *Deut.* 3: 23–26): God says "Seek my face!" and we reply, "Your face, Lord, I will seek" (*Ps.* 27: 8 cf. *Acts* 13: 1, 2).

(g) Prayer is a key to our experience of God's peace (*Phil.* 4: 6, 7), for a burden shared with God is far more than a burden halved—it is a burden lifted and carried by God (*I Pet.* 5: 7).

2. Some basic principles and rules of prayer.

(a) A first principle of prayer is that we must be in fellowship with God (*Prov.* 15: 8): reconciled to God through faith in our Lord Jesus Christ, our fellowship is with the Father and with the Son (*I John* 1: 3), and we may call God "Our Father" (*Luke* 11: 2; *Rom.* 8: 15).

(b) A second rule of prayer is the practice of obedience—by putting away sin (*Ps.* 66: 18; *I John* 1: 9), by maintaining right relationships with others (*Matt.* 5: 23, 24; *I Pet.* 3: 7), and by striving to abide in Christ (*John* 15: 7).

(c) A third rule of prayer is dependence upon the Lord Jesus Christ and His work on our behalf (*Eph.* 2: 13)—we pray in His Name (*John* 14: 13, 14; 15: 16; 16: 23, 24, 26).

(d) A fourth rule of prayer is the exercise of faith (*Heb.* 11: 6; *Jas.* 1: 6–8)—if we believe, we will receive whatever we ask for in prayer (*Matt.* 21: 22; *Mark* 11: 23, 24), and believing prayer has the assurance that we may receive beyond all our asking (*Eph.* 3: 20).

(e) A fifth rule of prayer is readiness for action, for faith and works go together (*Jas.* 2: 17): having prayed, we must be ready to be the instruments on occasions by means of which God answers our prayers (*Ex.* 14: 15; *Matt.* 9: 37, 38; cf. 10: 1 ff).

(f) A sixth principle of prayer is the honest desire for God's will to be done, and His Name to be glorified (*Matt.* 6: 10; *I John* 5: 14; cf. *Ex.* 32: 11–13; *Matt.* 26: 39).

(g) A seventh principle of prayer is sincerity: God has no time for hypocrites who make a lot of show without reality in their hearts (*Isa.* 29: 13; *Mark* 12: 40), but He promises to be near those who call upon Him in truth (*Ps.* 145: 18).

3. Prayer's parts.

(The Bible prescribes no set order for the different parts of prayer, and our daily circumstances will dictate a varying starting point. However, there is a natural order, although not binding, which Scripture suggests.)

(a) **Adoration** consists in reverencing God in a spirit of worship (*Ps.* 89: 7, 8; *Isa.* 6: 1, 2).

(b) **Praise** concerns itself with what God is, and it gives glory to God (*Ps.* 18: 3; 145: 3).

(c) **Thanksgiving** focuses upon what God has done for us (*Phil.* 4: 6), and, no matter what our circumstances, there is always cause for thanksgiving to God (*Ps.* 126: 3; *Eph.* 1: 3; *I Thess.* 5: 18).

(d) **Confession of sin** is a vital part of prayer for the maintenance of our fellowship with God (*I John* 1: 5, 6, 9), for "he who conceals his sins does not prosper, but whoever confesses and renounces them finds mercy" (*Prov.* 28: 13).

(e) **Prayer and supplication** are separate, yet related (*I Tim.* 2: 1; *Eph.* 6: 18): prayer has regard to the needs which are always present with us (as represented in the petitions of the Lord's Prayer—*Matt.* 6: 9–13) and **supplication** has regard to specific situations where special or emergency help is required (as illustrated in Mary's petition to Jesus at the wedding in Cana—*John* 2: 3—and Mary and Martha's message to Jesus about Lazarus—*John* 11: 3).

(f) **Intercession** approaches God for others (*Col.* 4: 12): we are to pray for all men without distinction of race, nationality or social position (*I Tim.* 2: 1, 2): when they are in need or are rebellious (*Ex.* 8: 12, 30; 32: 11, 13, 32; *Num.* 14: 13–19; cf. *Jer.* 15: 1); when they are ill (*Jas.* 5: 14); when they are unjustly treated, and perhaps imprisoned (*Acts* 12: 5; *Heb.* 13: 3); and even when they are our enemies (*Matt.* 5: 44; *Luke* 23: 34).

(g) Governments and rulers are not to be neglected in our intercession (*I Tim.* 2: 2).

(h) In praying for missionaries, for example, we should pray for their deliverance from malicious enemies, acceptance with God's people, health of mind and body, the ability to speak the right words boldly at the moment of opportunity, the turning of untoward circumstances to good, God-given opportunities for preaching Christ and progress in the establishment of the Church (*Rom.* 15: 30, 31; *II Cor.* 1: 11; *Eph.* 6:19; *Phil.* 1: 19; *Col.* 4: 3; *II Thess.* 3: 1).

(i) **Dedication to God** and to His will must be the background to all our prayers (*Rom.* 12: 1, 2; *Heb.* 10: 7).

4. **Characteristics of prayer at its best.**

(a) **Reverence** (*Gen.* 18: 25, 27; *Acts* 9: 31; 10: 2; *II Cor.* 5: 11; *Heb.* 12: 28).

(b) **Humility** (*Ps.* 10: 17; *Luke* 18: 9–14; *Jas.* 4: 6).

(c) **Boldness** (*Eph.* 3: 12; *Heb.* 4: 15, 16).

(d) **In accordance with Scripture** (*I Thess.* 4: 3; *I Tim.* 2: 1–3; *I John* 5: 14, 15).

(e) **Definiteness** (*I Chron.* 4: 10; *John* 17; *Eph.* 1: 16–23; 3: 14–21; *Phil.* 1: 3–11; *Col.* 1: 9–12).

(f) **Intelligence** (*I Cor.* 14: 15; cf. *Neh.* 1: 1–11).

(g) **Earnestness** (*Luke* 11: 5–13; *Mark* 7: 27; *Jas.* 5: 17).

(h) **Persistence** (*Gen.* 32: 26; *I Thess.* 5: 17).

(i) **Submission to God** (*Matt.* 26: 39; *Mark* 14: 39; *Luke* 22: 42; *Rom.* 12: 1, 2).

(j) Fasting (*Neh.* 1:4; *Matt.* 4:
2)—some situations are dealt
with satisfactorily only by
prayer and fasting (*Matt.* 17:
21; cf. *Acts* 14:21–23).

5. Our chief Helper in prayer is the Holy Spirit.

(a) In the gift of the Holy
Spirit (*Acts* 2: 38), God has
provided a perfect Helper who
is with us for ever (*John* 14:
16), and who attests to our
spirits that we are children of
God, helping us cry, "Abba"
(*Rom.* 8: 15; cf. *Gal.* 4: 6).

(b) He prompts us to pray by
bringing to our minds the
words and promises of our
Lord Jesus Christ (*John* 14:
26), and He urges us to pray
according to the will of God
which they reveal.

(c) He also prompts our concern for individuals (*Rom.* 10:
1; cf. 9: 1, 2), so that we feel
it to be sin if we do not pray
for them (*I Sam.* 12: 23).

(d) When the Holy Spirit ex-
cites our feelings, He also enables us to give utterance to
those feelings, in the right
manner—He intercedes for
us according to God's will
(*Rom.* 8: 26, 27).

(e) Prayer is to be in the Spirit

(*Eph.* 6: 18; *Jude* 20): praying
in the Spirit, we depend upon
Him as we ask for the things
we know to be right and in
accord with God's will (*Matt.*
6: 9–13; *Luke* 11: 2–4), and
the result is a renewed experience of God's peace, and an
attitude of complete sub-
mission to God's will, no
matter how He may choose to
answer our prayers (*Phil.* 4: 6,
7; *II Cor.* 12: 7–10).

(f) We must never forget that
the Holy Spirit is a Person
whom we both grieve (*Eph.*
4: 30) and quench (*I Thess.* 5:
19) by sin.

(g) By the Spirit's help we can
fulfil our Lord's instruction
that we should always pray
and not give up (*Luke* 18: 1;
Rom. 8: 26; *I Thess.* 5: 17).

17. THE STATE

Question: What is the relationship of Christians to the state
and what should be their attitude towards human authorities?

Answer: The relationship of
Christians to the state is determined by the understanding

the Bible gives of God's establishment of those in authority. The duty of Christians is to uphold all rightful authority and to strive to be good citizens, demonstrating by their exemplary conduct that their true citizenship is in heaven. On those infrequent occasions when the state demands an obedience contrary to God's commands, their duty then is to obey God.

1. God's establishment of those in authority.

(a) There is no authority except from God, and those that exist have been instituted by Him (*Rom.* 13: 1).

(b) God confers upon men the right to govern (*I Kings* 19: 15; *II Kings* 8: 9–13; *Jer.* 27: 6; *John* 19: 11).

(c) Men's rule is temporary, however, whereas God's rule is eternal (*Dan.* 4: 31), and He installs and removes kings (*Dan.* 2: 21), and at any moment He can bring their dominion to an end (*Dan.* 7: 12).

(d) God is like a potter who can do what He likes with the clay (*Rom.* 9: 21; cf. *Prov.* 8: 15; *Isa.* 26: 16; *Jer.* 18: 6); He can stir up the spirits of heathen kings so that they accomplish His purposes (*II Chron.* 36: 22, 23; *Ezra* 1: 1 ff; *Isa.* 44: 28; 45: 1).

(e) There are various institutions of government ordained for man's common good (*I Pet.* 2: 13). (Within every people or nation, permanently settled in a geographical area, there needs to be a public authority with the power of ultimate decision which exacts obedience, and is capable of enforcing its legislative and executive measures for the protection of all, both from internal and external enemies—cf. *Acts* 17: 26).

(f) There are supreme civil authorities, whether kings, emperors, dictators, presidents or central governments (*I Pet.* 2: 13).

(g) There are also local civil authorities, such as governors and local government officials (*I Pet.* 2: 14).

(h) These different sorts of authority are God's servants for the benefit of good citizens (*Rom.* 13: 4).

(i) They are established by God to punish those who do wrong and to praise those who do right (*I Pet.* 2: 14)—they are not, therefore, a terror to good conduct but to bad (*Rom.* 13: 3).

(j) They have the right to bear the sword—that is to say, to punish, and to execute God's punishment on the evil-doer (*Rom.* 13: 4; cf. *Acts* 16: 22, 23, 33, 37; 22: 24; *II Cor.* 11: 23, 25); they are entrusted by God with the office of avenger (*I Kings* 19: 16 f; *Isa.* 10: 5 ff).

(k) The state, for its necessary support and maintenance, has the right to command the payment of various dues and taxes, and to expect respect and honour (*Rom.* 13: 7)—it is, in fact, God's minister in attending to such duties (*Rom.* 13: 6).

(l) Whoever, therefore, resists the civil authorities in their God-given duties resists what God has appointed, and offenders must incur God's judgment (*Rom.* 13: 2).

2. The plain duty of Christians, therefore, is to uphold proper authority and to be good citizens.

(a) We are to be subject to every human institution of government (*I Pet.* 2: 13), respecting the most prominent people in the state and honouring all who hold public office (*Rom.* 13: 7), because of conscience (*Rom.* 13: 5).

(b) Our submissiveness is to express itself, whenever possible, in honest obedience to the laws and instructions of the state (*Tit.* 3: 1).

(c) We are to honour all men and in particular the supreme authority (*Rom.* 13: 7; *I Pet.* 2: 17).

(d) We are neither to curse those in authority (*Ex.* 22:28) nor to harm them (*I Sam.* 24: 6; *II Sam.* 1: 14).

(e) We are to pray for the supreme authority, and all who are in high positions, that we and others may lead a quiet and peaceable life, godly and respectful in every way (*I Tim.* 2: 2).

(f) We are to pay taxes to the government without complaint (*Mark* 12: 13–17; *Rom.* 13: 6, 7).

(g) We are to be good citizens by speaking evil of no one, avoiding quarrelling, being gentle and showing perfect courtesy toward all men (*Tit.* 3: 2).

(h) We are to be ready for any honest work (*Tit.* 3: 1).

74

(i) While it is true that we hold a dual citizenship (*Phil.* 3: 20), we are given no reason whatsoever for neglecting our civil responsibilities to the state (*Rom.* 13: 1 ff).

(j) Our desire to fulfil these duties is a direct consequence of our experience of God's salvation (*Tit.* 3: 1–7).

(k) For the most part at least, our duties to the state will not infringe the rights of God (*Mark* 12: 17).

3. When the state or other authorities command anything which is contrary to God's commandments, it is the duty of Christians to obey God.

(a) Rulers and civil authorities are always in danger of being intoxicated by power: they may attribute merit to themselves (*Isa.* 10: 7–11, 13 f), deify themselves (*Ezek.* 28: 2–5), elevate themselves against God (*Isa.* 14: 13), and even go so far as to offend Him by blasphemy (*Dan.* 11: 36).

(b) It is as well to remember, therefore, that the authority God entrusts to men is never absolute, but it is limited by moral obligations—for example, while in the Old Testa-

ment owners were given authority over their slaves, God's law regulated its exercise by stating precisely the rights of slaves (*Ex.* 21:1–6; 26 f.; *Deut.* 15: 12–18).

(c) Civil and other authorities sometimes choose to listen to the malicious accusations of enemies of the gospel who argue that Christian preaching is a political crime or that Christians are the causers of trouble (*Acts* 17: 6; cf. 19: 27; 24: 5).

(d) Religious authorities on occasions persecute Christians (*Luke* 12: 11), and in the days of the early Church it was the high priests who commanded the apostles not to speak and teach in the name of Jesus (*Acts* 4: 18; 5: 28, 40).

(e) The apostles' answer provides the classic answer when Christians are commanded to stop doing what God has plainly commanded: "We must obey God rather than men" (*Acts* 5: 29).

4. In usual circumstances, the fulfilment by Christians of their obligations to the state will be an essential part of their Christian testimony which

commends both them and the gospel to the powers that be.

(a) In Christ we are created for good works (*Eph.* 2: 10).

(b) We are urgently exhorted to bear fruit in good works (*Col.* 1: 10), to seek to do good (*I Thess.* 5: 15), and to do it for everyone (*Rom.* 15: 12; 16:19; *Gal.* 6: 6, 10).

(c) We may rest assured that the man who does right will generally receive praise from the authorities (*I Pet.* 2: 14).

(d) We are to live in society as the servants of God (*I Pet.* 2: 16).

(e) We are to be subject to the powers that be for the Lord's sake (*I Pet.* 2: 13).

(f) By our good citizenship we are to put to silence the ignorant criticisms of foolish men (*I Pet.* 2: 15).

18. SOCIAL RESPONSIBILITY

Question: What are the principles which should guide the Christian in the exercise of social responsibility and involvement in social action?

Answer: The Christian's responsibility for society is plainly taught in the Bible, and often indirectly. Social action on behalf of any who are in need is demanded by the rule: "Love your neighbour as yourself". The description of Christians as "the salt of the earth" implies the beneficial effect their behaviour should have upon society.

1. The pattern God Himself has set.

(a) God gave man a body as well as a soul, and He provided for the well-being of both (*Gen.* 1: 27–30).

(b) We may say that God inaugurated social action in the provision He made for man after his disobedience—"The Lord God made garments of skin for Adam and his wife and clothed them" (*Gen.* 3: 21); and the provisions of His law underlined its importance (e.g. *Ex.* 22: 25; *Lev.* 19: 10; 23: 22; *Deut.* 15: 11; 24: 12, 14, 15).

(c) God loves the world (*John* 3: 16), and He causes His sun to rise on the evil and the good, and sends rain on the righteous and the unrighteous (*Matt.* 5: 45).

(d) God's wrath is declared against extortion, robbery, oppression, and racial discrimination (*Jer.* 22: 13; *Ezek.* 22: 23–31, especially verses 29 and 31; *Amos* 2: 6, 7).

(e) God does not forget men's dishonest dealings at the expense of the helpless (*Amos* 8: 4–14).

(f) God forbids favouritism on the grounds of class, money and privilege (*Lev.* 19: 15; *Gal.* 3: 28; *Jas.* 2: 1–13).

(g) God has shown us what is good and what He requires of us as members of society; He requires us to act justly and to love mercy and to walk humbly with Him (*Micah* 6: 8; cf. *Amos* 5: 24).

2. God confirmed this pattern of social responsibility in the example of His Son, our Lord Jesus Christ.

(a) Our Lord Jesus Christ went about doing good (*Acts* 10: 38).

(b) He cared for all whose need confronted Him (*Matt.* 8: 28–34; *Luke* 7: 11–17).

(c) He was friendly with outcasts (*Matt.* 9: 10–11; *Mark* 2: 15–16; *Luke* 7: 39; 15: 2; 19: 7).

(d) He healed those who were ill (*Matt.* 11: 2–6; *Luke* 7: 21).

(e) He fed the hungry (*Matt.* 14: 14–21; *Mark* 6: 30–44; *Luke* 9: 10–17; *John* 6: 1–13).

(f) He taught the importance of good works: "let your light shine before men, that they may see your good deeds and praise your Father in heaven" (*Matt.* 5: 16).

(g) He spoke of His disciples' function as light and salt in the world (*Matt.* 5: 13, 14).

3. We have the example of the early Church.

(a) The early believers had everything in common (*Acts* 2: 44).

(b) They sold their possessions and goods, and gave to anyone as he had need (*Acts* 2: 45; 4: 32, 34, 35).

(c) They sought to look after widows and others in difficulty and there were no needy persons among them as a consequence (*Acts* 4: 34; 6: 1, 2).

(d) The early churches collected gifts for the impoverished Jerusalem Christians (*Acts* 24: 17; *Rom.* 15: 26; *I Cor.* 16: 3).

4. We have the teaching of the apostles.

(a) They took up our Lord's emphasis upon the continuing debt we have to love one another—"he who loves his fellow man has fulfilled the law" (*Rom.* 13: 8; cf. *Mark* 12: 29–33; *Jas.* 2: 8).

(b) They taught that a Christian does not cease to be an earthly citizen because he has become a citizen of heaven; rather he ought to be a better citizen (*Phil.* 1: 27; *I Pet.* 2: 13–17).

(c) They instructed Christians to do good to all people, especially to those who belong to the family of believers (*Gal.* 6: 10), to be kind to each other and to everyone else (*I Thess.* 5: 15).

(d) They made it plain that Christians are not to be afraid of exposing evil (*Eph.* 5: 11).

(e) They emphasised the importance of diligent work and honest dealings so that none would have just grounds for criticising believers' behaviour (*Eph.* 4: 28; *II Thess.* 3: 10–13).

5. Guidelines for Christian social involvement.

(a) We are to be good citizens (*Matt.* 17: 24–27): we have duties to the state and society as well as having a duty to God, and each must be fulfilled (*Matt.* 22: 15–22; *Rom.* 13: 1–7; *I Tim.* 2: 2; *I Pet.* 2: 17).

(b) We are to keep before us the priority of meeting man's spiritual need (e.g. *Luke* 3: 18, 19), and the unique trusteeship of the gospel our Lord Jesus Christ has committed to us (*Matt.* 28: 18–20; *I Thess.* 2: 4).

(c) By upholding the priority of the gospel, we do not neglect social action—in fact, where the gospel is genuinely received, it changes men's lives so that they influence society for good (*Luke* 19: 8; *John* 8: 11).

(d) Our commitment to the gospel, however, is not a commitment demanding callous indifference to people's material and physical needs—we must be willing to share not only the gospel but our very selves with them too (*I Thess.* 2: 8; cf. *Matt.* 25: 34–40; *I John* 3: 16–18).

(e) We are never to make our spiritual responsibilities an excuse for neglecting practical and social needs—this was the mistake of the priest and the Levite in the story our Lord told of the man who fell into the hands of robbers and who was helped by the good Samaritan (*Luke* 10: 30–37).

(f) When, however, we are involved in meeting people's material, physical and social needs, we must encourage them and ourselves to realise the importance of the right spiritual relationship with God we all need (*Mark* 2: 5, 11).

(g) We must not minimise the distinctive contribution we are able to make to social betterment by living the Christian life as we ought in all its aspects—especially within our home, among our neighbours, and at our daily employment (*Eph.* 5: 22–6: 9).

(h) As we show that we care about right relationships and that the individual counts and really matters, we make a contribution which the world desperately needs—it was in this way, for example, that Christianity brought about the freedom of slaves (cf. *Philemon*).

(i) Our primary concern should be with those social needs with which we are personally confronted day by day (*Luke* 10: 30–37; *Rom.* 15: 25, 26).

(j) When we are rightly involved in social action of any kind, we need to review periodically our involvement—and sometimes even to withdraw for a while to accomplish this review—to ensure that our proper priorities are being maintained (*John* 6: 15; *Acts* 6: 1–4).

(k) Love for God and love for man are never in conflict: loving God as we ought, we love our neighbour also (*Luke* 10: 27, 28).

19. WORK

Question: What does the Bible teach about work?

Answer: Work was an original purpose of God for man, but man's rebellion against God marred man's experience of God's purpose so that man finds his work all too often a burden rather than a pleasure.

Work is part of God's scheme for the support of the human race, and properly fulfilled it brings its own rewards.

While to avoid work is folly, life is not to be filled exclusively with work—God makes provision for rest and recreation. Christians should bear witness to their faith by the quality of their work.

1. There are many varieties of work.

(a) Work has taken a variety of forms from the beginning of God's creation (*Gen.* 4: 2; 9: 20).

(b) The Old Testament speaks of God filling men with His Spirit, giving them ability and intelligence, with knowledge and all craftsmanship, to be metal workers, carvers and embroiderers (*Ex.* 31: 2–11).

2. Work was an original purpose of God for man.

(a) Man was appointed by God as His "deputy" to co-operate with Him in the continuing work of harnessing and using the resources God provides in His creation (*Gen.* 1: 27, 28).

(b) Man was commanded to subdue the earth, and to have dominion over it (*Gen.* 1: 28; *Ps.* 8: 3–8)—a command clearly implying the necessity for work.

(c) Before man's fall, we see man happily at work (*Gen.* 2: 15).

(d) The principle of work is written into the whole of God's creation (*Prov.* 6: 6–11).

(e) It is always assumed that work constitutes part of God's pattern for man (*Ex.* 20: 9, 10; *Ps.* 104: 23).

(f) Work in all its different forms is a provision of God's wisdom for mankind (*Isa.* 28: 24–26).

(g) But God is not said to have commanded man to work, and the implication is present that it was pleasure for man to work prior to the Fall (*Gen.* 2: 15; cf. 3: 17–19).

(h) God intends that man should find enjoyment in his work (*Eccl.* 5: 18–20); indeed since the Fall, there is often more pleasure in work itself than in the achievements of our work (*Eccl.* 2: 10, 11).

(i) There is no disgrace in manual work; indeed its dignity is insisted upon (*Eph.* 4: 28; *I Thess.* 4: 11)—and, of course, our Lord Jesus Christ set an example by working as a carpenter (*Mark* 6:3).

(j) Work for all is a sign of God's blessing; sometimes unemployment in a nation may be a sign of God's judgment (*Zech.* 8).

3. Man's rebellion against God marred man's experience of God's purposes in the principle of work.

(a) The curse which followed the Fall of man was not the curse of work, but the pain and hardship connected with work by reason of the curse upon the ground (*Gen.* 3:17–19; 5:29).

(b) As a consequence of sin, and the disorder following in its wake, work becomes a burden all too often rather than a pleasure to man (*Gen.* 3:17-19).

(c) Daily work can be often just pointless and empty in meaning when performed without God (*Ps.* 127:2).

(d) There is a futile element in human work because, although the man who works may achieve something in life, his motive tends to be envy of his neighbour (*Eccl.* 4:4).

(e) Work has sometimes been an instrument of exploitation and oppression (*Ex.* 1:11–14; *Jas.* 5:4–6).

(f) Men's lives can be made bitter by hard service (*Ex.* 1:14).

4. The purpose which may be discerned behind the principle of work.

(a) The great incentive for daily work is our daily bread as the fruit of it (*Prov.* 16:26).

(b) Daily work is the means of building the home and sustaining it (*Prov.* 24:27).

(c) Daily work is part of God's scheme for the support of the human race (*Prov.* 27:25–27).

(d) By our work we are to make some return to our parents (*I Tim.* 5:4). Of course, such provision may not be necessary always, but it is a dreadful thing to work and not to provide for any member of our own family who may be in need (*I Tim.* 5:8).

(e) Our employment is not to be merely a means of gaining things for ourselves (*Mark* 8:36, 37).

(f) Giving to those who are not so well off as ourselves has a constant emphasis in the teaching of our Lord Jesus Christ (*Matt.* 19: 21; *Luke* 14: 13), and the early Church practised our Lord's teaching (*Acts* 2: 44, 45; 4: 32).

(g) The apostle Paul set an example of working, not only for his own support, but also for the benefit of those who were serving the Lord with him (*Acts* 20: 34); he also laid emphasis upon the provision of help for the poor (*Rom.* 15: 26, 27; *II Cor.* 8 and 9; *Gal.* 2: 10).

(h) No one should work for himself alone, but with the definite object of being able to help others (*Eph.* 4: 28), for those who are unable to work are entitled to aid.

5. Work, properly fulfilled, brings its rewards.

(a) Work brings the satisfaction of peaceful sleep, a benefit not to be despised (*Eccl.* 5: 12).

(b) Work, well done, is worthy of a reasonable wage (*Matt.* 10: 10; *Luke* 10: 7; *I Tim.* 5: 18).

(c) God chooses to reward men for good work, whatever their position or station in life (*Eph.* 6: 8).

(d) Diligence in daily work brings reward (*Prov.* 22: 29; 27: 23–27); whereas laziness in daily work makes the individual concerned dissatisfied (*Prov.* 13: 4).

(e) Ability eventually outruns privilege in employment, insofar that a diligent and wise employee will gain by conscientiousness what others may possess by birth or some special privilege of relationship (*Prov.* 17: 2).

6. Life is not to be all work.

(a) Work brings some reward, but too much work, or a total concern with work, can destroy its benefits (*Eccl.* 2: 10, 11, 24; 4: 6).

(b) Men can make an idol of their work and their achievements with disastrous consequences—for example, the rich fool in the parable (*Luke* 12: 16–21).

(c) Our daily work is not to be motivated by the desire to be rich for this can plunge us into ruin and destruction (*I Tim.* 6: 9, 10).

(d) It is better to have small

82

earnings when they are gained with a restful mind, than to gain a large income by worry and anxious work (*Eccl.* 4: 6).

(e) There is great gain in godliness with contentment; and godliness, of course, acknowledges happily the principle of rest which is so clearly written into God's commandments (*I Tim.* 6: 6).

(f) The cycle of work goes hand in hand with the cycle of rest: the fourth commandment safeguards the principle that man's life is not to be all work (*Ex.* 20: 8–11).

7. The folly of avoiding work.

(a) Idleness is condemned (*II Thess.* 3: 11).

(b) The man who does not work destroys himself (*Eccl.* 4: 5).

(c) Not to have proper work to do is a man's undoing if this state of affairs arises from laziness (*Prov.* 21: 25).

(d) Idleness destroys character (*Prov.* 18: 9).

(e) God will judge the slacker, and He makes no distinction between employer and employee (*Col.* 3: 25).

(f) No one who is able to support himself is entitled to be supported by others (*II Thess.* 3: 10).

8. Employers and employees.

(a) Employers are to pay wages readily (*Lev.* 19: 13; cf. *Deut.* 24: 14, 15); and to withhold proper wages is sin in God's sight (*Jas.* 5: 4).

(b) Employers are to remember their responsibility to be fair and just to those whom they employ, never forgetting that they are to view themselves as having Christ Himself as their Heavenly Employer (*Col.* 4: 1).

(c) Employers are not to misuse the power put in their hands; and they are to forbear threatening (*Eph.* 6: 9).

(d) Employers are to be as conscientious and responsible towards those who work for them as they expect employees to be towards employers (*Eph.* 6: 9).

(e) The Christian employee is to do his work, not with the idea of currying favour, but as a sincere expression of his devotion to the Lord (*Eph.* 6: 5, 6; *Col.* 3: 22).

(f) Whatever the Christian does, he is to put his whole heart and soul into it, as into work done for the Lord, and not for men (*Col.* 3: 23).

(g) The Christian is to know that his real reward, a heavenly one, will come from the Lord, since he is actually employed by the Lord Christ, and not just by his earthly employer (*Col.* 3: 24).

9. Christians should bear witness to their faith by the quality of their work.

(a) Knowing God through Jesus Christ makes a difference to the whole of life (*Rom.* 14: 7, 8): therefore, daily employment will be marked by this difference too.

(b) We are not to be conformed to the world's view of work, but we are to be transformed by the renewal of our mind, that we may prove what is God's will in our daily employment, as in everything else (*Rom.* 12: 2).

(c) Our daily work must be included within the sphere of the good works which God has prepared for us to do (*Eph.* 2: 10): our primary calling is to come to the Lord

Jesus Christ as sinners and to believe on Him, and to be set apart for God's possession (*I Cor.* 1: 2, 9); but our secondary calling is to discover those good works for which God has both fitted and chosen us (*Eph.* 2: 8–10).

(d) The principle of our acting as salt and light in society must surely have particular reference to the sphere of our daily employment (*Matt.* 5: 13–16).

(e) We are to earn our own living (*II Thess.* 3: 12), making the maximum use of our resources and talents, whether they are large or small (*Matt.* 25: 14–30).

(f) Our daily work is to be characterised by good behaviour (*I Pet.* 3: 16).

(g) We are to do our work quietly and efficiently (*II Thess.* 3: 12).

(h) It is important to do what may be described as "honest work" (*Eph.* 4: 28).

(i) Paul set an example of honest work by his tent-making, and the importance of such work featured in his teaching (*Acts* 18: 3; *I Thess.* 2: 9; *II Thess.* 3: 7–10).

(j) In all our work we are to see ourselves as serving the Lord (*Rom.* 12: 11; *Col.* 3: 22 –24).

(k) Work should be an act of worship—done "as to the Lord" (*Eph.* 6: 5, 6).

(l) We must take care not to discredit the faith whether by our standards of work or by our attitude to our work (*I Thess.* 4: 11, 12).

(m) The governing attitude and principle of the whole of the Christian life is that we should do all to the glory of God, and this goal must comprehend our daily employment (*I Cor.* 10: 31).

20. LEISURE

Question: What does the Bible teach about leisure?

Answer: The principle of rest and leisure is inherent in God's institution of the Sabbath, and the fourth commandment safeguards the principle that man's life is not to be all work.

The purpose of leisure is recreation and refreshment. The knowledge that God intends all His gifts to be received, used, and rejoiced in increases the Christian's appreciation and enjoyment of leisure. In a world marred by the fall, a Christian has to exercise discernment to ensure that his leisure enhances his appreciation of goodness, righteousness and truth, and genuinely refreshes him for renewed service of God in the world.

1. The basis for any consideration of the subject of leisure.

(a) Leisure is free time; time in which we are at liberty to choose our activity; the time available for other things after our daily work.

(b) The fundamental basis with which we begin and upon which we build is that everything God made is good (*I Tim.* 4: 4; cf. *Gen.* 1: 31).

(c) We must not fail to acknowledge that every good and perfect gift comes from God (*Jas.* 1: 17).

(d) God has provided in His creation satisfaction for men's bodies and gladness for men's souls (*Acts* 14: 17).

(e) God has given us a host of pursuits richly to enjoy (*I Tim.* 6: 17).

(f) The good things of God's creation are intended by God to be thankfully enjoyed by those who believe in Him and know the truth (*I Tim*. 4: 3).

(g) The creative and artistic gifts of men, as with all the other gifts given to man by God, are to be received gratefully (*I Tim*. 4: 3, 4, 5).

(h) But the fall of man means that these gifts can be abused and misinterpreted (*I Tim*. 4: 1–5), and the principles of goodness, righteousness and truth, uniformly laid down in the Scriptures, apply (*Eph*. 5: 9).

(i) Furthermore, there is a right time for everything (*Eccl*. 3: 1–8); and there is a right and a wrong time for relaxation or leisure (*Eccl*. 10: 16, 17).

2. The essential principle behind leisure.

(a) God rested on the seventh day, after His creative activity (*Gen*. 2: 2).

(b) On the pattern and basis of God's own "rest", it would seem to have been God's purpose for man from the beginning to have one day in seven for rest and recreation (*Gen*.

2: 2, 3), for God blessed and hallowed the seventh day.

(c) The principle of rest and leisure, as necessary for man, is inherent in the institution of the sabbath (*Gen*. 2: 3; *Ex*. 20: 8–11).

(d) The fourth commandment safeguards the principle that man's life is not to be all work (*Ex*. 20: 8–11).

(e) While the objective of the "sabbath" principle to animals is simply that of resting their bodies, for human beings the purpose is, in addition, recreation and refreshment (*Ex*. 23: 12).

(f) We need leisure and time to rest (*Mark* 6: 31).

3. The use of leisure.

(a) The early Christians chose to change from the Jewish sabbath (Saturday) to the Christian Sunday so as to combine the day of rest with the day they met together to remember Christ's death and resurrection (*Acts* 20: 7; *Rev*. 1: 10).

(b) The principle remains that the sabbath was made for man, and not man for the sabbath (*Mark* 2: 27).

86

(c) Worship of the Lord on a Sunday is part of a Christian's leisure because it is something he **chooses** to do: the Lord's Day is a day when believers choose to delight themselves in the Lord; instead of following selfish and unhelpful inclinations (*Isa.* 58: 13, 14).

(d) There are many different views of pleasure and leisure: for example, it is like sport to a fool to do wrong (*Prov.* 10: 23).

(e) The writer of *Ecclesiastes* sought to put human pleasures to the test, and he found them to be meaningless (*Eccl.* 2: 1 ff); men's wild pursuit of pleasure sometimes leads them into trouble (*Dan.* 5: 1 ff).

(f) The leisure of a lazy man can be his undoing (*Prov.* 21: 25).

(g) Leisure is not doing nothing, but, having time at our disposal, choosing to do with it what we will. Thus, for Christian believers, one of the most profitable uses of our leisure is enjoying fellowship with God's people (*Ps.* 16: 3), and we can say, "Better is one day in your courts than a thousand elsewhere" (*Ps.* 84: 10).

(h) The believer's pleasure is in the law of the Lord, and in the works of the Lord, and this pleasure leads him to study them (*Ps.* 1: 2; 111: 2).

(i) However leisure time is utilised, it should be used positively for, if the principle behind the sabbath—so far as man's body and mind is concerned—is that of refreshment, any leisure which debilitates is unhelpful, and outside of God's purpose (*Ex.* 23: 12).

4. Principles to govern the use of leisure.

(a) Any realistic consideration of lcisure recognises that the world in which we live offers many "pleasures" which compete for our attention and involvement (*I Pet.* 4: 3).

(b) We must always remind ourselves that sin offers transient pleasure; thus not every offer of pleasure is to be pursued (*Heb.* 11: 25).

(c) The desire for pleasures can be an unhelpful source of strife within ourselves (*Jas.* 4: 1), not least when they are of a purely sensuous kind (*Mark* 7: 21, 22).

(d) We are warned that in the

last days men will be lovers of pleasure rather than lovers of God (*II Tim.* 3: 4).

(e) Pleasure sought for pleasure's sake proves empty and unsatisfying (*Eccl.* 2: 10, 11).

(f) Our approach to leisure, therefore, must be sober—that is to say, we must know what we are doing and why (*I Pet.* 1: 13).

(g) We have to learn to discriminate so as to refuse the evil and choose the good (*Isa.* 7: 15).

(h) The Christian knows a better way than wine and excess to obtain satisfaction and joy—the fullness of the Spirit (*Eph.* 5: 18–20).

(i) Our use of leisure time is not to be contrary to the principle of our redeeming the time (*Eph.* 5: 15, 16; *Col.* 4: 5).

(j) The time we have at our disposal, after we have done our daily work and given ourselves opportunity for rest and necessary tasks, should include fruitful labour for God —the latter is a right use of our leisure, and properly entered into proves a means of refreshment (*Phil.* 1: 22; cf. *John* 4: 6, 8, 31–34).

(k) We need to have the fact of the shortness of life brought constantly before us so that we gain a heart of wisdom to use life properly (*Ps.* 90: 12).

(l) Living in a world where entertainment is automatically assumed to have a place in men's leisure, and in his times of resting, we need to relate Christian principles to the subject. Moral considerations are as relevant to the use of leisure time as to anything else: the Christian is to seek to do all to the glory of God (*I Cor.* 10: 31).

(m) Whatever we do, we are to do everything in the name of the Lord Jesus, thanking God the Father through Him (*Col.* 3: 17); at all times we are to put on the Lord Jesus, and make no provision for the flesh, to gratify its desires (*Rom.* 13: 14).

(n) We shall often find, not least in the sphere of entertainment, that all things are lawful, but not all things are helpful (*I Cor.* 6: 12; 10: 23); we have complete liberty as Christians, but we recognise that not everything is constructive and helpful.

(o) We must not allow any

pastime to make us its slave (*I Cor*. 6: 12).

(p) In our leisure, as in everything else, we should not merely go our own way, but our actions and activities should mean the good of others too (*Rom*. 15: 1–3).

(q) We are to keep in our thoughts all that is true and noble, all that is right and good, all that is lovable and attractive, whatever is morally excellent and worthy of praise—this positive and straight-forward directive provides us with tremendous scope, but with a careful yardstick to apply (*Phil*. 4: 8).

(r) Our leisure activities must not be moulded by the desires of our ignorant days, but must conform to the principle of holiness in every part of our life (*I Pet*. 1: 14–19).

(s) In our leisure activities we should abstain from the desires of our lower natures, for they are always at war with our souls (*I Pet*. 2: 11).

(t) Activities which include or tend towards licentiousness, passions, drunkenness, revels, carousing, and lawless idolatry are ruled out for the Christian (*I Pet*. 4: 3).

(u) Our former companions may think it strange that we will no longer join with them in their leisure pursuits, and accordingly say all sorts of unpleasant things about us (*I Pet*. 4: 4).

(v) Our aim to live no longer by human passions but according to the will of God will affect every use to which we put our time (*I Pet*. 4: 2), for we make it our ambition to please the Lord (*II Cor*. 5: 9), in whose presence we always find ourselves (*Ps*. 139; *Heb*. 13: 5).

21. GUIDANCE

Question: What does the Bible teach about guidance and the will of God?

Answer: The Bible teaches that the basic secret of guidance is commitment to the will of God, both before and after it is known and discovered. The will of God in general is given to us in the instruction of the Scriptures. The particular will of God for our lives is both discovered and worked out as we present our bodies to God as a living spiritual sacrifice,

and continue to do so, striving after daily obedience to His Word.

1. The choice before us.

(a) Human desires or the will of God? Our wishes or God's will (*I Pet.* 4: 2)?

(b) Rather than living for God's will, we have all lived much of our life according to our human desires; as Christians we should live the rest of our earthly life by the will of God (*I Pet.* 4: 2).

2. The truth concerning our own will.

(a) Our own will is always prone to evil; the things which our bodies and minds find congenial are often in marked contrast to what God wills for us (*Eph.* 2: 3).

(b) As Christians, we should aspire not to do our own will, but God's; wanting our own will to coincide always with His (*John* 5: 30a; *Luke* 22: 42).

3. Christians find within themselves a desire for God's will.

(a) Our new life or spiritual nature demands that we seek to do God's will (*Phil.* 2: 12, 13).

(b) That we desire to follow the will of God is the result of God's grace in our life through our Lord Jesus Christ (*Eph.* 2: 8–10).

(c) God's great mercy to us, rightly considered and meditated upon, stimulates us to seek the will of God, irrespective of the cost involved (*Rom.* 12: 1).

(d) Even as our body desires food, for its health, our soul requires obedience to God's will for its health (*John* 4: 34).

4. The Lord Jesus is our example of obedience to God's will.

(a) He came with the sole purpose of doing the Father's will (*Heb.* 10: 7, 9).

(b) He frequently spoke of His determination to seek not His own will but the will of the Father (*John* 5: 30a; 6: 38).

(c) Knowing the will of the Father, He spoke of it with assurance and He acted in perfect co-operation with it (*John* 6: 39, 40).

(d) At every crisis, obedience

to God's will was foremost (*Matt.* 26:42).

(e) The doing of God the Father's will was His food (*John* 4:34).

5. Fundamental facts regarding God's will.

(a) As we consider God's will with our limited human minds, there are two parts to it: there is that which is declared or published and that which is secret or hidden. God's declared or published will includes those events which have already taken place which are revealed to be His will—for example, the death of our Lord Jesus Christ to deliver us from our sins (*Gal.* 1:4)—and the whole of His written Word in which He tells man what to do. God's secret or hidden will, through which all things are ordered and done according to His plan and decision, concerns those things which are not revealed to us (*Eph.* 1:11).

(b) The published will of God relates to the whole of our lives: we should do all of it (*Col.* 4:12); and this is God's requirement of us (*Acts* 13:22).

(c) God's will is good and acceptable and perfect (*Rom.* 12:2).

(d) God's will is published supremely in the Lord Jesus Christ, and the dynamic for doing it, which we so desperately need, is found in Him alone, and our union with Him (*I Thess.* 5:18).

6. The fundamental importance of God's will in our life.

(a) What God looks for most is obedience to His will. He could say of David, "I have found in David the son of Jesse a man after my heart, who will do all my will" (*Acts* 13:33).

(b) Obedience to the will of God is more important than mere outward profession (*Matt.* 7:21); God requires not lip-service to His will, but action—the parable of the two sons (*Matt.* 21:28–32).

(c) Any profession of Christ's Lordship or religious activity, without obedience to God's will, are worthless to God, and are rejected by Him (*Matt.* 7:21–23).

(d) Obedience to the will of God is the condition and proof of a right relationship to our Lord Jesus Christ (*Matt.* 12: 50; *Mark* 3: 35).

(e) God wants us to be filled with the knowledge of His will (*Col.* 1: 9).

(f) Knowing God's will is the secret of achieving important goals: first, living as the Lord wants; secondly, doing what pleases Him; thirdly, producing in our lives all kinds of good deeds; and, fourthly, growing in our knowledge of God (*Col.* 1: 10).

7. Examples of God's published will.

First, with regard to our salvation.

(a) It is not the will of the Father that one of those who has trusted in our Lord Jesus Christ should perish (*Matt.* 18: 14).

(b) The will of the Father is that the Son should not lose any of all those He has given Him, but that the Lord Jesus should raise them all to life on the last day (*John* 6: 39, 40).

(c) By God's will all believers are made holy through the sacrifice of the body of Jesus Christ once for all (*Heb.* 10: 10).

Secondly, with regard to our growth in holiness.

(d) The will of God for our life may be summed up in the one word "sanctification" (*I Thess.* 4: 3, 7).

(e) It is God's will that by doing good things we should silence the ignorant talk of foolish people against Christianity (*I Pet.* 2: 15).

(f) It is God's will that, as Christian believers, we should always be joyful, pray constantly, and be thankful in all circumstances (*I Thess.* 5: 16–18).

(g) It is God's will that we should appreciate our need and obligation to be filled with the Spirit at all times (*Eph.* 5: 17–20).

8. Relating ourselves to God's will.

(a) Our purpose in life, like that of our Lord Jesus Christ, should be to do the will of the Father (*John* 6: 38).

(b) The will of God determines our place and function in the Church of Christ, and the direction of our life (*I Cor.* 12: 11; *Eph.* 2: 10).

(c) Doing the will of God

means obeying the instructions given in the Word of God (*I Thess*. 4: 1, 2).

(d) We should be testing and approving what God's will is for our life (*Rom*. 12: 2).

(e) The will of God should be the determining factor in all our movements (*Rom*. 15: 32).

(f) Knowing that God's will determines the things which happen to us, we should submit to them in a Christlike manner (*I Pet*. 3: 17).

(g) There may be, therefore, a battle within us for the submission of our will to God's will (*Matt*. 26: 42,) for the will of God often runs contrary to our natural feelings.

(h) In every circumstance, and in circumstances which are beyond our control, Christians may say, with confidence, "The Lord's will be done" (*Matt*. 26: 42; *Acts* 21: 14).

(i) The will of God should be sought and obeyed in small things as well as in large (*Phil*. 4: 6; *I Thess*. 5: 16–18).

9. Discovering God's will.

(a) When we really choose to do God's will, God never leaves us in ignorance of it (*John* 7: 17).

(b) He wishes to equip us with everything good that we may do His will (*Heb*. 13: 21).

(c) The knowledge we need of God's will does not come only from human wisdom for such so easily can make us proud (*I Cor*. 1: 20; 2: 5, 6, 13; 3: 19).

(d) Our knowledge of God's will comes from the illumination of the Holy Spirit: He gives the wisdom and understanding which enable us to know God's will (*Col*. 1: 9).

(e) The will of God in general and also on particular issues is given to us in the instruction of the Scriptures (*I Thess*. 4: 1; *Matt*. 12: 50; *Mark* 3: 35; cf. *Luke* 8: 21; *Rom*. 2: 18).

(f) The precise will of God for our individual lives, however, may be known only as we present our bodies as a living sacrifice, holy and acceptable to God (*Rom*. 12: 1, 2); to be in keeping with God's will we must dedicate ourselves to God (*II Cor*. 8: 5).

(g) This dedication involves the refusal to be conformed to this world, and the willingness for transformation of our life by the renewal of our minds (*Rom.* 12: 2).

10. Prayer has an important place both in our discovering God's will and our submission to it.

(a) The Lord Jesus Christ taught that God's will is to figure in our petitions to our Father (*Matt.* 6: 10).

(b) Our prayers should centre around our being filled with the knowledge of God's will in all spiritual wisdom and understanding, to lead a life worthy of the Lord, fully pleasing to Him, bearing fruit in every good work, and increasing in the knowledge of God (*Col.* 1: 10).

(c) Expressed another way, prayer should be directed at standing mature and fully assured in all the will of God (*Col.* 4: 12).

(d) Praying in this fashion, we may be sure that God will both hear and answer (*I John* 5: 14, 15).

(e) Prayer may be regarded as the surrendering of our wills to God's will (*II Cor.* 12: 7–10).

(f) Prayer's true motive is the desire for God's will to be done and His Name to be glorified (*John* 17: 1).

(g) All our petitions should be subject to God's will (*Rom.* 1: 10).

11. How we should do God's will when we know it.

(a) We should do what God wants with all our heart: this means doing God's will with our eye on God's approval, rather than man's (*Eph.* 6: 6).

(b) When we know God's will, we should live it out to the full (*Phil.* 1: 12–14, 22; 2: 17).

12. The practical outworking of God's will.

(a) Doing God's will means accomplishing the work He has chosen for us, whatever that may be (*John* 4: 34).

(b) Our obedience to God's will is bound to mean giving ourselves to God's people in very practical, and often costly, ways (*II Cor.* 8: 5).

(c) Doing God's will is closely associated with His working in us that which is pleasing in His sight (*Phil.* 2: 12, 13; *Heb.* 13: 21).

(d) Suffering of some kind

may often be in God's will for us (*I Pet.* 4: 19); our Lord's experience is an example (*Matt.* 26: 42.)

(e) Sometimes God takes something away from us that He may give it back to us for ever; but we cannot be sure that it will be so (*Philem.* 15).

(f) When God's will includes suffering , it is fundamentally important that we persist in doing right and that we should entrust our souls to our faithful Creator (*I Pet.* 4: 19).

(g) We need great patience at times to persist in doing the will of God in order to receive what God promises (*Heb.* 10: 36).

(h) But we may have the glorious assurance that where there is a will of God, there is a way of God: think of Joseph and Moses.

13. Finally, the blessing God's will is to us when we do it.

(a) When we do God's will we stand for ever, in marked contrast to the world around which passes away, together with all the desires we associate with the world (*I John* 2: 17).

(b) The nearest approach to heaven on earth is the doing of His will as it is done in heaven (*Matt.* 6: 10).

(c) The will of God is always identical with what is good and acceptable and perfect (*Rom.* 12: 2).

(d) When we know God's will we are in a position to choose what is right (*Rom.* 2: 18).

(e) Our spiritual life and Christian joy are fed and enriched as we are obedient (*John* 4: 34; *Ps.* 40: 8).

(f) When the will of God is the objective of our life, we discover tremendous peace (*Phil.* 4: 6, 7).

(g) As we do the will of God we receive all that He promises (*Heb.* 10: 36).

22. THE FAMILY

Question: What is the importance and function of the family?

Answer: The family begins with a husband and wife, living in a permanent marriage union, and with, generally, children as the natural consequence of that union. The

principal end of the family is the procreation, preservation, and education of children which makes it the primary unit of society. The family antedates all other human relationships and societies.

1. The family requires a high view of marriage as its foundation.

(a) Marriage has its basis and norm in God's act of creation, and is the original form of human fellowship (*Mark*. 10: 6, 7).

(b) When marriage takes place a fresh pattern of life is established, and a new family begins as a man leaves his own mother and father and is united to his wife, the two becoming one flesh (*Gen*. 2: 24; *Mark* 10: 8).

(c) It is good for a man to have a wife (*Gen*. 2: 18; *Prov*. 18: 22), and but one wife (*Gen*. 2: 24; *Mark* 10: 6–8; *I Cor*. 7: 2–4).

(d) A husband is the head of the wife as Christ is Head, and Saviour too, of the Church (*Eph*. 5: 23).

(e) A husband's principal duty is to love his wife (*Col*. 3: 19),

and to love her as he loves himself (*Eph*. 5: 28, 33).

(f) A husband should be faithful to his wife (*Prov*. 5: 19; *Mal*. 2: 14–15), respecting her (*I Pet*. 3: 7), and avoiding all harshness or bitterness in his dealings (*Col*. 3: 19).

(g) A husband should comfort his wife (*I Sam*. 1: 8), consult her (*Gen*. 31: 4–7), and be quick to praise and show his appreciation of her (*Prov*. 31: 28, 29).

(h) A wife is the principal helper of her husband (*Gen*. 2: 18).

(i) A wife's foremost duty is submission to her husband (*Gen*. 3: 16; *Eph*. 5: 22, 24; *I Pet*. 3: 1).

(j) A wife should love (*Tit*. 2: 4), honour (*Eph*. 5: 33), and obey her husband (*I Cor*. 14: 34; *Tit*. 2: 5), always striving to be faithful to him (*I Cor*. 7: 3–5, 10).

(k) An intelligent and capable wife is a gift from the Lord (*Prov*. 19: 14), her husband's crown (*Prov*. 12: 4), and, in fact, a priceless treasure (*Prov*. 31: 10 ff).

(l) Children are a gift from the Lord to a husband and wife

(*Gen.* 33: 5; *Ps.* 127: 3; *I Sam.* 1: 27), and as such enhance and deepen the marriage relationship.

2. The harmony of husband and wife is essential for the well-being of a family.

(a) The fact that disharmony in any area of married life can be disastrous and detrimental to a family's welfare is one of the reasons why a Christian should seek to have a Christian partner (*I Cor.* 7: 39; *II Cor.* 6: 14).

(b) Husband and wife are to be sensitive and thoughtful of the sexual needs and demands of each other (*I Cor.* 7: 3 f).

(c) For the physical relationship to cement regularly their unity and harmony, husband and wife must be faithful to one another in mind and thought as well as physically (*Matt.* 5: 27, 28).

(d) The original happiness of marriage has been sadly shattered by the corruption of the human heart (*Mark* 7: 20–23).

(e) Selfish disagreement, especially as it expresses itself in nagging, ruins harmony (*Prov.* 19: 13; 25: 24; 27: 15).

(f) Unhappy marriage brings about a total breakdown in happiness (*Prov.* 12: 4).

3. Parental duties.

(a) Parents should love their children (*Tit.* 2: 4), showing their love both in compassion (*Ps.* 103: 13) and in careful discipline (*Prov.* 3: 11 f; *Heb.* 12: 7).

(b) Parents should pray for their children, praying generally for their spiritual welfare (*Gen.* 17: 18; *I Chron.* 29: 19), and specifically for their well-being when tempted (*Job* 1: 5) or unwell (*II Sam.* 12: 16; *Mark* 5: 23; *John* 4: 46, 49).

(c) Parents should provide for their children (*Job.* 42: 15; *Isa.* 1: 2 f).

(d) They should save up for them and be prepared to spend everything they have, if necessary, for their welfare (*II Cor.* 12: 14, 15).

(e) They should know how to give good gifts to their children (*Matt.* 7: 9–11).

(f) Parents should educate their children (*Eph.* 6: 4), seeing themselves as their proper and primary instructors (*Prov.* 4: 1–4, 10–12).

(g) They should instruct them in God's ways (*Deut.* 31: 12–13), with the assurance that, as their children are trained up in the way that they should go, when they are old they will not depart from it (*Prov.* 22: 6).

(h) They should teach their children spiritual truth from the Scriptures, for children may share the promises of God (*Acts* 2: 39), and the Scriptures are able to make them wise for salvation through Jesus Christ (*II Tim.* 3: 15).

(i) They should teach their children most of all by example, remembering our Lord's solemn warning that if anyone causes a child who believes in Him to sin that it would be better for that person to have a millstone around his neck, and to be drowned in the depths of the sea (*Matt.* 18: 6).

(j) Parents should **discipline** their children (*Deut.* 8: 5).

(k) Children need discipline because folly is deep-rooted in their hearts (*Prov.* 22: 15;

29: 17); to neglect discipline is to throw away the family's security (*Prov.* 13: 24; 22: 6).

(l) Parental discipline, however, is to be careful and loving, and fathers in particular are instructed to be watchful lest they either discourage their children or make them resentful (*Col.* 3: 21; *Eph.* 6: 4).

(m) While discipline is never pleasant at the time, its fruits are good (*Heb.* 12: 10, 11).

(n) The experience children have of true human fatherhood should make it easy for them to appreciate God's greater Fatherhood (*Matt.* 7: 9–11; *Heb.* 12: 5–11).

4. Children's duties.

(a) Children should love their parents, not forgetting to be demonstrative in their love when appropriate (*Gen.* 46: 29).

(b) Children should respect their parents (*Lev.* 19: 3), honouring father and mother (*Ex.* 20: 12), and respecting too their parents' possessions as they respect other people's (*Prov.* 28: 24).

(c) To treat parents with

98

mockery or disrespect merits condemnation (*Gen.* 27: 12; *Prov.* 30: 17).

(d) The commandment to honour parents is obligatory (*Mark* 10: 19); any instruction which cuts across it is hypocrisy and transgression (*Matt.* 15: 4–7; *Mark* 7: 10–13).

(e) Children should obey their parents (*Eph.* 6: 1), listening deliberately to their advice and instruction (*Prov.* 6: 20; 23: 22).

(f) The ultimate prosperity of children may greatly hinge upon their obedience to their parents (*Deut.* 4: 40; 12: 25, 28; *Ps.* 128: 1–3).

(g) Children are to strive to obey their parents in everything (*Col.* 3: 20).

(h) Children, when adult, should provide, where necessary, for their parents, since they have a continuing responsibility towards them (*Matt.* 15: 5, 6; *Mark* 7: 11, 12).

(i) They must learn to do what is their Christian duty, and to repay those who have brought them up (*I Tim.* 5: 4; cf. *John* 19: 26, 27).

5. The common duties of the family in which all the members need to share.

(a) Love—the primary duty of the members of any family is love (*I Cor.* 13; *I John* 5: 1, etc.).

(b) Helpfulness—the life of the family is made harmonious by deliberate co-operativeness but it is made difficult by quarrelsomeness (*Prov.* 18: 19).

(c) Mutual forbearance—the members of the family are to be forgiving of one another (*Gen.* 50: 17–21; *Matt.* 18: 21–22).

(d) Submission—all members of the family must accept the need for the proper and firm management of household life, and the necessity, therefore, for the parents to give direction (*Prov.* 31: 27; *I Tim.* 3: 4, 5).

(e) Concern for unity—all need to see that they contribute by their behaviour and attitudes to the unity or disunity of the family, and that unity must be the goal always (*Gen.* 45: 24; *Ps.* 133: 1).

(f) Worship—the worship of God together, with the home seen as a place where

God's presence may be known, brings immeasurable help to the family (*Josh.* 8: 35; *I Cor.* 16: 19).

(g) **Concern for others**—the individual family unit is to look outside of itself and is to care for needy relatives, and especially grandparents (*I Tim.* 5: 3, 4), so that grandchildren become the crown of the old (*Prov.* 17: 6).

6. The Christian family has the benefits of the gospel which add immeasurably to its happiness and security.

(a) God is known to be the Giver of every good gift the family enjoys (*Jas.* 1: 17).

(b) God's Word becomes the final authority and guide so that the family has wise and consistent direction (*II Tim.* 3: 16, 17).

(c) Parents and children are encouraged to pattern their behaviour on the kingdom of heaven (*Phil.* 1: 27; 3: 20).

(d) The Holy Spirit makes love possible and effective in the most difficult of circumstances (*II Tim.* 1: 7).

(e) Husbands love their wives after the pattern of Christ's love (*Eph.* 5: 25).

(f) Wives submit themselves to their own husbands as part of their submission to the Lord (*Eph.* 5: 22).

(g) Children obey their parents with the desire to please the Lord by so doing (*Eph.* 6: 1; *Col.* 3: 20).

(h) Elderly relatives are cared for as part of Christian duty (*I Tim.* 5: 4).

(i) Relationships within the family are seen in the context of our relationship with God; a right relationship with God demands a right relationship with those to whom we are closest (*I Pet.* 3: 7).

(j) Marriage and the family are held in the highest possible honour because God so honours them (*Heb.* 13: 4).

23. EDUCATION

Question: What does the Bible teach about education?

Answer: Education aims at developing individuals' aptitude for every kind of learning so that they are well informed

100

quick to understand and qualified to serve. Education begins in the home, and all who teach children remain delegates of those children's parents, and nothing releases parents from their basic responsibility for the teaching and discipline of their own children. The principal lesson to be taught is that the fear of the Lord is the beginning of wisdom.

1. Education is a subject worthy of study.

(a) We are to attribute all that is good in this world to God: (*Jas.* 1: 17): the study of everything which is good, therefore, is a worthy pursuit. Both the natural processes of the earth and the course of historical events are governed by God's wisdom (*Isa.* 28: 23–29; 31: 2); thus by a proper understanding of these things we are caused to acknowledge God more worthily.

(b) God has given man special responsibilities in His creation which demand the education of man's mind (*Gen.* 1: 28; *Ps.* 8: 5, 6, 7, 8).

(c) God has given all kinds of abilities to men which need to be discovered, drawn out, and used (*Ex.* 31: 3–5).

(d) The intellect is not to be despised: more can be done by proper education than by authoritarianism and force (*Eccl.* 9: 17, 18).

2. The aims of education.

(a) The first aim of education is the **imparting of understanding**, or insight (*Prov.* 4: 1, 7); and basic to this understanding or insight is the truth that "the fear of the Lord is the beginning of wisdom" (*Prov.* 1: 7).

(b) The second aim of education is **knowledge**—the person who has understanding seeks knowledge (*Prov.* 15: 14).

(c) Knowledge is gained constantly by those who have understanding, to be used at the appropriate time in the future (*Prov.* 10: 14).

(d) Knowledge helps a man to make the right and best choices (*Phil* 1: 9, 10).

(e) The third aim is **wisdom**—that is to say, the ability to use knowledge in a way pleasing to God and helpful to man (*Prov.* 2: 1–6; 14: 33).

(f) The man who possesses wisdom does not profess to know everything, but is ever ready to take advice, and shows a willingness to learn from any who will teach him (*Prov.* 13: 10).

(g) The fact that education is not speedily achieved is generally recognised (*Dan.* 1: 4, 5): our Lord Jesus Christ is said to have grown in wisdom, as part of His human development from boyhood to manhood (*Luke* 2: 40, 52).

(h) The aims of the educative purpose may be expressed as follows: to make a man skilful in all wisdom, endowed with knowledge, understanding learning, and competent to serve (*Dan.* 1: 4).

3. The education of children.

(a) Children are a gift from God (*Ps.* 127: 3–5; 128: 3, 4; cf. *Gen.* 11: 30; 17: 16).

(b) Children are necessarily of limited understanding (*I Cor.* 14: 20).

(c) Children are naturally limited in their outlook (*I Cor.* 13: 11).

(d) Children are easily swayed (*Eph.* 4: 14).

(e) A basic factor in our approach springs from the knowledge that folly is bound up in the heart of a child, and this fact must always be borne in mind (*Prov.* 22: 15).

(f) Children are to be viewed not only as immature, but as sinful by nature (*Ps.* 51: 5).

(g) God-centred education should begin from the earliest days of the child's life, training the child in the way that it should go (*Prov.* 22: 6).

(h) Such education and training must include careful discipline (*Prov.* 22: 15; 29: 17).

(i) The administering of discipline is not to be abhorrent for true discipline is a mark and proof of love (*Heb.* 12: 5–11).

(j) To withhold discipline can all too easily mean setting a child's course for destruction (*Prov.* 19: 18).

(k) Education begins in the home, for parents are to give their children instruction (*Prov.* 4: 1), particularly by providing them with good precepts (*Prov.* 4: 2). We must not lose sight of the parental responsibility for the education of children: parents may delegate parts of their responsibility, but other teachers are to be regarded as their delegates.

(l) Parents are commanded to instruct their children (*Gen.* 18: 19; *Ex.* 10: 2; 12: 26, 27; 13: 14–16; *Deut.* 4: 9, 10; 6: 6–9; 11: 19; *Isa.* 38: 19).

(m) In particular, parents are to be diligent in the religious or spiritual education of their children (*Deut.* 6: 6–9), seizing the casual as well as the formal opportunities for instruction.

(n) Parents are to give their children the commands of God that they may be careful to do all the words of the law (*Deut.* 32: 46); the way of wisdom should be heard first from parents' lips, and in their parents' lives children should find living examples to follow (*Prov.* 4: 11, 12).

(o) By their actions parents are to prompt the right sort of questions from their children which will enable the parents to instruct the children in the mighty redeeming acts of the Lord (*Ex.* 12: 26, 27; 13: 14–16).

(p) Education, whether provided by parents or others, requires wise teachers: the lips of the wise spread knowledge (*Prov.* 15: 7, 12).

(q) Wise teachers reprove (*Prov.* 15: 12), and are refreshing in their candour and clarity (*Prov.* 18: 4).

(r) Wise teachers have insight and discernment to recognise the character and intentions of those whom they teach (*Prov.* 20: 5), and they know how to draw out those whom they teach.

4. The requirements for success in education.

(a) To arrive at wisdom by way of understanding and knowledge, we have to begin by acknowledging that **discipline is necessary** (*Prov.* 23: 13, 14; 29: 15).

(b) Open rebuke is better than hidden (*Prov.* 27: 5).

(c) The second requirement is that **correction should be heeded** (*Prov.* 10: 17): progress comes through teachableness, and teachableness includes the readiness to accept rebuke.

(d) If an individual is often reproved, and still chooses to resist, he will suddenly be done for (*Prov.* 29: 1).

(e) To love discipline and correction is to love knowledge (*Prov.* 12: 1); the prudent heed admonition (*Prov.* 15: 5, 32).

(f) A rebuke goes deeper into a man of understanding than a hundred blows into a fool (*Prov.* 17: 10).

(g) Character benefits and is made attractive by receiving constructive criticism with genuine joy (*Prov.* 25: 12).

(h) The third requirement is that **the person under instruction should be receptive** (*Prov.* 12: 15): the wise man knows that he can always increase his learning (*Prov.* 1: 5; 18: 15).

(i) Application to work, and concentration are to be urged upon those who are under instruction (*Prov.* 23: 12).

(j) Education requires attentiveness to instruction (*Prov.* 4: 1, 13; 17: 27, 28)—wisdom is a long-term investment (*Prov.* 19: 20).

(k) The fourth requirement is that **knowledge must be practically applied** (*Prov.* 19: 27).

(l) The purpose of having an understanding mind is to be able to do successfully what has been committed to one to do in life, including the ability to discern between good and evil (*I Kings* 3: 9).

5. The value of education.

(a) Education is an adornment (*Prov.* 1: 8, 9), in that the properly educated person is attractive in character, a profitable addition to anyone's acquaintances.

(b) Education benefits the individual no end: the man who obtains wisdom loves himself (*Prov.* 19: 8).

(c) Education is satisfying, because it gives the individual hopes for a happy future (*Prov.* 23: 13–18).

(d) Education is better than material wealth (*Prov.* 16: 16): wealth can be deceptive, whereas education of the right sort foils deception (*Prov.* 28: 11).

(e) Wise speech comes from true education, and when a man can use his tongue wisely, he has overcome one of the main causes of friction and trouble in human relationships (*Prov.* 15: 7, 21; 16: 23).

(f) Goodwill on the part of all right-thinking men, and success, come as the results of education arising from understanding, knowledge, and wisdom (*Prov.* 13: 15, 16; 21: 22; 24: 3–6).

6. Basic to the whole subject of education, from the biblical viewpoint, is the truth that proper education is based upon the fear of the Lord.

(a) Ideally, education should be God-centred (*Prov.* 1: 7; 9: 10).

(b) The purpose of God-centred education is the reverencing of God: this is the whole duty of man (*Eccl.* 12: 13).

(c) Wisdom, counsel and understanding, in the fullest sense, belong to God (*Job* 12: 13); the truly wise are those to whom God has graciously imparted wisdom (*Matt.* 12: 42; *Acts* 6: 10; 7: 10; *Jas.* 3: 17; *II Pet.* 3: 15).

(d) True wisdom stems from the fear of the Lord (*Job* 28: 28; *Ps.* 111: 10; *Prov.* 1: 7; 9: 10).

(e) As Christianity is the only true religion, and God in Christ the only true God, the only possible means of an entirely profitable education is Christian discipline and instruction (*Eph.* 6: 4).

(f) To educate fallen man, we must remember his fallen nature: he is darkened in his understanding and alienated from the life of God because of the ignorance that is in him, due to his hardness of heart (*Eph.* 4: 18).

(g) If education is divorced from God's revelation, it can soon become impoverished and unproductive (*I Cor.* 1: 17; 2: 4; *II Cor.* 1: 12), and at its worst both foolish and devilish (*I Cor.* 1: 19–25; *Jas.* 3: 15–16).

(h) Wisdom, without a reverence for God, easily becomes a source of human pride (*Isa.* 5: 21), and, having no anchor in God, it is doomed to failure (*Isa.* 19: 11–15).

(i) When men deny God, they become, in fact, futile in their thinking (*Rom.* 1: 21, 22).

(j) We need to be aware of the limitations of the intellect, even at its very best (*Eccl.* 8: 17; 12: 12).

(k) The fear of the Lord is the beginning of wisdom (*Prov.* 1: 7).

(l) Where there is a reverence for God, God is pleased to prosper the whole course of an individual's education, irrespective of the teachers who may be involved (*Dan.* 1: 17).

24. SEX

Question: What does the Bible teach about sex?

Answer: Sex is a gift of God, and is properly appreciated as we have a right understanding of marriage. As with all of God's gifts to mankind, the gift of sex can be abused. Self-knowledge, therefore, is to govern a Christian's attitude to sex; and this knowledge means the control of the thought-life and the recognition of the dignity of the Christian's body as the temple of the Holy Spirit. God's call to sanctification is the test of all behaviour between the sexes.

1. Sex is a gift of God.

(a) Sex is a creation of God (*Gen.* 1: 27; *Matt.* 19: 4; *I Tim.* 4: 3).

(b) Sex, as created by God, was good (*Gen.* 1: 31; *I Tim.* 4: 3, 4).

(c) God's purpose in the creation of sex was the procreation of children (*Gen.* 1: 28a): that is to say, the coming of children was intended to be always a cause of joy (*John* 16: 21).

(d) Sexual desire is one of the reasons, therefore, that men and women come together in marriage (*I Cor.* 7: 9).

(e) To fulfil this desire within marriage is right, but outside of marriage is wrong (*I Cor.* 7: 8, 9).

2. We must appreciate the importance of marriage.

(a) Marriage is a calling of God to some and not to others (*I Cor.* 7: 7, 17).

(b) Marriage has higher ends than merely the fulfilment of the sexual desire: one of its pre-eminent purposes is the bearing of children (*Ps.* 127: 3–5; *I Tim.* 5: 14) and their rearing in the discipline and instruction of the Lord (*Eph.* 6: 4)— for this reason among others marriage for the Christian is to be "only in the Lord" (*I Cor.* 7: 39).

(c) Marriage is further intended for the mutual help of husband and wife by means of friendship and companionship (*Gen.* 2: 18, 20).

(d) Marriage is to be entered upon not in the passion of lust but in holiness and honour (*I Thess.* 4: 4, 5).

(e) Marriage is to be received

with thanksgiving, as with all of God's gifts (*I Tim*. 4: 3, 4).

(f) Marriage has special enjoyment and meaning for those who believe and know the truth of God (*I Tim*. 4: 3; *Eph*. 5: 22–23).

(g) Marriage is consecrated by the Word of God and prayer (*I Tim*. 4: 3, 4, 5).

(h) When a man and woman come together they are one flesh (*Eph*. 5: 31; note also *I Cor*. 7: 16); thus those who are married cease to have exclusive rights over their own bodies (*I Cor*. 7: 1–6).

(i) Within marriage the full enjoyment of the sexual relationship is encouraged within the bounds of self-control and holiness (*I Cor*. 7: 3–6).

(j) The marriage bond is indissoluble (*Gen*. 2: 24; *Matt*. 19: 3–9; Mark 10: 3–9; *Eph*. 5: 31): what God has joined together, no man should dare to put asunder (*Matt*. 19: 6).

(k) Marriage is to be held in honour by all (*Heb*. 13: 4): to violate the sanctity of marital intercourse is great wickedness and sin against God (*Gen*. 39: 9; *I Thess*. 4: 6; *Heb*. 13: 4).

3. We must also appreciate the honourableness of the unmarried state.

(a) The unmarried state is recognised to be God's call to some (*Matt*. 19: 10–12; *I Cor*. 7: 7).

(b) Celibacy or virginity is a gift of God to some, even as marriage is to others (*I Cor*. 7: 7, 17).

(c) There are definite advantages in the unmarried state so far as service for God is concerned: undivided attention to the Lord is possible in a manner which is impossible to the married (*I Cor*. 7: 32–35).

(d) The unmarried should regard themselves as married to Christ (*I Tim*. 5: 11)—their first pledge is to Him (*I Tim*. 5: 12).

4. Self-knowledge is to govern a Christian's attitude to sex.

(a) The Christian's old nature is corrupt through deceitful lusts (*Eph*. 4: 22): the lusts of the flesh are at war with the soul (*I Pet*. 2: 11), and the danger attaching to these lusts is never to be overlooked (*I Cor*. 9: 27).

(b) The Christian's new nature

is in conflict with the old; and he is to live according to the new and not according to the old (*Eph*. 4: 17–24).

(c) Satan's temptations centre especially around the sexual urge (*I Cor*. 7: 5): some aspects of sex are particularly tempting and trying in youth (*II Tim*. 2: 22).

(d) The recognition of this problem inherent in man's nature means that the body is to be disciplined and subdued (*I Cor*. 9: 27).

(e) Knowledge of human nature makes plain that physical desire and attraction are often confused with love, whereas they are by no means the same (*II Sam*. 13); and physical desire, mistaken for love, once acceded to, frequently leads to lack of respect and hatred (*II Sam*. 13: 15).

(f) Of ourselves we cannot control the passion of our sinful hearts and flesh (*Rom*. 7: 19, 20, 24); only by the grace of the Holy Spirit can we overcome (*Gal*. 5: 16).

5. The control of the thought-life.

(a) Doubtless we have all sin-ned with regard to sex, in thought if not in deed, at some time (*John* 8: 1–9).

(b) Sin begins with the thoughts (*Mark* 7: 21; *Matt*. 5: 28).

(c) Evil thoughts, fornication, adultery, coveting, foolishness come naturally and easily to our old nature (*Mark* 7: 21).

(d) Jesus condemned as adultery of the heart the adulterous desire, even if no adulterous designs attach themselves to the desire (*Matt*. 5: 27, 28).

(e) We need to be ruthless in dealing with those things which would lead us astray sexually (*Matt*. 5: 27–30).

(f) We need to fill our thoughts with things which are honourable, just, pure, lovely and gracious (*Phil*. 4: 8), rather than occupying ourselves at all with things which are unpleasant (*Eph*. 5: 12).

6. God's warnings with regard to the misuse of sex.

(a) Men are solemnly forewarned that God will judge all who abuse sex (*I Thess*. 4:

108

6): the immoral and the adulterous He will judge (*Heb.* 13: 4).

(b) All who live according to human passions and not according to God's will shall give account to God who is ready to judge the living and the dead (*I Pet.* 4: 2–5).

(c) No immoral or impure person has any inheritance in the kingdom of Christ and of God (*Eph.* 5: 5, 6).

7. The Christian's body.

(a) The Christian is not to regard his body as his own—it has been bought with a price (*I Cor.* 6: 19, 20).

(b) The Christian is to have a reverence for his body: it is a temple of the Holy Spirit (*I Cor.* 6: 19).

(c) The Christian is to glorify God in his body (*I Cor.* 6: 20).

(d) The body is to be continuously presented to God as a living sacrifice (*Rom.* 12: 1).

(e) By immorality a man sins against his own body (*I Cor.* 6: 18), and against Christ (*I Cor.* 6: 15, 17).

8. Principles are laid down in the Bible to govern and guide man-woman relationships.

(a) The Christian is to know how he should behave with regard to sex whether married or unmarried (*I Thess.* 4: 3, 4, 5).

(b) The Christian's attitude to sex will surprise the non-Christian, and especially those who knew him before he became a Christian (*I Pet.* 4: 3, 4).

(c) Christians are to recognise that the fulfilment of fleshly lusts is not the most important thing in life: more important is their heavenly citizenship (*I Pet.* 2: 11).

(d) The Christian must not be deceived by those who try to make him think that Christian standards are too high (*Eph.* 5: 6).

(e) Perfect propriety is to characterise the Christian's relationships with those of the other sex (*I Tim.* 5: 1, 2).

(*f*) Courtesy is to dominate the Christian man's relationship to the woman, remembering that she is the weaker vessel (*I Pet.* 3: 7; *I Tim.* 5: 2, 3).

(g) The Christian is to be wise

and careful in his relationships with those of the other sex (*Eph.* 5: 15).

(h) The Christian should beware of foolishness in his approach to members of the other sex (*Eph.* 5: 15–17).

(i) The Christian should beware of silly talk or levity about sex, because such leads all too often to foolish action (*Eph.* 5: 3–5).

(j) The Christian should beware of allowing his emotions to be excessively aroused—this is Paul's argument against strong drink in this very chapter (*Eph.* 5: 18).

(k) Sexual temptation is to be avoided where possible (*II Tim.* 2: 22): it is no disgrace to run away from sexual temptation—indeed it is commended (*Gen.* 39: 12; *II Tim.* 2: 22).

(l) There is to be nothing unclean in the Christian's experience of sex (*I Thess.* 4: 7).

(m) Self-control is to be exercised ruthlessly before marriage: if this is impossible, then marriage should take place (*I Cor.* 7: 9, 36)—it is recognised that the sexual urge is more powerful in some than in others (*I Cor.* 7: 8–9, 36–38).

9. **The general principles of Christian conduct taught in the Bible must be applied also to sex.**

(a) The Christian must not allow his attitude to sex to be governed by the moral climate of his day (*Eph.* 4: 14–21); he is not to form close associations with those who reject Christian teaching on the subject (*Eph.* 5: 7), and he must be ready to speak out against wrong views of sex (*Eph.* 5: 11).

(b) The Christian should endeavour to learn from the Scriptures what is pleasing to God with regard to sex (*Eph.* 5: 10, 17; *I Pet.* 4: 2).

(c) The Christian is called to sanctification (*I Thess.* 4: 7): his use of sex is to be consistent with holiness (*I Thess.* 4: 7).

(d) There is a right time and place for everything one needs to do (*Eccl.* 3: 1–8).

(e) There are circumstances where it is necessary to refrain from things which are right in themselves (*I Cor.* 7: 29–31).

110

(f) All appearance of evil in relationships between the sexes should be avoided (*I Thess.* 5: 22).

(g) Whatever the Christian would wish others to do to him, he should do to others (*Matt.* 7: 12).

(h) The Christian should not provoke others to envy by reason of some special relationship (*Gal.* 5: 26; *I Thess.* 4: 10, 11).

(i) The well-being of the Christian's soul will be a guide as to his attitude in particular situations to sex (*I Pet.* 2: 11).

(j) The Holy Spirit is given to enable the Christian to gain victory over sin in the body (*Rom.* 8: 13; *II Tim.* 1: 7; *Gal.* 5: 23): as the Holy Spirit's help is sought sincerely, His help is received (*Luke* 11: 13).

(k) The right attitude to sex is maintained as Christians are filled with the Spirit, have fellowship with one another sincerely and spiritually, and endeavour at all times and in all places to give God the thanks for His gifts (*Eph.* 5: 18–20; read these verses in the light of the earlier verses of the chapter).

25. GIVING

Question: What does the Bible teach about giving?

Answer: Giving, modelled upon the Old Testament tithe, and calculated to forward God's work by the support of His servants, is to be regular, systematic and according to how God has prospered us. However, the New Testament does not lay down the principle of the tithe, but it presupposes that our giving will more than equal the tithe because of the inward compulsion of the Holy Spirit moving us to respond to the generosity of God with similar generosity.

1. Any consideration of Christian giving must begin with God's giving.

(a) Every good and perfect gift comes from God the Father (*Jas.* 1: 17).

(b) When God gives, He gives with an abundant fullness, e.g. in His blessing of creation (*Gen.* 1: 22, 28; cf.

111

Ps. 104), in His promises to His people (*Gen.* 17: 1–24; 22: 17; *Ex.* 1: 7, 20; 32: 13), in His bestowal of rich blessings (*Deut.* 28: 11) and in His gift of salvation (*Ps.* 5: 7; 31: 19; 51: 1).

(c) God's giving is limitless— He has given us His Son, and in His Son He gave Himself (*John* 3: 16; 1: 14; *Acts* 20: 28; *II Cor.* 9: 15).

(d) Our Lord Jesus Christ, though rich beyond all telling, became poor for our sakes, so that we through His poverty might become rich (*II Cor.* 8: 9): He gave His life as a ransom for many (*Matt.* 20: 28), and His flesh for the life of the world (*John* 6: 32, 51; cf. Luke 22: 19).

(e) He makes us rich with every spiritual gift (*I Cor.* 1: 5 ff), with a variety of spiritual gifts (*I Cor.* 12), the gifts of His ascension (*Eph.* 4: 7–12).

(f) God's giving is part of the outflow of His love towards us (*I John* 3: 17).

(g) He gives to us that we may be in a position to give and to be generous in our giving (*II Cor.* 9: 11).

2. **Tithing was the basic pattern of giving in the Old Testament.** (A tithe is a tenth part, and it may have to do with the ancient custom of counting by tens, a system made easy by the ten fingers and toes common to man.)

(a) The Jews were instructed to tithe their cereal and fruit crops and their livestock (*Lev.* 27: 30–33).

(b) Underlying the tithe was the basic idea that the earth is the Lord's and all that is in it (*Ps.* 24: 1).

(c) Tithing came to mean an expression of thanksgiving to God for His generosity (*Gen.* 28: 20–22).

(d) The Jews paid their tithes to the Levites (*Num.* 18: 20–24), or later to the Levites who served as priests (cf. *Heb.* 7: 5), in return for the service they rendered at the sanctuary (*Num.* 18: 21), and as compensation for their lack of landed possessions.

(e) Payment was made in Jerusalem (*Deut.* 12: 5, 6, 11, 17, 18) or each third year in their home communities (*Deut.* 14: 28–29; 26: 12).

(f) The Levites, in turn, were required to give one tenth of the tithe to the priests (*Num.* 18: 26, 28; *Neh.* 10: 38–39).

(g) In times of spiritual decline the people neglected often to pay their tithes, so that Hezekiah, for example, found it necessary to call authoritatively for their payment (*II Chron.* 31: 4–12).

(h) Nehemiah discovered a similar position of neglect (*Neh.* 13: 12).

(i) Malachi was obliged to rebuke the people for robbing God by withholding tithes and offerings (*Mal.* 3: 7–12).

(j) In the Old Testament, as in the New, giving is no substitute for justice, mercy and faithfulness (*Micah.* 6: 8; *Matt.* 23: 23; *Luke* 11: 42; 18: 9–14).

(k) If we ask, Is tithing an obligation under the new covenant? the New Testament maintains an eloquent silence on the matter (for example, see *I Cor.* 9: 13).

3. **The New Testament has much to say about the characteristics of Christian giving.**

(a) It will be, pre-eminently, a reflection of God's dealings with us (*Matt.* 18: 32, 33), and an outflow of the giving of ourselves to the Lord (*II Cor.* 8: 15).

(b) It will be according to our means (*Acts* 11: 29), as God has prospered us (*I Cor.* 16: 2).

(c) At the same time it will be undeterred by our means, whether large or small, because giving will be counted a privilege (*II Cor.* 8: 3, 4).

(d) It will be regular, systematic, and without fuss or ostentation (*I Cor.* 16: 2; cf. *Matt* 6: 2–4).

(e) It will often be costly (*Luke* 21: 4), frequently generous beyond measure (*II Cor.* 8: 2), and to the limit of our resources (*II Cor.* 8: 3)—in fact, it will set no limits (*I John* 3: 16).

(f) It will be joyful, cheerful, ungrudging, an act of the will, without external pressure, and a matter of individual determination (*Luke* 21: 4; *II Cor.* 8: 2–4, 8; 9: 5, 7).

(g) It will look for nothing in return (*Luke* 14: 12 ff), and it will take every possible form (*II Cor.* 9: 11).

(h) It will be seen as one of the reasons why we go to work

and earn money and have possessions—we gain in order to give away (*Eph.* 4: 28).

4. The secret of generous giving is correct motivation.

(a) The desire to respond to the grace and generosity of God, and our thanksgiving to God for the gift of His Son, and the love we feel for Him (*II Cor.* 8: 7–9; 9: 15).

(b) The desire to acknowledge that God Himself is our true wealth rather than the sum total of our material possessions, as the world would have us think (*Ps.* 73: 25; *II Cor.* 6: 10).

(c) The desire to be a good steward of what God has given us (*Rom.* 14: 12; *I Pet.* 4: 10 f).

(d) The desire to show our love for God by love for others (*I John* 5: 1–2), as we respond to Him in good deeds by the generous use of our material resources (*I Tim.* 6: 18).

(e) The desire to help and relieve those who are in need, and especially fellow-Christians (*Acts* 11: 29; *I Cor.* 16: 1; *II Cor.* 8: 4; *Gal.* 6: 10): we share our surplus so that their deficit may be met, and on occasions vice versa (*II Cor.* 8: 14, 15; *Eph.* 4: 28; *I Tim.* 6: 18).

(f) Our desire to be faithful in supporting God's work by providing adequately and generously for the support of those who serve Christ in the gospel at home and overseas (*I Cor.* 9; *Gal.* 6: 6; *I Tim.* 5: 17).

5. There are inevitable consequences of proper giving.

(a) God is pleased by our giving (*II Cor.* 9: 7): it is a spiritual sacrifice (*Heb.* 13: 16).

(b) God more than makes up to us what we give (*II Cor.* 9: 8; *Phil.* 4: 15–19).

(c) God is thanked and praised for our giving by those who benefit from it (*II Cor.* 9: 13), and so He is glorified (*II Cor.* 8: 19).

(d) God encourages us by it too: it is a proof of our faith by our works (*II Cor.* 8: 13; *Jas.* 2: 15, 16), and evidence of God's grace at work in us (*II Cor.* 8: 1).

(e) By giving in a way which pleases God, we lay up for

ourselves a good foundation for the future (*I Tim.* 6: 19).

(f) We discover too in the present a unique happiness (*Acts* 20: 35) and unexpected blessings (*Mal.* 3: 10).

26. PRIDE

Question: What is pride? and why is it sinful?

Answer: The pride we have in view is that which shows itself in our having too high an opinion of ourself. It constitutes sin because it leads us to think we can be independent of God as well as superior and often indifferent to our fellowmen.

1. The nature of pride.

(a) It comes from within our heart (*Mark* 7: 22; *Luke* 9: 46, 47): it is described as the imagination of a man's heart (*Luke* 1: 51), arrogance of heart (*Isa.* 9: 9), and the lifting up of the heart (*Ps.* 131: 1; *Dan.* 5: 20).

(b) It is our seeing ourselves as different from others in some respect, and feeling superior (*I Cor.* 4: 7); it is a false sense of our own importance (*Matt.* 26: 33; *Mark* 14: 29).

(c) It is an inappropriate love of self (*II Tim.* 3: 2), and the exaltation of self (*Luke* 18: 9–14).

(d) It is our departing from our proper position before God and our fellows (*Jude* 6), thinking of ourselves more highly than we ought to think (*Rom.* 12: 3).

2. Forms of pride.

(a) It may take the form of pride in **appearance** (*Mark* 12: 38; *I Pet.* 3: 3).

(b) It may take the form of pride in **position** or **prestige** (*Mark* 9: 33–37; *Luke* 9: 46–48; *Mark* 12: 38, 39; *I John* 2: 16).

(c) It may take the form of pride in **power** (*Lev.* 26: 19; *Ezek.* 30: 6; cf. *Acts* 8: 18, 19).

(d) It may take the form of pride in **achievements** and **success** (*II Chron.* 26: 15, 16).

(e) It may take the form of pride in **possessions** (*II Kings* 20: 13; *Luke* 12: 13–21).

(f) It may take the form of pride in **knowledge** (*I Cor.* 8: 1) and of **intellect** (*Isa.* 5: 21).

(g) It may take the form of pride in **abilities** and **spiritual gifts** (*I Pet.* 4: 10–11; cf. *I Cor.* 12: 4 ff).

(h) It may take the form of pride in **men,** and the **human relationships** we possess (*I Cor.* 3: 21).

(i) It may take the form of pride in **spiritual blessing** (*II Cor.* 12: 7).

3. **The expression of pride.**

(a) It expresses itself in attitudes (*Eccl.* 7: 8), in excessive self-confidence (*Matt.* 26: 33–35; *Mark* 14: 29–31; *Luke* 22: 33), in an unwillingness to take advice (*Prov.* 13: 10), in contempt for others (*Ps.* 123: 4), in presumptuous planning for the future (*Jas.* 4: 15, 16), and in arrogance (*Prov.* 8: 13).

(b) It expresses itself in our **eyes**: we may have haughty eyes (*Prov.* 6: 17; 21: 4), and such may first be demonstrated in regard to our parents (*Prov.* 30: 17).

(c) It expresses itself in our **objectives** and **ambitions**: pride always wants more of that of which it is proud (*Hab.* 2: 5), which is another way of saying that it is greedy.

(d) It expresses itself in **words** (*I Sam.* 2: 3; *Luke* 9: 46): particularly in boasting (*Isa.* 10: 12, 13), exaggeration (*Dan.* 4:1; *II Pet.*2: 18; *Jude* 16), and argumentativeness (*II Tim.* 2: 24, 25).

(e) It expresses itself in **actions** and **reactions**: it does not rejoice in the success of others (*I Cor.* 13: 4); it prompts anger and violence (*Gen.* 4: 6 ff).

4. **The effects of pride.**

(a) It encourages arrogance (*Prov.* 21: 24).

(b) It inflates or puffs up (*I Cor.* 4: 6); it lifts us up to a false sense of our importance (*I Tim.* 3: 6).

(c) It brings strife in its wake (*Prov.* 13: 10; 28: 25).

(d) It breeds a false self-confidence (*Matt.* 26: 33–35; *Mark* 14: 29–31; *Luke* 22: 33).

(e) It makes us foolishly feel we can be independent of everyone, even including God (*Ps.* 10: 4; *Hos.* 7: 10).

(f) It provides a false sense of security (*Obad.* 3, 4).

(g) It leads to contempt and rejection of God's Word (*Jer.* 43: 2).

(h) It leads to self-deception (*Jer.* 49: 16); the pride of our heart deceives us (*Prov.* 26: 12; *Obad.* 3).

(i) It becomes an obstacle to our worship of God, and acceptance with Him (*Gen.* 4: 3–5; *Jas.* 4: 6).

(j) It cuts us off from God because it constitutes part of our inner defilement (Mark 7: 20–23).

(k) It ultimately brings both a fall (*I Cor.* 10: 12) and disgrace *Prov.* 16: 18; cf. 18: 12).

5. **Examples of pride in the Bible.**

(a) The angels who did not keep their own position (*Jude* 6; cf. *Isa.* 14: 12; ff).

(b) Pharaoh, who was proud in his dealings with the Israelites (*Neh.* 9: 10).

(c) Hezekiah, who was too proud to show his gratitude to God for His goodness to him (*II Chron.* 32: 25).

(d) Nebuchadnezzar, who was proud of his might and majesty (*Dan.* 3; 4: 30; 5: 20).

(e) Belshazzar, whose heart was proud in that he refused to humble himself (*Dan.* 5: 22, 23).

(f) Haman, who desired respect for himself from men (*Esth.* 3: 5).

(g) Moab, whose pride was seen in arrogance and empty boasting (*Isa.* 16: 6).

(h) Tyre, whose pride was in their achievements and their commerce (*Isa.* 23: 8, 9).

(i) Edom, whose pride misled her to feel she was not vulnerable from attack (*Obad.* 3).

(j) Babylon, whose pride led her to be defiant against the Lord (*Jer.* 50: 29, 32).

(k) Assyria, whose pride gave her a sense of superiority over all others (*Ezek.* 31: 3, 10).

(l) Israel, whose pride was intoxicating and without justification (*Isa.* 28: 1; *Hos.* 5: 5, 9).

(m) Judah, whose pride caused her not to give glory to God (*Jer.* 13: 15, 19).

(n) The Pharisees, whose pride caused them to trust in themselves that they were righteous and to despise others (*Luke* 18: 9–14).

(o) The scribes, whose pride was seen in their delight in

outward show and public acknowledgement (*Mark* 12: 38, 39).

(p) Peter, who felt he was stronger than others and able to withstand temptation (*Matt.* 26:33–35; *Mark* 14:29–31; *Luke* 22: 33).

(q) Herod Agrippa, who thought he could take glory to himself which was God's alone (*Acts* 12: 21–23).

(r) The Laodiceans, whose pride made them blind to their spiritual poverty (*Rev.* 3: 17).

6. The guilt of pride.

First, it causes us to sin against God.

(a) It is declared to be sin (*Prov.* 21: 4).

(b) When we are proud we have lost sight of our indebtedness to God, that we have nothing good which we have not, in fact, received (*I Cor.* 4: 7).

(c) We ascribe to ourselves the success which we really owe to God (*Judg.* 7: 2).

(d) We refuse to hear God's words and stubbornly follow our own heart's inclination (*Jer.* 13: 10).

(e) We think we can be independent of God when, in fact, the opposite is the case (*Jer.* 13: 8–11).

(f) We trust not in God but in ourselves, believing that we can build our life on what we think we can accomplish and control ourselves (*Ps.* 52: 1; 75: 4; 94: 3, 4).

Secondly, the guilt of pride is that it also causes us to sin against others.

(g) Puffed up, we favour one person against another (*I Cor.* 4: 6).

(h) Conceited, we ignore and despise those whom we think inferior to us (*Rom.* 12: 16; cf. *Luke* 18: 9).

(i) Proud, we think little of the interests of others and are often inconsiderate of them (*Ps.* 10: 2; *Prov.* 21: 24).

7. The condemnation of pride.

(a) One of the factors that should condemn pride in our own eyes is that it is Satan's pre-eminent sin (*I Tim.* 3: 6; *Rev.* 13: 5).

(b) God has no pleasure in our foolish pride (*Jer.* 13: 15; *Zeph.* 3: 11).

(c) Pride is part of those

characteristics which mark men out as opposed to God (*II Tim.* 3: 2 ff).

(d) God hates pride (*Amos* 6: 8; *Jer.* 13: 9) and He resists the proud (*Jas.* 4: 6; *I Pet.* 5: 5).

(e) Pride makes God's judgment inevitable (*Jer.* 13: 15–17;), so that He will put an end to pride (*Ps.* 18: 27; *Isa.* 2: 12; 13: 11; 23: 9; *Jer.* 13: 9).

(f) Those who walk in pride, God is well able to abase (*Dan.* 4: 37).

8. The cure of pride.

(a) Its cure begins when we realise that there is no place at all for pride in ourselves in the presence of God (*I Cor.* 1: 29).

(b) Its cure proceeds as we see ourselves as sinners, and individually as "the worst" of sinners (*I Tim.* 1: 15), in stark contrast to how we once viewed ourselves (*Phil.* 3: 4–6).

(c) Its cure is about to be effected when we abandon all claims to self-righteousness and depend utterly and completely on Jesus Christ for both salvation and righteousness before God (*Phil.* 3: 7–11), so that we glory in Jesus Christ (*Phil.* 3: 3), and in His Cross (*Gal.* 6: 14).

(d) The cure must never be taken for granted, for the danger of pride will not be removed until we are changed perfectly into our Lord's likeness (*II Cor.* 12: 7; Phil. 3:21).

(e) Pride is kept under control as we realise that the only true pride is pride of the Lord (*I Cor.* 1: 31): paradoxically, having humbled ourselves before God, we can boast in the Lord (*Jer.* 9: 23 f), in His divine intervention and help in the past, and in the assurance we have of the same benefits in the future (*I Chron.* 16: 27 f; 29: 11; *Ps.* 5: 11; 32: 11; 89: 17 f).

(f) The cure of pride is assisted by our being mindful of the proverbs of Scripture concerning pride (*I Kings* 20: 11; *Prov.* 25: 14; 27: 1).

(g) Its cure is further assisted by our being mindful of the words of Scripture which warn against pride and encourage instead the pursuit of humility (*Jas.* 4: 6; *I Pet.* 5: 5).

(h) If we do not allow pride to be cured now, it will be finally cured at the day of judgment:

God has a day reserved for the proud and lofty (*Isa*. 2: 12, 17; *Mal*. 4: 1). and His judgment is directed at the extinction of all false pride (*Dan*. 4: 37; *Matt*. 23: 12).

(j) Safety for the Christian lies in the active pursuit of humility, following the example of our Lord Jesus Christ without compromise (*Phil*. 2: 1–13).

27. WRATH

Question: What is wrath? and why is it sinful?

Answer: Wrath is our reaction of indignation and displeasure at the deeds, words or intentions of others. It is not always sinful in that wrath may be a just reaction to wrong but it is very often sinful either because selfishness prompts our anger or because our anger, though justly stirred, runs away with itself and leads us to wrong words and actions.

1. Wrath and anger.

(a) Wrath describes passionate rage which boils up suddenly in an angry outburst, sometimes to disappear almost as quickly, but at other times to become a lasting bitterness.

(b) Wrath and anger are almost synonymous words in the Bible. In the New Testament wrath comes from a Greek root which means "to boil up" or "to well up" and originally denoted violent movement. Wrath, therefore, indicates a rage which quickly bursts forth, often uncontrollably, and as quickly disappears. Anger, however, describes that angry attitude and temper which lasts and is nursed.

(c) In man wrath and anger are especially sins of the tongue (*II Cor*. 12: 20; *Jas*. 3: 3–18), but they find their place on our tongues and in our actions because they are often cherished in our hearts (*Eccl*. 7: 9; *Amos* 1: 11).

2. Wrath and anger are not always out of place and sinful.

(a) We ought to be angry when good is put aside and evil exalted, and we have examples in the Bible of just and holy anger:

(i) Moses was angry at the

120

Israelites' lack of trust in God (*Ex.* 16: 20), and at their apostasy in making a golden calf (*Ex.* 32: 19, 22);

(ii) David was angry at the unjust rich man about whom Nathan told him, not realising at first that it was at himself his anger was rightly directed (*II Sam.* 12: 5);

(iii) Nehemiah was angry at the abuses which had taken place in Jerusalem (*Neh.* 5: 6);

(iv) Paul's spirit was provoked to anger in Athens when he witnessed its idolatry (*Acts* 17: 16).

(b) We have evidence too of God inducing a proper anger in His people for good purposes (*Rom.* 10: 19; *II Cor.* 7: 11).

(c) Our Lord Jesus Christ was angry at men's indifference to human need (*Mark* 3: 5), and His wrath was the revelation of God's wrath.

(d) God's holy and just wrath and anger are described in the Bible in various aspects:

(i) God's wrath is slow (*Ps.* 103: 8; *Isa.* 48: 9; *Jonah* 4: 2; *Nah.* 1: 3);

(ii) God's wrath is righteous (*Ps.* 58: 10, 11; *Lam.* 1: 18;

Rom. 2: 6, 8; 3: 5, 6; 9: 18, 20, 22; *Rev.* 16: 6, 7);

(iii) God's wrath is **perfectly controlled**—e.g. our Lord's cleansing of the temple was not done on impulse, but the night before He inspected the temple (*Mark* 11: 11).

3. But more often than not we do wrong to be angry because of the selfish motives and attitudes which prompt our anger (*Jonah* 4: 4).

(a) Pride—and especially hurt pride—promotes anger (*Gen.* 4: 3–5; *II Kings* 5: 11; *Esth.* 3: 5; *Dan.* 3: 13).

(b) Unwillingness to accept rebuke spurs on anger (*II Chron.* 26: 19).

(c) Jealousy kindles anger (*I Sam.* 17: 28; *Acts* 5: 17, 18).

(d) Resentment encourages anger (*Luke* 4: 28).

(e) Selfishness sparks off anger (*I Kings* 21: 4).

(f) Touchiness provides ready opportunity for anger (*Gen.* 40: 1 f).

(g) Malice is the companion often of anger (*Gen.* 27: 41, 45; *Col.* 3: 8).

4. Wrath and anger do harm and easily lead to other sins.

(a) When we lose control of ourselves on account of wrath or anger sin crouches at the door (*Gen.* 4: 7).

(b) Like a wind or hurricane that arises swiftly or unexpectedly, or a fire that gets out of control, wrath and anger can do immeasurable harm (*Eccl.* 10: 4; *Ps.* 124: 3) and mischief (*Prov.* 6: 34; 15: 1; 16: 14), besides being overwhelming (*Prov.* 27: 4).

(c) They tear us apart (*Amos.* 1: 11).

(d) They show on our face (*Gen.* 4: 5).

(e) They have physical repercussions (*Acts* 7: 54)—to harbour anger or resentment is as bad for the body as it is for the soul (*Prov.* 14: 30).

(f) They mar prayer and fellowship with God (*I Tim.* 2: 8).

(g) They spoil Christian fellowship and the life of the church (*II Cor.* 12: 20).

(h) They give the devil a foothold which he will use to his own evil advantage (*Eph.* 4: 26 f).

(i) They can be the first step even to murder, and they can certainly constitute the spirit of murder for murder is only anger full-grown (*Matt.* 5: 22).

(j) They are accompanied frequently by quarrelling and harsh words (*Prov.* 15: 18; *Eph.* 4: 31).

(k) They lead often to cruelty (*Gen.* 49: 7; *II Chron.* 16: 10; *Prov.* 27: 4) and injustice (*Prov.* 14: 17; 29: 22).

(l) They issue all too often in strife and contention (*Prov.* 21: 19; 29: 22; 30: 33), violence (*Dan.* 2: 12) and murder (*Gen.* 4: 8; 49: 6; *Ex.* 2: 12; *Matt.* 2: 16–18).

5. The condemnation of wrath and anger.

(a) They *are* a characteristic of fools (*Prov.* 12: 16; 14: 17, 29; 27: 3, 4; *Eccl.* 7: 9).

(b) They provide sufficient grounds for terminating friendship, for keeping friendship with a man whose temper is uncontrolled can lead us in the same direction (*Gen.* 49: 6; *Prov.* 22: 24).

(c) They reveal the state of a man's heart (*Luke* 6: 45).

(d) They are a work of the flesh, and are opposed to God's Spirit (*Gal.* 5: 20).

(e) They never work the will of God (*Jas.* 1: 19, 20).

(f) They are an infringement of the sixth commandment (*Matt.* 5: 21, 22).

(g) They bring their own punishment (*Job*. 19: 29; *Prov.* 25: 28).

(h) They are frequently an infringement of God's prerogative of judgment for wrath and anger so easily make us take judgment into our own hands (*Rom.* 12: 19).

(i) They put us in danger of God's judgment (*Matt.* 5: 22).

6. The Christian attitude to wrath and anger.

(a) We recognise wrath and anger, arising from bitterness, as belonging to the old life we once lived before our conversion, and that they are among the many things we are to put away from us (*Eph.* 4: 31).

(b) We are to be slow to be angry (*Ps.* 37: 8; *Prov.* 15: 18; 16: 32; 19: 11; *Tit.* 1: 7; *Jas.* 1: 19).

(c) Aiming at the avoidance of wrath and anger, we also try to placate those who are carried away by wrath and anger, where it is right and possible to do so (*Prov.* 15: 1, 18; 16: 32; 29: 8, 11).

(d) Our aim when anger is justifiable is neither to allow it to cause us to sin (*Eph.* 4: 26), nor to allow Satan to gain a foothold by means of it (*Eph.* 4: 27).

28. ENVY

Question: What is envy? and why is it sinful?

Answer: Envy is basically ill-will occasioned by looking at someone else's superior position or advantages. It is sinful because, besides indicating discontent with God's providence, it is contrary to love for our neighbour in that love rejoices at the good of others.

1. The characteristics of envy.

(a) Envy begrudges the honour and the advantages others enjoy (*Gen.* 26: 14).

(b) It fails to see God's providence in the ordering of gifts, honours and abilities (*Deut.* 8: 17, 18; *Prov.* 30: 8, 9).

(c) It is sad at the happiness of others (*Luke* 15: 25–30).

(d) It makes us hostile to those who have never injured us (*Gen.* 37: 3, 4).

(e) It seeks the destruction of others rather than their welfare (*Matt.* 27: 18; *Mark* 15: 10).

(f) It may even break through every restraint in order to bring about the ruin of the person who is envied (*Gen.* 4: 3–8).

2. The incitement of envy.

(a) It is incited by the attractiveness and commendation given to the virtues of others (*I John* 3: 12; cf. *Gen.* 4: 3–8).

(b) It is stirred up by the success of others (*I Sam.* 18: 8, 9; *Dan.* 6: 3, 4; *Acts* 13: 45; 17: 4, 5).

(c) It is prompted by pride (*I Tim.* 6: 4, 5).

(d) It is encouraged by the existence of both bitterness (*Jas.* 3: 14) and malice (*Tit.* 3: 3) in our hearts towards others.

3. The prevalence of envy.

(a) It was behind man's first rebellion, for by means of the encouragement of envy Satan caused man to lose his enjoyment of unspoiled fellowship with God (*Gen.* 3: 1–6).

(b) It was envy which brought about the first shedding of blood in human history (*Gen.* 4: 5, 8).

(c) It is one of the evil things which is characteristic of the human heart and which marks man's defilement before God (*Mark* 7: 20–23; *Jas.* 3: 14).

(d) It is very often the explanation why people work so hard to succeed, in that they envy their neighbours and want to exceed them (*Eccl.* 4: 4).

(e) It is behind practically all coveting (*I Kings* 21: 1–4).

(f) It can fill a life in company with other sins (*Rom.* 1: 29).

4. The condemnation of envy.

(a) God hates envy (*Prov.* 3: 31, 32).

(b) Envy is a characteristic of the world, as it chooses to live without reference to God (*I Cor.* 3: 3; *Tit.* 3: 3).

(c) In terms of the great conflict there is between light and darkness, envy and jealousy belong to the darkness (*Rom.* 13: 12–13).

(d) Envy is an evidence of a corrupted mind (*Rom.* 1: 28, 29), and is a work of the flesh in contrast to the fruit of the Spirit (*Gal.* 5: 19–23).

(e) Envy is the opposite of fellowship: moved by envy, we desire to have what others have; in fellowship, however, we desire to share with others what we ourselves possess (*Mark* 14: 3–9).

(f) Envy is the opposite of love (*I Cor.* 13: 4; *I John* 3: 11, 12) so that it makes us unlike God (*I John* 4: 8).

(g) Envy makes us like Satan, whose work we further when we allow envy to rule our hearts and actions (*John* 8: 44; *I John* 3: 12).

5. **The dangerous consequences of envy.**

(a) It is more cruel and destructive than anger (*Prov.* 27: 4).

(b) It is like a cancer, doing harm to both the body and the mind, because it takes away our peace of mind (*Prov.* 14: 30).

(c) It ruins spiritual appetite (*I Pet.* 2: 1 f) and fellowship with God (*Ps.* 66: 18).

(d) It quickly leads to insulting language (*I Pet.* 2: 1 f).

(e) It breeds a destructively critical spirit (*Dan.* 6: 3, 4; *Acts* 17: 5).

(f) It gives birth to unwarranted suspicion and anger (*I Sam.* 18: 8, 9).

(g) It can give vent to itself in spiteful actions (*Gen.* 26: 14, 15).

(h) It can suddenly escalate into disorder and every kind of evil (*Jas.* 3: 16; *Gen.* 37: 11; *Acts* 7: 9): conspiracy (*Gen.* 37: 18), mockery (*Gen.* 37: 19), thoughts of murder (*Gen.* 37: 20), violence (*Gen.* 37: 23), cruelty (*Gen.* 37: 24), betrayal (*Gen.* 37: 26–28), lies (*Gen.* 37: 32) and immeasurable hurt to others (*Gen.* 37: 34).

29. LUST

Question: What is lust? and why is it sinful?

Answer: Lust is either uncontrolled, overmastering desire or desire willingly allowed to go beyond that which is lawful and legitimate. Lust is sinful because it puts pleasure

before pleasing God, and it places self-gratification before the good of others.

1. The distinction between desire and lust.

(a) Desires—whether physical, mental, spiritual or sexual —were given by God to man at his creation and were wholly good (*Gen.* 1: 31; *I Tim.* 4: 3, 4; *Jas.* 1: 17).

(b) Sin, however, acting like a poison, mars all men's desires, and left to itself would use them to increase the corruption that is in the world (*II Pet.* 1: 4).

(c) Desire is necessary, for example, if appetite is to ensure that the body is fed (*Matt.* 4: 2), and if the human race is to be continued by procreation (*Gen.* 3: 16; *Heb.* 13: 4).

(d) Our Lord Jesus Christ had an eager desire to eat the Passover with His disciples (*Luke* 22: 15), and Paul had a desire to depart and be with Christ (*Phil.* 1: 23): these desires were wholly commendable.

(e) Our desires, however, can so easily be set on evil things and then they become lusts (*I Cor.* 10: 6).

(f) Desire becomes lust when its object is unlawful (*II Sam.* 11: 3, 4; *Ex.* 20: 14).

(g) Desire becomes lust when it gains control of us rather than our controlling it (*I Thess.* 4: 5)—thus looking becomes covetousness (*Josh.* 7: 21), eating becomes gluttony (*I Sam.* 2: 12–17), attraction leads to mental adultery (*Matt.* 5: 27, 28), and burning sexual desire becomes immorality (*II Sam.* 11: 2, 4).

2. The source of lust.

(a) Desires—both good and bad—find their origin in our heart (*Ps.* 37: 4; *Matt.* 15: 19, 20; *Rom.* 1: 24, 29). (In Biblical language, the heart covers the whole inward life of a man: his thinking, feelings and will.)

(b) Lust is part of our nature as fallen men and women, and that nature may be described as being corrupt through deceitful lusts (*Eph.* 4: 22).

(c) Lust springs from the passions of our mortal bodies which demand satisfaction in unlawful, and therefore sinful ways (*Rom.* 6: 12).

(d) Lust finds its home in our flesh which pleads for the

gratification of its desires (*Rom.* 13: 14; *Gal.* 5: 16).

(e) Lusts reflect the kinship of fallen men and women with the devil (*John* 8: 44).

(f) Lust is a manifestation of the sin which dwells in man and which controls him (*Rom.* 7: 7, 8).

3. Lust's characteristics and objectives.

(a) Lust is deceitful in that it promises happiness but it brings, in fact, misery (*Eph.* 4: 22).

(b) Lust shows itself in uncontrolled passion (*I Thess.* 4: 5) leading to sexual immorality and sometimes perversion (*Rom.* 1: 29; *Jude* 7).

(c) Lust reveals itself in covetousness whether of money (*Acts* 20: 33), other people's material possessions (*Ex.* 20: 17), or another person's body (*Prov.* 6: 25; *Matt.* 5: 28).

(d) Lust's pre-eminent stimulus is what comes to men and women through their eyes (*I John* 2: 16): Eve, for example, was tempted by what she *saw* of the tree in the midst of the garden (*Gen.* 3: 6), and Achan was tempted by what he saw among the spoils of the city of Jericho (*Josh.* 7: 21).

(e) Lust finds itself stirred by what it sees, whether in the form of another person's attractiveness (*II Sam.* 11: 3, 4; *Job* 31: 1; *Matt.* 5: 28) or in terms of the pleasures of the world (*Matt.* 4: 8; *Luke* 8: 14).

(f) Lust can be stimulated by harmful friendships and bad company (*II Tim.* 2: 22).

(g) Lust keeps company with sins such as debauchery, drunkenness, orgies, carousing and idolatry (*I Pet.* 4: 3).

(h) Lust is linked often with filthiness, silly talk and levity (*Eph.* 5: 4).

(i) Lust desires our surrender to it (*I Thess.* 4: 5) through its strong enticements (*Jas.* 1: 14; *Jude* 16).

(j) Lust listens only to what it wants to hear (*II Tim.* 4: 3): men who follow after their own evil desires choose to scoff at all presentations of truth which might make them uncomfortable (*II Pet.* 3: 3).

4. Lust's consequences.

(a) Lust never stands still;

once conceived it gives birth to sin; and sin, when it is is full-grown gives birth to death (*Jas.* 1: 15).

(b) Lust dishonours the body (*Rom.* 1: 24; *I Cor.* 6: 17–20).

(c) Lust ruins the good things of life (*II Pet.* 1: 4).

(d) Lust breeds inward conflicts and outward strife (*Jas.* 4: 1).

(e) Lust chokes the influence of God's Word in the individual's life (*Mark* 4: 19).

(f) Lust leads to transgression and offending one's brother (*I Thess.* 4: 5).

(g) Lust makes us the world's friend and God's enemy (*Jas.* 4: 4): God demands our total obedience and love from the whole heart (*Deut.* 6 : 5).

(h) Lust brings upon itself the judgment of God (*I Thess.* 4: 6): it merits God's wrath (*Col.* 3: 6).

5. The antidote to lust.

(a) The only true antidote to lust is the grace of God that brings salvation and which teaches us to say "No" to ungodliness and worldly passions, and to live self-controlled, upright and godly lives in this present age while we await the return of Jesus Christ (*Tit.* 2: 11–13).

(b) Realising that the Lord Jesus gave Himself for us to redeem us from all wickedness, and to purify for Himself a people that are His very own (*Tit.* 2: 14), prompts gratitude (*Rom.* 12: 1, 2) and the desire to live for Him and not for ourselves (*II Cor.* 5: 15).

(c) We say "No", therefore, to worldly passions (*Tit.* 2: 12); we flee evil desires, if necessary, and pursue righteousness (*II Tim.* 2: 22); we put off our old self with its wrong desires and put on the new self, created to be like God in true righteousness and holiness (*Eph.* 4: 23, 24).

(d) We aim at living self-controlled lives (*Tit.* 2: 12): the godly man is not passionless, but controlled in his passions (*Gal.* 5: 23, 24).

(e) We find strength for these things from knowing that they are God's will (*I Thess.* 4: 3; *I Pet.* 4: 2 f).

(f) We find power for these things by the indwelling of the Holy Spirit (*Gal.* 5: 16).

(g) We find daily encouragement from God's very great and precious promises to persevere in proving the reality of the antidote that His salvation provides against lust (*Heb.* 13: 21; *II Pet.* 1: 4).

30. GLUTTONY

Question: What is gluttony?

Answer: Gluttony is excessive eating, so that a man lives to eat rather than eating to live. It is sinful because by it a man makes a god of his stomach, and harms both his body and his usefulness to others.

1. Gluttony in general.

(a) The Greek word for "glutton" in the New Testament represents someone who eats too much (*Matt.* 11: 19; *Luke* 7: 34).

(b) Food and drink can become a foolish preoccupation of life (*Luke* 21: 34).

(c) Gluttony is greedy over-indulgence in food—or eating for eating's sake (*Prov.* 23: 20).

(d) Gluttony goes beyond what is enough (*Prov.* 25: 16), in that it eats more than the body requires for satisfaction (*Ps.* 78: 29, 30); and special occasions are thought of often as a particular opportunity for excess (*Prov.* 23: 1, 2).

(e) The glutton also tends to eat too frequently, and at the wrong times (*Eccl.* 10: 16); he eats not for strength but for the enjoyment of excess (*Eccl.* 10: 17).

(f) Gluttony pays undue attention to the desire for food, and allows the desires of the flesh to dominate life (*Rom.* 13: 13, 14).

(g) Gluttony is accompanied in many instances by excessive drinking (*Prov.* 23: 20, 21), and is to be regarded as equally vicious as drunkenness (*Deut.* 21: 20; *Prov.* 23: 20).

2. The effects of gluttony.

(a) Gluttony leads to our surrender to natural appetites with their bias to excess and sin. Desires naturally characterise the body and mind of man (*Eph.* 2: 3), and because of sin those desires can often be deceitful (*Eph.* 4: 22), and Satan may endeavour to lead us astray, if he can, by the necessary appetite we have for food (*Matt.* 4: 3).

(b) Gluttony leads to lethargy and drowsiness (*Prov.* 23: 20, 21).

(c) Gluttony leads to sleep at the wrong times all too often (*Prov.* 23: 20, 21).

(d) Gluttony leads to laziness and sloth (*Eccl.* 10: 16–18).

(e) Gluttony leads to the dulling of a man's senses (*Prov.* 23: 21) so that he can become oblivious of moral and spiritual issues (*Amos* 6: 4, 7), and lacking in all spiritual alertness (*Luke* 21: 34–36).

(f) Gluttony can prove a great snare to a man because it can blunt his awareness of spiritual and moral issues (*Gen.* 25: 29–34; *Heb.* 12: 16, 17).

(g) Gluttony can lead to other associated evils (*Deut.* 21: 20; *Prov.* 23: 21; *Ps.* 141: 4), including glorying in excess (*Phil.* 3: 19).

(h) Gluttony can prove ruinous in its influence upon others (*Prov.* 28: 7; *Eccl.* 10: 16, 17).

(i) Gluttony tends to lead to a feeling of self-sufficiency and independence of God (*Deut.* 32: 15; *Prov.* 30: 8, 9; *Isa.* 22: 13).

(j) Gluttony injures health in that the body becomes fat and bloated (*Deut.* 32: 15), and may bring physical complications which could have been avoided (*Eccl.* 11: 10).

(k) Gluttony can be the first step to poverty (*Prov.* 23: 21).

(l) Gluttony has ruin as its end (*Phil.* 3: 19), and a self indulgent person can be described as "dead while alive" (*I Tim.* 5: 6).

(m) Esau (*Gen.* 25: 29–34), Eli's sons (*I Sam.* 2: 12–17) and the rich man called Dives (*Luke* 16: 19–31), are illustrations of some of the sad effects of gluttony.

3. The sinfulness of gluttony.

(a) Gluttony is, in effect, waste of food, and waste of food is contrary to God's intention (*Lev.* 19: 9; 23: 22; *John* 6: 12).

(b) Gluttony ignores truths and obligations God has plainly revealed. For example, the glutton forgets that it is not mere food that gives life (*Deut.* 8: 3); the glutton fails to see that God is concerned with the daily practicalities of life (*I Cor.* 10: 31), and he certainly does not seek God's

130

blessing on his eating (*I Tim.* 4: 4, 5).

(c) Gluttony is frequently part of a hedonistic approach to life, that is to say, the theory of ethics in which pleasure is regarded as the chief good or the proper end of action (*Isa.* 22: 13; *Luke* 12: 19; *I Cor.* 15: 32).

(d) Gluttony is a form of slavery because a man makes himself a slave of food rather than a servant of God (*I Cor.* 6: 12, 13); instead of ruling his body, a man's body rules him (*Rom.* 13: 13, 14).

(e) Gluttony makes a god of food and of the stomach (*Phil.* 3: 19).

(f) Gluttony is a manifestation of worldliness, of loving the world rather than God in that lavish and expensive eating habits are something of which men can be foolishly proud (*I John* 2: 15–17; cf. *Phil.* 3: 19).

(g) Gluttony often offends the principle and commandment that we should love our neighbour as ourselves. Gluttony is frequently the sin of the person who lives only for himself (*Luke* 16: 19), so that while he eats, others whom he could help go hungry (*Luke* 16: 19, 20).

(h) Gluttony causes a man to sin against his body, forgetful of the fact that his body is a wonderful gift of God (*Ps.* 139: 14).

(i) God judges gluttony (*Num.* 11: 33, 34; *Ps.* 78: 31), and we shall all be judged for our use of the body (*II Cor.* 5: 10).

4. **Correctives for the avoidance of gluttony.**

(i) *A proper perspective and sense of priorities.*

(a) One day God will put an end to food and to the stomach (*I Cor.* 6: 13).

(b) There are deeper dimensions to human life than physical hunger (*Deut.* 8: 3): the food we more urgently need is that which nourishes spiritual life.

(c) The needs of the body are not as important as the requirements of the soul (*Matt.* 9: 1–8; *Mark* 2: 1–12; *I Cor.* 5: 5).

(d) God's kingdom is not a matter of eating and drinking but of the righteousness, peace and joy which the Holy Spirit gives (*Rom.* 14: 17).

(e) For the man who knows

131

God, eating and drinking are not secular activities: whether he eats or drinks, he wants to do all to the glory of God (*I Cor.* 10: 31).

(f) True satisfaction is found neither in food nor in other physical pleasures but in doing God's will (*John* 4: 34).

(ii) *An understanding of the proper place of food in human life.*

(a) Food is a just necessity for life: every man needs to take nourishment both of proper quality and sufficient quantity to maintain his physical life and well-being (*I Tim.* 6: 8); food is meant for the stomach, and the stomach for food (*I Cor.* 6: 13).

(b) All of God's creatures depend on Him for food (*Ps.* 104: 27, 28), and we are encouraged to pray for our daily bread (*Matt.* 6: 11), and to regard it as the proper objective of our daily work (*Eccl.* 6: 7; *II Thess.* 3: 10).

(c) Food is good since God created foods to be received with thanksgiving by those who believe and know the truth (*I Tim.* 4: 4 ff). He desires that we should enjoy His gifts (*I Tim.* 6: 17), for His goodness is illustrated to us in terms of the good things He has given us to eat (*Deut.* 32: 13, 14).

(d) Health, however, does not depend on living upon delicacies (*Dan.* 1: 5–16).

(e) Food should be eaten principally for the sake of maintaining strength (*Eccl.* 10: 17), and while enjoyment of eating is lawful, slavery to that enjoyment is not (*I Cor.* 6: 12).

(iii) *An appreciation of the Christian teaching concerning his body.*

(a) The body is the sphere or activity in which we do either good or evil (*II Cor.* 5: 10).

(b) The body is fearfully and wonderfully made (*Ps.* 139: 14) but sadly can be the subject of abuse (*Eccl.* 11: 10).

(c) The Christian's bodily life should be determined by what God has done for him in Jesus Christ (*Rom.* 12: 1, 2; *I Cor.* 6: 12–14, 20): the body is not meant for lust but for the Lord (*I Cor.* 6: 13).

(d) The body is the instrument, in which, and by which, we may honour Christ (*Phil.* 1: 20).

(e) The highest dignity is given to the body in that the Christian's body is a temple of the Holy Spirit within, which he has of God (*I Cor.* 6: 19).

(f) Hence the Christian is to know how to possess, control and manage his own body in holiness and honour (*I Thess.* 4: 3, 4).

(iv) *A rightful maintenance of self-discipline.*

(a) Restraint is to be put upon a big appetite (*Prov.* 23: 2), so that enough is eaten rather than too much (*Prov.* 25: 16).

(b) Part of the fruit of the Spirit is self-control (*Gal.* 5: 23).

(c) Fasting may find a place in this self-discipline and God's people throughout the centuries have set an example of fasting: David (*II Sam.* 12: 16, 22; *Ps.* 109: 24), Esther (*Esther* 4: 16), Nehemiah (*Neh.* 1: 4), Daniel (*Dan.* 9: 3), Anna (*Luke* 2: 37), the disciples of John (*Matt.* 9: 14), Cornelius (*Acts* 10: 30), the early Christians (*Acts* 13: 2), and the apostles (*II Cor.* 6: 5; 11: 27).

(d) It is important to remember, however, that Christianity brought an end to ritual fasting (*Mark* 2: 18–22).

(e) Our Lord Himself fasted (*Matt.* 4: 2), and He made clear that certain situations are satisfactorily dealt with only by prayer and fasting (*Matt.* 17: 21).

(f) Fasting is linked, therefore, with prayer in special situations (*Mark* 9: 29): it is part of worship (*Luke* 2: 37; *Acts* 13: 1, 2) and a symbol of self-humbling before God (*Ps.* 69: 10; 35: 13).

(g) Fasting, however, is never to be a matter of display, but is to be in secret (*Matt.* 6: 16–18).

(v) *A genuine concern for the needs of others.*

(a) We avoid gluttony by exercising a proper concern for the material needs of others (*I Tim.* 6: 17, 18).

(b) We are to be generous and share our food with those who are hungry (*Prov.* 22: 9).

(c) We should discipline our intake of food so that we can assist the poor (*Isa.* 58: 6, 7).

(d) We are not to neglect the needs of people's bodies to be fed (*Jas.* 2: 16; cf. *Matt.* 25: 42).

(e) Even in the way we eat, we are to have the good of others in view before our own good (*I Cor*. 10: 31–33).

(vi) *The pursuit of the true satisfaction God intends for us.*

(a) The Christian knows that there is a better way to joy and happiness than excess in the satisfaction of his physical appetites: he is to find it in the continuous experience of God's Spirit filling his life (*Eph*. 5: 18).

(b) The Christian's "food" should be to do the Father's will (*John* 4: 34; cf. *II Cor*. 5: 9).

31. AVARICE

Question: What is avarice and why is it sinful?

Answer: Avarice is the love of money and greed for gain, the opposite of contentment. It is sinful because it is a form of idolatry in that money and what it may secure become a man's god, leading him not only to dishonour God his Creator but to neglect and abuse his fellow man.

1. **Avarice defined.**

(a) One of the principal features of human life is the amassing of earthly property (*Matt*. 6: 19 ff).

(b) Avarice is the love of money and greed for gain (*I Tim*. 3: 3).

(c) Avarice means that a man never has enough (*Hab*. 2: 5).

(d) Avarice is the opposite of contentment with what a man already possesses (*Heb*. 13: 5).

(e) Avarice is not limited to material possessions: its focus, for example, can be upon power (*III John* 9) or sexual immorality (*II Pet*. 2: 14).

(f) Avarice often takes the form of covetousness (*Josh*. 7: 20, 21).

(g) Avarice is laying up treasure upon earth to the total neglect of being rich toward God (*Luke* 12: 21).

(h) Avarice can become the attitude of a whole nation in that everyone is greedy for unjust gain (*Jer*. 8. 10).

2. **How avarice manifests itself.**

Avarice manifests itself in opinions and viewpoints.

(a) *The meaning of life.* Avarice finds the meaning of life in the acquisition of money and possessions (*Luke* 12: 18, 19), encouraged by false ideas about money and what it can do.

(b) *Profit.* Avarice always keeps foremost the personal profit motive (*Tit.* 1: 11), so that each action and enterprise is looked at from the viewpoint of personal advantage.

(c) *Security.* Avarice regards wealth as the principal symbol of security (*Jas.* 5: 2, 3).

(d) *Happiness.* Avarice views wealth as the main source of happiness (*Luke* 12: 18, 19).

Avarice manifests itself in actions.

(e) *Miserliness.* Avarice can make a person stingy in his dealings with others (*Prov.* 28: 22).

(f) *Selfish luxury and pleasure.* Avarice can, on the other hand, make a man lavish in his own enjoyment of luxury and pleasure (*Jas.* 5: 5; *Luke* 16: 19).

(g) *Dishonesty.* Avarice can prompt a man to seek wealth by dishonest means (*Ezek.* 22: 27; *I Pet.* 5: 2).

(h) *Indifference to the rights of others.* The unrestricted longing for possessions can cause a man to set aside the rights of others, especially if he is in a position of power or influence (*Amos* 2: 6; *Luke* 16: 20, 21).

(i) *Division.* The desire for wealth can divide relatives and spoil relationships (*Gen.* 13: 5, 6), and particularly is this the case in families over wills (*Luke* 12: 13).

(j) *Injustice.* Greed can lead a man to become unjust, e.g. an employer giving insufficient wages in order to save himself money (*Jas.* 5: 4).

(k) *Violence.* Striving for unlawful wealth can lead to violence and even murder (*Ezek.* 22: 27; *Mic.* 6: 12).

Avarice manifests itself in attitudes of mind.

(l) *Arrogant complacency.* Wealth easily breeds a harmful complacency (*Prov.* 18: 23; 28: 11), and the false conviction that the future is in the wealthy man's hands (*Jas.* 4: 13–17).

(m) *Gloating satisfaction.*

135

Wealth is simply hoarded often and gloated over (*Luke* 12: 18, 19; *Jas.* 5: 2, 3).

(n) *Anxiety.* Satisfied as an avaricious man may be in some respects with what he has, he will, at the same time, find that his wealth and its preservation bring anxiety (*Eccl.* 5: 12).

(o) *Discontent.* The man who loves wealth will never be satisfied by it (*Eccl.* 5: 10), and his eyes will always be greedy (*I Sam.* 2: 29; cf. 2: 12–17).

3. The sinfulness of avarice.

(a) *It breaks the first great commandment*: "Love the Lord your God with all your heart and with all your soul and with all your mind" (*Matt.* 22: 37).

(b) Avarice makes a man give his heart to material treasures, and to be so devoted to his possessions that he ceases to love God (*Matt.* 6: 21, 24).

(c) Avarice is a form of idolatry in that money becomes a man's god (*Col.* 3: 5).

(d) Avarice denies the truth that man's proper and true happiness is in having the Lord as God (*Ps.* 144: 15), and having Him as one's helper (*Ps.* 146: 5; *Heb.* 13: 5, 6).

(e) *It breaks the second great commandment*: "Love your neighbour as yourself" (*Matt.* 22: 39).

(f) Avarice causes men to hoard money and possessions selfishly rather than use them for personal good and the proper good of others (*Jas.* 5: 2–4).

(g) The love of money proceeds from the love of self (*II Tim.* 3: 2), and always has personal gain in view even in the discharge of the seemingly most honourable of tasks (*Tit.* 1: 11).

(h) It ravages human relationships: greed occurs in a group of four nouns which comprehensively describe the power of sin in spoiling human relationships, wickedness, evil, greed and depravity (*Rom.* 1: 29).

(i) It hurts other people as, for example, by neglect (*Luke* 16: 19 ff) or by example—for instance, if parents take the alluring road to wealth they may find their family overwhelmed by the ways of the world (*Gen.* 13: 10–13; cf. *Gen.* 19: 12–26).

(j) *Avarice is the first step to all kinds of sin* (*I Tim.* 6: 10).

(k) Greed is linked frequently in the Bible with fornication and idolatry, in that greed in one form quickly leads to greed in another, so that a man ends up worshipping the objects of his greed (*I Cor.* 5: 10 f).

(l) It is behind many of the works of the flesh, all of which are in direct opposition to the will of God for man (*Gal.* 5: 19–21).

(m) It finds deceit easy in that greed may be the real motivation of what seem to be good and kind actions (*I Thess.* 2: 5; *I Pet.* 5: 2; *II Pet.* 2: 3).

(n) It is the most obvious form of worldliness, in that two of worldliness' preeminent characteristics are the desire to buy everything that appeals to man, and the pride that comes from wealth and importance: such love of the world is the opposite of love for God (*I John* 2: 15, 16).

4. The folly of avarice.

(a) The happiness and enjoyment avarice promises are often illusory (*Eccl.* 2: 8 f, 26; *Luke* 19: 2).

(b) Wealth is a totally insufficient source of security for the future, because God may not give a man the opportunity to enjoy it (*Eccl.* 6: 2).

(c) Avarice loses sight of the temporary hold man has on all material possessions (*Prov.* 27: 24; *Luke* 12: 20).

(d) It forgets, too, that even man's earthly hold of them is subject to circumstances over which he has no control (*Jas.* 5: 2, 3).

(e) It brings a man into the unenviable position of not really being sure who his true friends are, although his wealth attracts many apparent friends (*Prov.* 14: 20; 19: 4).

(f) Avarice makes the big mistake of thinking that man's life consists in the abundance of his possessions (*Luke* 12: 15).

(g) Avarice neglects the fact that there are many important things money cannot do: wealth can take care of a man's burial but not his destiny thereafter (*Luke* 16:

23), so that it cannot save him from eternal separation from God; wealth of a material nature will be of no use on the day of judgment (*Isa.* 10: 3).

(h) Avarice can cost a man his eternal well-being (*Matt.* 16: 26), in that his pursuit of money leads him to forget that his greatest need is to be rich before God (*Luke* 12: 19, 20).

(i) Avarice can lead to a man possessing immense outward wealth and at the same time knowing an inner poverty (*Prov.* 28: 22).

(j) Avarice shuts a man out of God's kingdom (*Matt.* 19: 23 f; *Mark* 10: 23 f; *Luke* 18: 24 f).

(k) Avarice brings God's judgment, in that the man who thinks all the time about getting rich will be punished (*Prov.* 21: 13; 28: 20; *Jas.* 5: 1).

(l) The proceeds of avarice will be evidence against men on the day of judgment so that wrongly accumulated wealth will prove to be a liability rather than an asset (*Jas.* 5: 3): the store of accumulated wealth becomes, in effect, a store of divine wrath from which God will draw on the day of judgment (*Jas.* 5: 3).

(m) Those whose lives are governed by avarice may be compared to cattle feasting themselves while, all unknowingly, they are living in the shadow of the day of their slaughter (*Jas.* 5: 5).

5. Proper correctives to avarice.

The corrective of an eternal perspective.

(a) The danger of wealth is that it may be a wealth limited to this world alone (*I Tim.* 6: 17–19).

(b) The true value of material possessions is seen when we appreciate that at the judgment of the world they will all disappear (*Rev.* 18: 11–19).

(c) Our view of wealth is determined by what we consider to be true currency (*II Cor.* 6: 10), in that there is a wealth which has nothing to do with this world's wealth (*Rev.* 2: 9).

(d) Real wealth does not consist in the abundance of our possessions but in the state of our soul, upon whether or not

138

we are rich toward God (*Luke* 12: 15–26; cf. *Ps.* 73).

(e) The knowledge of God's salvation through Jesus Christ is more profitable than wealth and more relevant to our basic needs (*Acts* 3: 6).

(f) True wealth is spiritual wealth such as pardon (*Eph.* 1: 7), peace with God (*Rom.* 5: 1), the support of God's Spirit (*John* 14: 16) and the assurance of heaven (*John* 14: 2, 3).

(g) Christians may be poor but in fact they have everything worthwhile (*II Cor.* 6: 10; *Heb.* 10: 34).

The corrective of the Bible warnings given by way of sad examples of what avarice has caused men to do: things happened to people in the past as a warning and were then written down for our instruction (*I Cor.* 10: 11).

(h) Avarice has made men turn away from following the Lord Jesus Christ (*Matt.* 19: 22).

(i) It has made them neglect human need on their doorstep (*Luke* 16: 20).

(j) It has made them think that all is well with them when

the opposite has been the case (*Luke* 12: 19).

(k) It has caused men to betray friends and commit suicide (*Matt.* 26: 15, 16; *Acts* 1: 18).

(l) It has caused men to exploit those who work for them (*Jas.* 5: 4).

(m) It has caused men to tell lies and practise deceit (*Acts* 5: 3, 4, 8).

The corrective of the genuine pursuit of Christian discipleship.

(n) Our Lord's chosen lifestyle involved the loss of any financial security (Luke 9: 58), and He warned His disciples against all active striving for the increase of material possessions as a means of security (*Luke* 12: 15).

(o) The Christian is not to be a lover of money (*I Tim.* 3: 3), and those who assume Christian leadership must be outstanding examples of those who neither love money nor are greedy for it (*I Tim.* 3: 3, 8; *Tit.* 1: 7).

(p) The Christian is to live with the assurance that his material needs are of concern to God and he is encouraged to bring them to God day by day as he prays (*Matt.* 6: 11; Luke 11: 3).

(q) The Christian's aim must be contentment (*Heb.* 13: 5).

The corrective of putting wealth to use.

(r) The Lord can make us rich (*I Sam.* 2: 7), and there is no sin in wealth providing it is acquired honourably and used wisely (*II Cor.* 9: 8).

(s) If material wealth is used rightly it can add to our heavenly wealth which is much more important (*Matt.* 6: 19–21; *Luke* 12: 33, 34).

(t) Used to benefit others, our possessions are a means of showing our love not only to others but to God Himself (*I John* 3: 17).

32. SLOTH

Question: What is sloth?

Answer: Sloth is laziness and wrongful inactivity, the opposite of hard work, diligence and self-discipline. It is sinful because it abuses time, wastes life and leads to neglect of our duty to God, our fellow man, and self.

1. **Sloth's characteristics.**

(a) Sloth is laziness and disinclination to action, exertion or labour; and, persevered in, it amounts to a slow death (*Prov.* 21: 25).

(b) Sloth can be manifested in many different spheres of life: in the home (*Eccl.* 10: 18), the garden (*Prov.* 24: 30, 31), daily employment (*Prov.* 20: 4), the exercise of responsibility for others (*Isa.* 56: 9–12), and in the care of one's soul (*II Pet.* 1: 5–11).

(c) *Inactivity.* Sleep is a mark of the lazy (*Prov.* 6: 11; 19: 15; 24: 33): the lazy man gets little further than a door swinging on its hinges (*Prov.* 26: 14).

(d) *Soft options.* Sloth makes a habit of the soft choice (*Prov.* 20: 4): it encourages a man to stay at home when he ought to be out and doing (*Prov.* 22: 13).

(e) *Lack of resolution.* Sloth describes the situation of the individual who for one reason or another does not have the resolution to act: for example, he lacks discipline to get down to hard work or to begin something which needs to be done (*Prov.* 6: 6, 9, 10).

(f) *Excuses*. Sloth encourages a man to make excuses for his laziness: for example, he suggests that he is not at his best in the morning (*Prov.* 26: 14) or that he cannot do anything well if he is hurried (*Prov.* 26: 15, 16).

(g) *Pessimism*. Sloth meets difficulties everywhere (*Prov.* 15: 19), and some of them are quite exaggerated and imaginary (*Prov.* 26: 13).

(h) *A world of wishing*. Sloth causes a man to live in a world of wishing (*Prov.* 21: 25, 26): he seldom moves from the will to the deed.

(i) *Dissatisfaction*. Laziness results in dissatisfaction with life (*Prov.* 13: 4).

(j) *Conceit*. Sloth is accompanied often by conceit: a lazy man will think he is more intelligent than seven men who can give reasons for their opinions (*Prov.* 26: 16).

(k) *Blind to itself*. Sloth is sometimes completely unaware of itself (*Prov.* 26: 16); the slothful man believes his own excuses (*Prov.* 22: 13), and the shirker deceives himself into believing that he is a realist (*Prov.* 26: 13).

2. Sloth's consequences.

(a) Laziness has its price (*Prov.* 12: 24).

(b) *Self-indulgence*. Sloth leads to physical softness, and following the dictates of natural desires (*Prov.* 20: 4).

(c) *Untidiness of life*. Sloth breeds a general untidiness of life (*Prov.* 15: 19).

(d) *Deficient convictions*. The lazy man is too lazy to develop and possess genuine convictions (*Prov.* 26: 16); he may pretend that he is simply open-minded, although laziness is the principal cause of his lack of conviction.

(e) *Apathy*. Sloth makes a man apathetic about the most necessary duties (*Prov.* 12: 27; 26: 15).

(f) *Mischief*. Sloth leads all too easily to unhelpful and harmful activity, such as meddling in other people's affairs (*II Thess.* 3: 11) and gossip (*I Tim.* 5: 13).

(g) *Unfinished tasks and lack of achievement*. Sloth makes a man miss his opportunities: for example, failing to sow at the right time, he has no harvest to gather (*Prov.* 20: 4); he puts things beyond his reach by his laziness (*Prov.* 13: 4).

(h) *Disappointment.* Disappointment is the inevitable accompaniment of laziness (*Prov.* 13: 4; 21: 25).

(i) *Gradual deterioration.* Sloth is a creeping, spreading disease (*Prov.* 19: 15), so that a little laziness quickly becomes habitual laziness (*Prov.* 6: 10, 11).

(j) *Poverty of various sorts.* Sloth can lead to various forms of poverty (*Prov.* 6: 11), especially to material need (*Prov.* 20: 4; 21: 25) and hunger (*Prov.* 19: 15; 24: 34).

(k) *Bondage or wrongful indebtedness to others.* Sloth leads a man to bondage in that he lives at the expense of others and puts himself in their debt, frequently in a way which will prove detrimental to him (*Prov.* 12: 24).

(l) *Uselessness.* Sloth is synonymous with a somewhat expensive uselessness (*Prov.* 18: 9).

(m) *Destructiveness.* The lazy man's sluggishness eventually overwhelms him (*Prov.* 24: 30–34). When God's gifts and benefits are not properly used,

they may be lost (*Luke* 19: 26).

(n) *Ruin.* A lazy man's ease is his own undoing and ruin (*Prov.* 21: 25; 24: 30, 31; *Eccl.* 10: 18).

3. Sloth's sinfulness.

The abuse of time.

(a) Sloth makes a man a bad steward of time, in that time is short (*I Cor.* 7: 29), and is to be redeemed (*Col.* 4: 5).

(b) The slothful man forgets that every day is the day the Lord has made for good purposes (*Ps.* 118: 24).

The waste of life.

(c) Human existence should mean fruitful labour (*Phil.* 1: 22).

(d) Life is to be lived with zest and purposefulness (*Col.* 3: 23).

The contradiction of God's image in which man was made.

(e) God is always working (*John* 5: 17), and His Son set us an example in that He went about doing good (*Acts* 10: 38).

(f) Our Lord's earthly life was the complete opposite of sloth: His meat was to do the Father's will (*John* 4: 34).

*The neglect of duty to God,
our fellowman and ourselves.*

(g) By sloth we neglect to
serve God with the whole-
heartedness which alone satis-
fies Him (*Deut.* 1: 36; *Josh.*
14: 8, 9, 14; Matt. 25: 26).

(h) By sloth we neglect to
serve our fellowman with the
diligence such service requires
(*Luke* 10: 30–37; 16: 19–21;
II Cor. 8: 16).

(i) By sloth we neglect our
duty to ourself in that our
spiritual well-being requires
diligence (*II Pet.* 1: 5), as does
our usefulness by the exercise
of our God-given gifts (*I Pet.*
4: 9–11).

4. Correctives to sloth.

A Christian understanding.

(a) Sloth is contrary to Christian instruction (*II Thess.* 3:
6), and the apostles set a
deliberate example of avoiding all idleness (*II Thess.* 3: 7,
8).

(b) The Christian is not to flag
in zeal but rather is to be
aglow with the Spirit in his
service of the Lord (*Rom.* 12:
11).

(c) The Christian is to make
good use of the time between
now and the Lord's second
advent (*Matt.* 25: 1–30), making sure that he fulfils the
ministry the Lord has given
to him (*Col.* 4: 17).

(d) The Christian is to serve
the Lord in newness of spirit
(*Rom.* 7: 6).

*A proper stewardship of
time.*

(e) There are many evil pressures encouraging the misuse
of time, so that proper stewardship is all the more important (*Eph.* 5: 16).

(f) The shortness of life's opportunities should make us
wise in the use of our time
(*Ps.* 90: 12).

(g) There is a right time for
everything (*Eccl.* 3: 1 ff).

*An appreciation of the pur-
pose of life.*

(h) Whatever our hands find
to do, we should do with all
our might (*Eccl.* 9: 10).

(i) We may be sure that God
has a programme of good
works for us to fulfil at every
stage of our life (*Eph.* 2: 10).

*A proper place for, and con-
trol of, sleep and relaxation.*

(j) Restful sleep is a gift from
God (*Ps.* 127: 2), and it is intended that sleep should be

the reward of a diligent worker (*Eccl.* 5: 12).

(k) Our Lord practised retirement from activity (*Matt.* 14: 13, 23), and called upon His disciples to do the same (*Mark* 6: 31).

(l) There is a right and wrong time both for sleep and relaxation and wisdom knows the difference (*Eccl.* 10: 16, 17).

An understanding of the place of diligence in right living.

(m) The ant is an example of diligence: ants have no leader, chief, ruler, but they store up their food during the summer, getting ready for winter (*Prov.* 6: 6, 7).

(n) Diligence is necessary if we would gain understanding and wisdom (*Prov.* 17: 24).

(o) Diligence should characterise our activity no matter how uncertain we are of the future (*Eccl.* 11: 6).

(p) All the responsibilities which come to us in life are to be exercised diligently (*Rom.* 12: 8; *Col.* 3: 17).

(q) Diligence brings its own reward and wealth (*Prov.* 13: 4; 12: 27).

33. LOVE

Galatians 5: 22: "The fruit of the Spirit is love."

Question: What is the love required of us?

Answer: The love required of us is a totally unselfish love, a matter of will and action, expressed in service of the unworthy as much as of the worthy, based upon the pattern of the love set forth in the Cross of our Lord Jesus Christ.

1. God is the source of love.

(a) Love comes from God (*I John* 4: 7).

(b) God is love (*I John* 4: 8, 16), and is called "the God of love" (*II Cor.* 13: 11).

(c) Love characterises every aspect of God's relationship to His people (*Hos.* 2: 19).

(d) God has demonstrated His love to us: He sent His one and only Son into the world (*Rom.* 8: 32; *Col.* 1: 13)—He sent Him to be the atoning sacrifice for our sins (*John* 3: 16: *Rom.* 5: 8; *Gal.* 2: 20; *I John* 4: 9, 10).

(e) God the Father has lavished the greatest possible love upon us as believers by letting us be called God's children (*Eph.* 1: 4; *I John* 3: 1; *Jude* 1).

(f) We both know and rely upon the love God has for us (*I John* 4: 16).

(g) God has given us the Spirit of love to indwell us (*Gal.* 5: 22; *II Tim.* 1: 7).

(h) God has poured out His love into our hearts by the Holy Spirit (*Rom.* 5: 5)—His love holds us captive (*II Cor.* 5: 14).

(i) Our love for God is the response of gratitude (*Luke* 7: 47; *I John* 4: 19).

(j) We are to show to the world that we are God's children, and Christ's disciples, by the display and practice of love (*John* 13: 35; *I John* 3: 14; 4: 7).

(k) The love of Christ's people for others for His sake is something quite different from the love with which the world is familiar (*John* 13: 34).

2. The priority of love.

(a) Love has priority over spiritual gifts (*I Cor.* 13: 1–3).

(b) To be specific, love has priority over the gift of tongues (*I Cor.* 13: 1).

(c) Love has priority over the gift of prophecy (*I Cor.* 13: 2).

(d) Love has priority over the gift of knowledge and teaching (*I Cor.* 13: 2, 8)—knowledge without love so easily puffs a man up with a sense of his own importance (*I Cor.* 8: 1).

(e) Love has priority over the special gift of faith that can accomplish miracles (*I Cor.* 13: 2; cf. 12: 29; *Mark* 11: 22 f).

(f) Love has priority over the special gift of generous giving (*I Cor.* 13: 3; cf. *Rom.* 12: 8).

(g) Love has priority over complete dedication to an ideal, even if that dedication involves death for its sake (*I Cor.* 13: 3).

(h) Love's priority is seen in that it is to be the aim of *all* believers, whereas this is not true of God's others gifts (*I Cor.* 14: 1; cf. 12: 27–31).

(i) Besides being part of the fruit of the Spirit, love takes first rank among that fruit (*Gal.* 5: 22; cf. *Rom.* 15: 30; *Col.* 1: 8; 3: 14).

(j) Love's priority is seen in that our Lord has given love as a new commandment (*John*

13: 34; *I John* 4: 21): it is one of the first commandments we receive after we have come to faith in the Lord Jesus (*I John* 3: 23; cf. *Matt.* 28: 20).

(k) Love is the one perpetual debt we owe to one another (*Rom.* 13: 8).

(l) Its priority is all the greater when we realise that the true love we express to others is really love expressed to Jesus Christ Himself (*Matt.* 25: 33 ff).

3. The foremost characteristics and activities of love.

(a) Patience (*I Cor.* 13: 4).

(b) Kindness (*I Cor.* 13: 4): love strives to be honest (*Mark* 10: 21), and in speaking the truth endeavours to do so without offence (*Eph.* 4: 15).

(c) Joy (*I Cor.* 13: 6).

(d) Forbearance (*I Cor.* 13: 7): love makes allowances for people (*Eph.* 4: 2), and covers over a multitude of sins (*I Pet.* 4: 8).

(e) Faith: the outflow of genuine faith is love (*Gal.* 5: 6; *I Thess.* 3: 6; 5: 8; *I Tim.* 1: 14).

(f) Hope (*I Cor.* 13: 7).

(g) Endurance (*I Cor.* 13: 7), after the pattern of our Lord's love for His disciples (*John* 13: 1).

(h) Service: love is active in good works (*Heb.* 10: 24), prompt in willing service (*Gal.* 5: 13), and anxious to fulfil God's law towards a neighbour (*Rom.* 13: 10).

(i) Generosity (*II Cor.* 8: 8–12, 24): love goes out of its way to share and meet another's need (*I John* 3: 17).

(j) Constructiveness: love builds up (*I Cor.* 8: 1), unites believers (*Col.* 2: 2), and binds all other virtues together in perfect unity (*Col.* 3: 14).

(k) Reflective of God's love: love shows kindness even to its enemies (*Matt.* 5: 44, 45; Luke 6: 27, 35), always endeavouring to show to others the love the Lord Jesus has shown to us (*John* 13: 34).

4. The opposites of love.

(a) Jealousy (*I Cor.* 13: 4).

(b) Boastfulness (*I Cor.* 13: 4).

(c) Arrogance (*I Cor.* 13: 5).

(d) Rudeness (*I Cor.* 13: 5).

(e) Selfishness (*I Cor.* 13: 5).

(f) Irritability (*I Cor.* 13: 5).

(g) Resentment (*I Cor.* 13: 5).

(h) Maliciousness (*I Cor*. 13: 6).

(i) Hatred (*I John* 3: 11–18).

5. The consistent aims and objectives of love.

(a) Love aims at growth (*Phil.* 1: 9), that it may abound, increase and overflow (*I Thess.* 3: 12; *II Thess.* 1: 3).

(b) Love aims at being non-selective in its objects and to love all in the same way (*Phi.* 2: 2)—Christian love loves all other Christians as brothers and other men as neighbours (*Gal.* 6: 10).

(c) Love aims at sincerity and genuineness (*Rom*. 12: 9; *II Cor*. 6: 6; *I Pet*. 1: 22; *I John* 4: 18).

(d) Love aims at consistency: its objective is to *walk* in love (*Eph.* 5: 2); it wants to be unfailing (*I Pet.* 4: 8).

(e) Love aims at building others up in the things of God (*I Cor.* 8: 1), with no thought of self-interest (*Rom.* 15: 1–4).

(f) Love's objective is to follow the pattern of Christ's love even if that means great personal sacrifice (*John* 13: 34; *Eph.* 5: 2, 25, 28).

(g) Love's objective, therefore, is to mix love with every action (*I Cor.* 16: 14).

6. The permanence of the priority of love.

(a) It is basic to all Christian ethics (*I John* 2: 7).

(b) It remains the principal test of a Christian profession (*I John* 2: 9, 10; cf. *John* 13: 35).

(c) It never ends (*I Cor*. 13: 8).

(d) When spiritual gifts pass away, and are unnecessary, love will remain (*I Cor.* 13: 8–12).

(e) Faith, hope and love are the principal priorities of the Christian life, but the greatest of these is love (*I Cor*. 13: 13).

34. JOY

Galatians 5: 22: "The fruit of the Spirit is . . . joy."

Question: What is the joy required of us?

Answer: The joy required of us is not the seldom found result of an agreeable set of circumstances but an inward joy springing up within us, irrespective of what our difficulties

may be. It is a gift of God through our Lord Jesus Christ, and is one of the principal consequences of the experience of salvation.

1. Defining joy.

(a) Joy is virtually synonymous with gladness or delight (*Matt.* 5: 12; *Luke* 1: 14), and has to do with a man's heart (*Ps.* 16: 9; 33: 21; *Acts* 2: 26, 46; 14: 17) or soul or spirit (*Luke* 1: 47), that is to say, his innermost being (*John* 7: 38).

(b) God Himself is the author of the joy a man's heart or soul needs to know (*I Thess.* 3: 9), and it is His gift to believers (*Rom.* 15: 13).

(c) Christian joy has God as its object (*Ps.* 9: 2; 33: 21; 149: 1; *Joel* 2: 23)—God Himself becomes our exceeding joy (*Ps.* 43: 4).

(d) Joy focuses its attention on the contemplation of God—His power, His holiness and His mercy (*Luke* 1: 49, 50)—and on His habitual acts (*Luke* 1: 51–53); it finds its rest in God's character and attributes (*Rev.* 19: 6, 7).

(e) Christian joy is always joy in God's saving acts (*Isa.* 44: 23)—His salvation is its supreme joy (*Rev.* 19: 7).

(f) The distinctive feature of Christian joy is that it is joy in God through our Lord Jesus (*Rom.* 5: 11; cf. *I Cor.* 1: 31; *Phil.* 3: 3; 4: 4, 10)—in fact, He has been the anticipated joy of the ages in that Abraham and others rejoiced at the thought of seeing His day (*John* 8: 56; cf. *I Pet.* 1: 10–12).

(g) God the Holy Spirit conveys this joy in Christ to the individual believer's soul (*John* 7: 38; cf. *Luke* 10: 21; *Rom.* 14: 17; *I Thess.* 1: 6; *Gal.* 5: 22)—a joy which is a foretaste of heaven (*I Pet.* 4: 13; *Jude* 24).

(h) Christian joy is a *secure* joy: since it does not find its source in man, man cannot take it away (*John* 16: 22).

(i) Christian joy is a *glorious* joy for it already has something of heaven's touch upon it (*I Pet.* 1: 8).

(j) Christian joy is an *inexpressible* joy since it is incapable of declaration by words (*I Pet.* 1: 8).

(k) Christian joy is an *everlasting* joy (*Isa.* 35: 10; 51: 11).

2. Defining some of the foundations of Christian joy.

(a) Christian joy is the joy which the gospel of our Lord Jesus Christ provides (*Luke* 2: 10, 11; *I John* 1: 1–4; *I Thess.* 1: 6): for example, the joy of being found by the Heavenly Father through the Good Shepherd (*Luke* 15), or the joy of finding Christ and His kingdom as a treasure without price (*Matt.* 13: 44, 45).

(b) Christian joy is the joy of faith (*Ps.* 33: 21; *Acts* 16: 34; *Phil.* 1: 25)—faith and joy in a crucified (*Gal.* 2: 20; 6: 14), risen (*Matt.* 28: 8; *John* 16: 20, 22) and ascended Saviour (*Luke* 24: 50–53), whom we have not yet seen, but believing in Him we are filled with joy (*I Pet.* 1: 8).

(c) Christian joy is the joy of salvation (*Ps.* 51: 14; *Isa.* 35: 10; 51: 11; *Hab.* 3: 18; *Acts* 8: 39; 13: 48), with the particular joys that salvation brings of forgiveness (*Ps.* 51: 1–12; cf. *Eph.* 1: 7), reconciliation to God (*Rom.* 5: 11), justification through faith (*Rom.* 5: 1, 2), and acceptance with God (*Jude* 24).

(d) Christian joy is the joy of a new life (*Rom.* 6: 4; *II Cor.* 5: 17; cf. *Luke* 19: 6–9).

(e) Christian joy is the joy of fellowship with the Father and with His Son Jesus Christ (*I John* 1: 3, 4; cf. *John* 14: 21, 23).

(f) Christian joy is the joy of fellowship with one another (*Ps.* 133: 1; *II Cor.* 2: 2) because that fellowship is based on fellowship with the Father and the Son (*I John* 1: 1–7).

(g) Christian joy is the joy of future and certain glorious prospects—of rewards (*Matt.* 5: 12; 25: 21, 23), but most of all of the hope of the glory of God (*Rom.* 5: 2) and sharing in our Saviour's triumph (*Heb.* 12: 2; cf. *Phil.* 2: 9–11; *II Tim.* 2: 11, 12.

(h) One important way of defining Christian joy is that it is Jesus Christ's joy in us (*John* 15: 11).

3. The joy our Lord Jesus Christ exhibited.

(a) He possessed a full and unique joy (*John* 15: 11; 17: 13).

(b) His joy expressed itself in praise and thanksgiving (*Luke* 10: 21).

(c) He was full of joy through the Holy Spirit (*Luke* 10: 21).

(d) His joy was to do the Father's will (*Ps.* 40: 8; *John* 4: 34).

(e) He endured the Cross, despising the shame, for the joy that was set before Him (*Heb.* 12: 2).

(f) His prayer for His disciples to His Father was that they should have the full measure of His joy within them (*John* 17: 13).

(g) Christian joy at its best, therefore, is the Lord Jesus sharing His joy with us to the full as He completely shares our life (*John* 17: 13; cf. 14: 21, 23; *Rev.* 3: 20).

4. How joy expresses itself.

(a) It expresses itself in contentment and pleasure in ordinary everyday things (*Acts* 2: 46) because God is recognised as the source and author of all that is good and all in which we can rejoice (*I Thess.* 3: 9; *I Tim.* 4: 4; 6: 17; *Jas.* 1: 17).

(b) It expresses itself in praise and thanksgiving (*Ps.* 27: 6; 33: 1; *Luke* 1: 46, 47; 10: 21; *Acts* 2: 46, 47; *Rev.* 19: 7).

(c) It expresses itself in singing (*Ps.* 5: 11; 9: 2; 84: 2; *Isa.* 12: 6; 35: 10; 44: 23; 49: 13) as the Holy Spirit aids that expression through psalms, hymns and spiritual songs (*Eph.* 5: 18, 19).

(d) It expresses itself in confidence in God and in His supplies of strength (*Neh.* 8: 10), so that Christian joy not only survives difficult circumstances but almost seems to thrive on them (*Matt.* 5: 12; *Acts* 5: 41; *Col.* 1: 11), because of the joyful perspective of faith that God uses every difficulty and obstacle to mature and perfect the development of the character of His Son in us (*Rom.* 5: 3; *Heb.* 12: 11; *Jas.* 1: 2).

(e) Joy expresses itself in confident prayer (*John* 16: 24).

(f) Joy expresses itself in Christian fellowship (*Rom.* 12: 15; *II Tim.* 1: 4; *II John* 12).

(g) Joy expresses itself in generous giving (*II Cor.* 8: 2).

5. The maintenance of the Christian's joy.

(a) There is no doubt that God intends that it should be

150

maintained (*I Thess.* 5: 16), and outward trials (*I Pet.* 1: 6), and earthly considerations which affect ordinary human happiness (*Hab.* 3: 17, 18; *Ps.* 73: 25, 26; *Phil.* 4: 11–13; *II Cor.* 6: 10; *Heb.* 13: 5, 6) should make no difference since the One in whom our joys are found is always the same (*Heb.* 13: 8).

(b) Joy is maintained as faith grows (*Phil.* 1: 25).

(c) Joy is maintained as hope abounds (*Rom.* 15: 13): we are ever to have before us our living hope (*I Pet.* 1: 3) and the prospect of our sharing Christ's glory (*I Pet.* 4: 13).

(d) Joy is maintained as identification with the Lord Jesus is practised (*I Pet.* 4: 13; cf. *Col.* 1: 24).

(e) Joy is maintained as we continually rediscover the perfection of God's peace through the exercise of prayer (*Ps.* 34: 5; *John* 16: 24; *Rom.* 15: 13; *Phil.* 4: 6, 7).

(f) Joy is maintained as we honestly face the obstacles. Joy is maintained as we are filled with the Holy Spirit day by day (*Acts* 13: 52; *Eph.* 5: 18–20).

6. Obstacles and impediments to Christian joy.

(a) Failure to progress in the faith (*Phil.* 1: 25).

(b) Neglect of practical righteousness (*Rom.* 14: 17; cf. *Matt.* 5: 6).

(c) Omitting to seek peace in human relationships with diligence (*Rom.* 14: 17; cf. *Matt.* 5: 9).

(d) Breakdowns in loving each other as commanded by our Lord Jesus Christ (*John* 15: 10–12).

(e) Unbelief (*Phil.* 1: 25; *I Pet.* 1: 6, 7).

(f) Disobedience (*John* 15: 10, 11).

(g) The neglect of prayer (*John* 16: 24).

(h) Broken fellowship with God and His people in any way (*I John* 1: 1–7).

(i) Unconfessed sin (*Ps.* 51: 3, 8, 9, 12; *I John* 1: 1–10).

(j) All that grieves the Holy Spirit (*Eph.* 4: 30), for His ministry is the key to our experience of our Saviour's joy.

35. PEACE

Galatians 5: 22: "The fruit of the Spirit is . . . peace."

Question: What is the peace required of us?

Answer: The peace required of us is peace in the sense of peaceableness. The peaceableness, however, is the direct consequence of our discovery of peace with God through our Lord Jesus Christ, and the disposition this new relationship with God brings.

1. The priority of peace with God, and the way to it.

(a) The world has lost true peace because of man's sin: there is no peace for the wicked (*Isa* 48: 22; 57: 21).

(b) Fallen rebellious man does not know the way of peace (*Rom.* 3: 17).

(c) When we lack peace, we soon forget what real happiness is like (*Lam.* 3: 17).

(d) God alone can give His creatures true peace (*Ps.* 4: 8).

(e) In order to provide peace for His creatures, God had to make the great provision of a Saviour (*Luke* 2: 9–14).

(f) No peace with God was possible without the just demands of His wrath against sins being satisfied, and God accomplished this by the death of His Son upon the Cross for our sins (*Rom.* 5: 1; *Col.* 1: 20).

(g) Christians are those who, like all men by nature, were once enemies of God, but whom God has reconciled to Himself (*Rom.* 5: 11; *Eph.* 2: 16).

(h) The Lord Jesus Christ, therefore, came into the world to guide our feet into the way of peace (*Luke* 1: 79), and His saving work is the sole foundation of our peace (*Eph.* 2: 14–17).

(i) Justified by faith, we have peace with God through our Lord Jesus Christ (*Rom.* 5: 1) —peace follows upon faith (*Mark* 5: 34; *Luke* 7: 50; *Rom.* 15: 13).

(j) Peace, therefore, is completely inseparable from the experience of God's grace in Christ (*Gal.* 1: 3; *I Thess.* 1: 1) —it is through God's steadfast love and mercy that we can know true peace (*Jer.* 16: 5).

(k) Peace is God's free gift to His people (*Num.* 6: 26), and He delights in their enjoyment of peace (*Ps.* 35: 27; 147: 14).

(l) God's peace is like a river (*Isa.* 48: 18); it is a peace which passes understanding (*Phil.* 4: 7).

(m) The Lord Jesus Christ, our Saviour and Lord, is the Guarantor and Guardian of our peace (*Isa.* 9: 6), and He can give us peace at all times and in many different ways (*II Thess.* 3: 16).

(n) His peace is quite different from that which the world provides, for it can quieten troubled hearts and dismiss anxious fears (*John* 14: 27).

(o) Obedience to God, and in particular to His commandments, is a key to the maintenance of our experience of God's peace (*Ps.* 119: 165; *Isa.* 48: 18).

(p) The active pursuit of righteousness is a second condition of the maintenance of our peace (*Ps.* 85: 10; *Rom.* 12: 17, 18).

(q) The third condition is maintained fellowship with God (*Ps.* 73: 21–28), es-

pecially as that fellowship expresses itself in prayer (*Phil.* 4: 6, 7).

(r) The peace we know with God, and from God, brings the obligation to know too the peace between man and man which was one of the purposes for which our Lord Jesus Christ died (*Eph.* 2: 14).

2. **The peaceableness which flows from finding our peace with God and the peace He gives.**

(a) When we lack peace with God, and thus peace within, we also lack peace in our personal relationships (*Jas.* 4: 1–4).

(b) Finding in our Lord Jesus peace with God, however, we also find a meeting place and concord with one another, whatever may have been our divisions of race, colour, class or circumstances beforehand (*Eph.* 2: 14).

(c) Peace or peaceableness is part of the outflow of spiritual and eternal life (*Rom.* 8: 6).

(d) Peaceableness is a consequence of having the salt of the gospel in our life (*Mark* 9:

153

50)—all our relationships are significantly affected for the good (*Rom.* 14: 17, 19).

(e) Peaceableness is the out-working of love (*Col.* 3: 14, 15; *I Thess.* 5: 13), and love is not easily provoked (*I Cor.* 13: 5).

(f) Reconciled to God, we are able to benefit from God's heavenly wisdom, and peaceableness is a fundamental aspect of that wisdom (*Jas.* 1: 5; 3: 17, 18).

(g) Reconciliation to God brings a commitment to righteousness (*I Pet.* 2: 24), and peace is the normal fruit and gift from God of persevering in doing the right thing (*Rom.* 14: 17; *Jas.* 3: 18; cf. *Isa.* 32: 17).

(h) Reconciliation to God is synonymous with membership of God's family, and God carefully disciplines the characters of His spiritual children to make them more peaceable (*Heb.* 12: 11).

(i) Filled with the Spirit (*Eph.* 5: 17)—a further great gift of reconciliation—we develop His fruit of peaceableness in our characters (*Gal.* 5: 22; *Rom.* 8: 6).

(j) Peaceableness is a fundamental aspect of the kingdom of God (*Rom.* 14: 17), so much so that the Lord Jesus said, "Blessed are the peacemakers" (*Matt.* 5: 9).

3. The expression of peaceableness.

(a) Peaceableness expresses itself in the determination to maintain a clear conscience (*I Pet.* 3: 10–16), and this resolve involves the regular and genuine pursuit of practical righteousness (*Heb.* 12: 14)—peacemakers so sow peace that they raise a harvest of righteousness (*Jas.* 3: 18).

(b) Peaceableness expresses itself in the active pursuit of good works (*Jas.* 3: 17), even in the face of opposition from those who regard themselves as our enemies (*Matt.* 5: 43–48; *I Pet.* 2: 20; 3: 13, 14).

(c) Peaceableness expresses itself in forbearance (*II Tim.* 2: 22, 24) mercifulness (*Jas.* 3: 17) and gentleness (*I Pet.* 3: 15; *Tit.* 3: 2), especially where correction has to be given by us (*II Tim.* 2: 22, 25).

(d) Peaceableness expresses itself in courtesy (*Tit.* 3: 2), considerateness (*Jas.* 3: 17),

154

kindliness (*II Tim*. 2: 22, 24), and respect to all without discrimination or prejudice (*I Pet*. 3: 15).

(e) Peaceableness expresses itself in the active pursuit of peace, even if it means relinquishing our rights (*Gen*. 13: 8; 21: 22–24)—although that does not mean pretending problems do not exist but rather dealing with them peaceably (*Gen*. 21: 25 ff).

(f) Peaceableness expresses itself by coming between contending parties and trying to make peace (*I Sam*. 25: 18–35; *Matt*. 5: 9).

(g) Peaceableness expresses itself particularly in the words and language we employ (*Prov*. 18: 6, 7), seeking that its words should be righteous (*Prov*. 16: 13), wise (*Prov*. 25: 11, 12), calm (*Prov*. 15: 1; 17: 27), and sometimes very few (*Prov*. 11: 12, 13).

(h) Peaceableness expresses itself in the home (*Prov*. 17: 1), for a lack of peace there brings misery (*I Sam*. 1: 3–7).

(i) Peaceableness in marriage has as its secret the concentration of each partner upon his or her duties to the other rather than what he or she may expect from the other as his or her rights (*Eph*. 5: 22, 25).

(j) Peaceableness for parents means being sensitive and realistic in their demands and expectations of their children (*Eph*. 6: 4).

(k) Peaceableness within the church fellowship means striving always for peace and agreement (*Col*. 3: 15; *I Thess*. 5: 13; *Heb*. 12: 14).

4. **Appreciating peaceableness by identifying its opposites.**

(a) Envy (*Prov*. 14: 30; *Gal*. 5: 21; *I Tim*. 6: 4; *Jas*. 3: 14, 16, 17).

(b) Jealousy (*Mark* 10: 37, 41; *II Cor*. 12: 20; *Gal*. 5: 20; *Jas*. 3: 16, 17).

(c) Pride and conceit (*Gen*. 4: 5; *Ps*. 131: 1; *Jas*. 4: 1–6).

(d) Arrogance (*II Cor*. 12: 20).

(e) Selfish ambition (*Jas*. 3: 14, 16, 17).

(f) False loyalties (*I Cor*. 1: 10–12).

(g) Uncontrolled desires (*Jas*. 4: 1, 2), such as coveting (*Jas*. 4: 2).

(h) Hatred (*Gal*. 5: 20).

(i) Uncontrolled behaviour,

especially that brought about by drunkenness (*Esth.* 1: 12; *Gal.* 5: 21; *I Tim.* 3: 3).

(j) The desire for vengeance (*Esth.* 2: 21).

(k) Harshness (*Prov.* 15: 1).

(l) Evil-speaking, gossip and malicious talk (*II Cor.* 12: 20; *I Tim.* 6: 4; *Tit.* 3: 2; *I Pet.* 3: 10–12).

(m) Unhealthy interest in controversies and arguments (*I Tim.* 6: 4; *II Tim.* 2: 23).

(n) Quarrelling (*I Cor.* 1: 11; *II Cor.* 12: 20; *I Tim.* 3: 3; 6: 4; *Tit.* 3: 2).

(o) Factions, dissensions, and conspiracy (*Esth.* 2: 21; *II Cor.* 12: 20; *Gal.* 5: 20).

(p) Some activities lead to peace, and others do not (*Luke* 19: 42; *Rom.* 14: 19): those which lead to peace are to be pursued, and those which do not are to be fled from without debate (*II Tim.* 2: 22).

5. The fundamental importance of peaceableness.

(a) God is slow to anger (*Jonah* 4: 2), and His spiritual children should be the same (*Matt.* 5: 9).

(b) Peaceableness characterised the life and ministry of our Saviour (*Zech.* 9: 9; *Matt.* 21: 3; *John* 12: 14, 15), and His mind is to be in us (*Phil.* 2: 5), and His example ever before us (*I Pet.* 2: 21).

(c) God the Holy Spirit would have peaceableness as one of His pre-eminent fruits in our life (*Gal.* 5: 22).

(d) Our experience of spiritual joy is intimately linked with our pursuit of righteousness and peace (*Rom.* 14: 17).

(e) Furthermore, a tranquil mind gives physical health (*Prov.* 14: 30).

(f) Peaceableness is one of the conditions of God's presence and of His blessing upon us (*II Cor.* 13: 11)—and often we shall find Him making up to us in spiritual peace what we may appear to have lost in preserving neighbourly peace (*Gen.* 13: 14–18; *I Pet.* 3: 9).

(g) The body of Christ, the Church, can function properly only as it knows peace (*I Cor.* 14: 33): without peace there can be no mutual edification (*Rom.* 14: 19).

(h) Peaceableness helps to bind God's people together in unity (*Eph.* 4: 3).

(i) Peaceableness is sometimes

used by God to win surprising victories, victories which might not have been won in any other way (*Prov.* 25: 15; *I Sam.* 24: 17; *I Pet.* 3: 15, 16).

(j) Peaceableness is a matter for active pursuit in the Christian life (*I Pet.* 3: 12).

36. PATIENCE

Galatians 5: 22: "The fruit of the Spirit is . . . patience."

Question: What is the patience required of us?

Answer: Of the two Greek words translated often as patience, that chosen to describe this aspect of the fruit of the Spirit is the one used of God's patience, forbearance and steadfastness. It particularly expresses restraint in the face of opposition. Our patience, like God's, is to be the outflow of love, shown to everyone, and demonstrated most of all in forgiveness. The patience God has shown to us is to be reflected directly in the patience we show to others.

1. God is patient.

(a) Patience was part of God's amazing revelation of His character to His people in the Old Testament (*Ex.* 34: 6; *Num.* 14: 18); it was a fact of certain knowledge among them (*Jonah* 4: 2).

(b) The same truth concerning God's patience is presented to us in the New Testament (*Rom.* 9: 22; *I Tim.* 1: 16; *I Pet.* 3: 20; *II Pet.* 3: 15): He is rich in patience (*Rom.* 2: 4).

(c) God's patience has been seen throughout the history of mankind, most of all in His dealings with Israel (*Judg.* 3: 7, 9, 12, 15; *Rom.* 10: 21), in spite of all her spiritual adultery and backsliding (*Hos.* 2: 14–23; *Amos* 4: 6–11).

(d) God's patience is regularly linked with His constancy (*Num.* 14: 18; *Ps.* 86: 15; *Jonah* 4: 2), goodness and forbearance (*Ex.* 34: 6; *Rom.* 2: 4).

(e) God's patience is not in opposition to His righteous wrath: His patience means that His wrath's operation is postponed until something takes place in man which justifies the postponement; if, however, a change does not take place, then wrath

157

executes its judgment (*Num.* 14: 18).

(f) God's patience allows the development of either obedience or disobedience, resulting either in deliverance or destruction (*I Pet.* 3: 20); and the potential of wrath necessarily increases with the patience shown (*Rom.* 9: 22).

(g) God's patience is seen in that He waits to be gracious to us (*Isa.* 30: 18).

(h) It is plain, therefore, that God's patience should lead men to repentance (*Rom.* 2: 4), and they should be urged not to abuse God's patience and the opportunity it gives for finding salvation (*II Pet.* 3: 15).

(i) We may find God's patience difficult to understand, particularly when the implementation of His justice seems to be delayed (*Jer.* 15: 15); one of the reasons for this problem in our minds is our very human concept of time (*II Pet.* 3: 8).

(j) We are called to be like God in all His attributes which can be shared by us, and this includes, therefore, His patience (*Matt.* 5: 48).

2. **God has given us example of patience.**

(a) The foremost example i our Lord Jesus Christ wh displayed amazing patienc with His disciples: in thei slowness to understand (*Mar.* 4: 10–20); in their earthl mindedness (*Mark* 10: 35 45), and in their desertion o Him in His hour of nee (*Matt.* 26: 56; *Mark* 16: 7 *John* 11: 15–19).

(b) The supreme example o His patience was His conduc in His trial and crucifixio: (*Matt.* 26: 59–68; 27: 29–50 *I Pet.* 2: 21–25).

(c) His continuing patience i seen in His present dealing with men: Paul knew himsel to be an example of Christ' waiting patience which bor with him as a persecutor unt it won him over—a waitin patience which continues t wards men to this day (*I Tir* 1: 13–16).

(d) Abraham (*Gen.* 22: 1' 18; *Heb.* 6: 15), Job (*Jame* 5: 11), the prophets (*Jas.* : 10), and so many of ou spiritual forefathers are e> amples to us of patience (*Hel* 11: 13); and the things th: happened to them are obje

lessons to help us (*I Cor.* 10:
11).

(e) The example of patience
the apostle Paul was to
Timothy helps us also (*II Tim.*
3: 20).

3. The patience God has shown to us is the patience we are to show to others.

(a) The pattern of God's
dealings with us is to be the
pattern of our dealings with
others (*Luke* 6: 36; *Matt.* 5:
7).

(b) Our patience must most of
all be shown in forgiveness
(*Matt.* 18: 23–35).

(c) Our patience must be the
expression of love (*I Cor.* 13:
4).

(d) Our patience is to be
evident in our relationships
to everyone, whether we are
warning, encouraging or supporting them (*I Thess.* 5: 14).

4. The necessity of patience.

(a) It is essential to a life
worthy of our calling as
Christians, enabling us to
preserve the unity the Spirit
gives, for patience encourages
that peace which binds us
together (*Eph.* 4: 1–3; *Col.*
1: 11).

(b) It is an essential part of
the Christian's spiritual
"dress" or "clothing" (*Col.* 3:
12).

(c) It is a necessary condition
of claiming God's promises
(*Heb.* 6: 12).

(d) It is a priority in the teaching of and preaching to others
(*II Tim.* 4: 2).

(e) It is a key to victory in the
battle against the world, the
flesh and the devil (*I Pet.* 2:
11; 5: 8–10; see the repeated
use of the verb "stand" in
Eph. 6: 11, 13, 14).

(f) It is an essential part of the
Christian's testimony, when
persecuted or unjustly treated,
that he patiently refuses to
retaliate (*I Pet.* 2: 18–23; 3:
13, 14).

5. The rewards of patience.

(a) It can bring people to an
experience of salvation (*II
Pet.* 3: 15).

(b) It gains its end in fruitfulness (*Jas.* 5: 7).

(c) It adds beauty to character
(*Gal.* 5: 22).

(d) It marks us out as true
servants of God (*II Cor.* 6:
6).

6. The achievement of patience.

(a) First and foremost, we must focus our attention upon the example God has given us in His Son Jesus Christ (*Heb.* 12: 1–3).

(b) We should pray for patience, being realistic in facing up to the challenges to our patience (*Col.* 1: 11).

(c) We are to make it a deliberate objective (*Col.* 3: 12).

(d) As we grow in grace, and in the knowledge of our Lord Jesus Christ (*II Pet.* 3: 18), so the fruit of the Spirit will grow, which includes patience.

37. KINDNESS

Galatians: 5 22: "The fruit of the Spirit is . . . kindness."

Question: What is the kindness required of us?

Answer: The kindness required of us is the outflow of love in goodness and forgiveness, after the pattern of God's kindness to us. Such kindness is sympathetic, down-to-earth in practical concern and help, and uninfluenced by either the mer-its or gratitude of those to whom it is extended.

1. The nature of kindness.

(a) Kindness is linked with tender-heartedness (*Eph.* 4: 32); it follows upon compassion in the spiritual garments believers are to wear (*Col.* 3: 12).

(b) Kindness is love in action (*Eph.* 2: 7; 4: 32; *Tit.* 3: 4).

(c) Kindness is the reaction of love with goodness towards those who may ill-treat it (*I Cor.* 13: 4): it is goodness in action (*II Cor.* 6: 6).

(d) Kindness is love in practice, doing good to others (*Luke* 6: 35).

(e) Kindness is almost synonymous with forgiveness (*Eph.* 4: 32; *Col.* 3: 12, 13).

(f) Kindness is uninfluenced by the gratitude or ingratitude of those to whom it is extended; it does not stop when it gets no return (*Luke* 6: 32–35).

2. The declared opposites of kindness.

(a) Bitterness (*Eph.* 4: 31, 32).

(b) Anger (*Eph.* 4: 31, 32).

(c) Insults (*Eph.* 4; 31, 32; *I Pet.* 2: 1–3).

(d) Hateful feelings of any sort (*Eph.* 4: 31, 32).

(e) Lying (*I Pet.* 2: 1–3).

(f) Hypocrisy (*I Pet.* 2: 1–3).

(g) Jealousy (*I Pet.* 2: 1–3).

3. The fundamental example of kindness.

(a) God Himself is the supreme example of kindness: His kindness never fails (*Ps.* 118: 1–14, 29), and we are instructed to consider it well (*Rom.* 11: 22).

(b) God is rich in kindness, a truth displayed in His tolerance and patience to the ungrateful and the wicked (*Rom.* 2: 4; *Luke* 6: 35).

(c) God's kindness is seen in the way in which God delays the Judgment, giving men an opportunity for repentance (*Rom.* 2: 4).

(d) Salvation is the fruit of God's kindness exercised through our Lord Jesus Christ (*Tit.* 3: 4): not only has He saved us from the punishment of sin but He has raised us up with Christ and made us to sit with Him in the heavenly places (*Eph.* 2: 4–6).

(e) Furthermore, in the ages to come, He is going to show the immeasurable riches of His grace towards us in Christ Jesus, so that Christians are examples of how very, very rich God's kindness is (*Eph.* 2: 7).

(f) Everything the Lord Jesus Christ said and did revealed the kindness of God: when He said, "My yoke is easy", He used the adjective derived from the noun "kindness" used in Galatians 5: 22. The burdens He puts upon us when we become His disciples are never too much for us; to serve Him is to find ourselves experiencing His kindness (*Matt.* 11: 30).

(g) God's kindness does not come to an end (*Ruth* 2: 20).

(h) Men should not presume, however, upon God's kindness (*Rom.* 2: 4), for His kindness provides no evidence that He will not punish the guilty (*Rom.* 11: 22); rather God's kindness should lead men to repentance (*Rom.* 2: 4).

4. The outworkings of kindness (Luke 6: 35).

(a) Kindness means loving our enemies, and doing good

to those who hate us (*Luke* 6: 27).

(b) Kindness involves blessing those who curse us, and praying for those who mistreat us (*Luke* 6: 28).

(c) Kindness means that if anyone hits us on one cheek, we let him hit the other one too; if someone takes our coat, then we let him have our shirt as well (*Luke* 6: 29).

(d) Kindness finds expression by giving to everyone who asks us for something, and when someone takes what is ours, not asking for it back (*Luke* 6: 30).

(e) Kindness works by doing to others just what we want them to do for us (*Luke* 6: 31).

(f) Kindness is not loving only the people who love us but loving our enemies and doing good to them, lending and expecting nothing back (*Luke* 6: 32–36).

(g) Kindness refrains from judging others (*Luke* 6: 37).

(h) Kindness is marked by generous giving (*Luke* 6: 38).

(i) Where kindness is at work, after the pattern of our Lord Jesus Christ, people are not chafed, irked or galled un- necessarily; burdens are not unsympathetically placed upon them (*Matt.* 11: 30).

(j) Where kindness is really at work, its expressions are the same to all men, even when the person showing kindness may himself be under strain (*II Cor.* 6: 6).

5. The necessity of kindness in the Christian.

(a) God requires kindness to others: it is a condition of pleasing Him, and of walking humbly with Him (*Micah* 6: 8), and without it the Lord has a controversy with us (*Hos.* 4: 1).

(b) Kindness is a proof of our new birth, in the possession of the divine nature, for in genuine kindness we reveal the same attitude as our heavenly Father (*Luke* 6: 27, 35).

(c) Kindness is a characteristic of the new man which is renewed in knowledge after the image of its creator (*Col.* 3: 10); it is an essential part of the spiritual clothing of God's people to be put on deliberately (*Col.* 3: 12).

(d) Kindness is one of the

marks of God's servants (*II Cor.* 6: 6).

(e) Kindness also has a converting power (*Rom.* 2: 4; *Luke* 22: 61, 62; cf. *I Pet.* 2: 12).

(f) The measure of kindness we use towards others is the one we may expect God to use towards us (*Luke* 6: 38).

38. GOODNESS

Galatians 5: 22: "The fruit of the Spirit is . . . goodness."

Question: What is the goodness required of us?

Answer: When we affirm that God is good, we are declaring that He is all that He as God ought to be. The goodness required of us is that we should always strive to live as the members of God's family ought to live, with high moral standards and the active practice of good works. The basic content of the Christian's life is to be goodness.

1. God's goodness.

(a) God is good (*II Chron.* 30: 18; *Ps.* 86: 5; 106: 1; 107: 1; 118:1), and He alone is worthy of that description (*Matt.* 19: 17; *Mark* 10: 18).

(b) His goodness is seen in that His steadfast love endures for ever (*I Chron.* 16: 34).

(c) His goodness is displayed in His creation (*Gen.* 1: 4, 10, 12, 18, 21, 25, 31; *I Tim.* 4: 4).

(d) His goodness is demonstrated in all His works (*Ps.* 104: 24–31; 119: 68; *Acts* 14: 17).

(e) His goodness is witnessed by His gifts (*Neh.* 9: 20; *Ps.* 85: 12; *Luke* 1: 53; 11: 13; *Jas.* 1: 17).

(f) The commandments and directions God gives are good (*Ps.* 119: 39; *Mark* 3: 4; *Rom.* 7: 12; *Heb.* 6: 5).

(g) God's promises are good (*I Kings* 8: 56), not least in the salvation (*Heb.* 9: 11; 10: 1) and hope (*II Thess.* 2: 16) He grants to those who believe on His Son Jesus Christ.

(h) God's message to mankind in Jesus Christ is *good* news (*Rom.* 10: 15).

(i) God's will and purposes for our lives are good (*Ps* 84: 11; *Rom.* 12: 2) and the work He begins in Christians' lives at their new birth is "a good work" (*Phil.* 1: 6).

(j) Even when God needs to discipline Christians it is always for their good (*Ps.* 119: 67, 71; *Heb.* 12: 10).

(k) There is no limit to God's goodness and the good He gives to His spiritual children in Christ (*Rom.* 8: 32; *Eph.* 1: 3).

(l) Goodness finds its model and example in our Lord Jesus Christ (*I Pet.* 2: 19–24), who is the visible image of the invisible God (*Col.* 1: 15): He went about doing good (*Acts* 10: 38).

2. God's goodness teaches us truth about ourselves.

(a) Goodness is the test of a man's life (*Matt.* 7: 15–20; Luke 6: 43–45), and God judges everyone by the same standard of goodness (*Rom.* 2: 10, 11).

(b) By nature no one consistently does good (*Rom.* 3: 12): evil things rather than good things are the more natural fruit of human lives (*Matt.* 12: 34).

(c) The more we know ourselves, the more we know that good does not naturally dwell in us (*Rom.* 7: 18).

(d) Even though we may possess the desire to do good, we are not able to do it; instead of doing the good we want, we find ourselves doing the evil we do not want to do (*Rom.* 7: 18, 19).

(e) The call God gives to salvation, therefore, is not based upon man's goodness but entirely upon God's grace (*Rom.* 9: 11, 12; *Eph.* 2: 8): God has shown how much He loves us in that while we were still sinners the Lord Jesus Christ died for us (*Rom.* 5: 7, 8).

(f) God's goodness should make us continually thankful (*Ps.* 118: 29), so that we recognise that the only proper response to it is the offering of ourselves to Him (*Rom.* 12: 1).

(g) Real goodness begins when we hear God's message of salvation, retain it in a good and obedient heart, and persist until fruit is born (*Luke* 8: 8, 15)—the fruit of the Spirit which includes goodness (*Gal.* 5: 22, 23).

3. Defining goodness.

(a) Goodness is to do justice, love kindness and to walk

humbly with God (*Micah* 6: 8).

(b) Goodness is genuine obedience to the law of God (*Ps.* 34: 14 ff; 37: 27).

(c) Goodness is the outflow of love (*Gal.* 5: 22; *I Cor.* 13).

(d) Goodness is the putting aside of our own will and pleasure so as to please our neighbour for his good in order to build him up in the faith (*Rom.* 15: 2).

(e) Goodness is the opposite of evil (*I Thess.* 5: 15; *I Pet.* 3: 11; *III John* 11), disobedience (*Tit.* 1: 16), selfishness (*Rom.* 2: 7, 8) and hypocrisy (*Jas.* 3: 17).

(f) Goodness always helps rather than harms (*Luke* 6: 9; *Acts* 9: 36), delights in giving rather than receiving (*Matt.* 7: 11; *Acts* 20: 35; *II Cor.* 9: 8), and concerns itself with the need that requires to be met rather than with the merits of the person in need (*Luke* 6: 33; *Gal.* 6: 10).

(g) Real goodness is consistent goodness (*Tit.* 2: 10), flowing from a life full of the Holy Spirit and of faith (*John* 7: 38, 39; *Acts* 11: 24).

4. Goodness in us is the fruit of the Spirit.

(a) The word translated "goodness" in "the fruit of the Spirit" (*Gal.* 5: 22) conveys the idea of moral excellence and belongs with righteousness and truth to "the fruit of light" (*Eph.* 5: 9).

(b) The fruits of the Christian life are all fruits of goodness (*Matt.* 7: 17–20).

(c) Born again by God's Spirit into God's family, we find within ourselves new desires after goodness (*II Thess.* 1: 11).

(d) Goodness is a reflection of our heavenly Father's character being reproduced in us (*Matt.* 5: 45; *III John* 4, 11).

(e) Practical goodness is part of the transformation to be expected of converted men and women (*Eph.* 4: 28).

(f) Christians should be full of goodness (*Rom.* 15: 14), being wise about what is good but innocent about what is evil (*Rom.* 16: 19).

(g) Goodness is essentially living and behaving in the world as true servants of God (*I Pet.* 2: 15, 16).

(h) One of its principal demonstrations is in the general principle of submission to others: to civil authorities (*I Pet.* 2: 13–17), to employers (*I Pet.* 2: 18–25), of wives to husbands (*I Pet.* 3: 1–6), of children to parents (*Eph.* 6: 1, 2), and to one another (*Eph.* 5: 21; *I Pet.* 3: 8).

(i) Goodness responds to opposition and suffering with patience (*I Pet.* 2: 20), and does not allow anything to put it off from pursuing the right course (*I Pet.* 3: 6).

(j) Goodness on the part of Christians is God's chosen answer to men's unjust opposition to Christian witness (*I Pet.* 2: 15; 3: 1 ff).

(k) Our lives are meant to bear fruit in every good work (*Col.* 1: 10).

5. Goodness and good works.

(a) True religion and good works go together (*I Tim* 2: 10; *Matt.* 5: 16).

(b) Good works have no place in the obtaining of salvation (*Eph.* 2: 9; *Tit.* 3: 5), but they are a principal evidence of the experience of salvation (*Jas.* 2: 17): we are born again to do good works God has planned (*Eph.* 2: 10).

(c) Works cannot be divorced from words (*II Thess.* 2: 17), and goodness manifests itself in speech (*Matt.* 12: 34; *Luke* 6: 45; *II Thess.* 2: 17)—speech that builds up (*Eph.* 4: 29) and avoids speaking evil (*Tit.* 3: 1, 2).

(d) Goodness never pays back wrong for wrong but always tries to be kind (*I Thess.* 5 15), not only to fellow-Christians but to everyone (*Gal.* 6: 10).

(e) Our income is intended to enable us to be rich in good works (*I Tim.* 6: 17, 18), so that there should be a harvest of good works in our lives as we wisely use what God has given (*II Cor.* 9: 8–10).

(f) Goodness is displayed in all kinds of good deeds such as bringing up children well, showing hospitality, doing menial tasks for others, helping those in trouble, and being available to do good whenever the opportunity presents itself (*I Tim.* 5: 10; *Tit.* 3: 1).

(g) Good works do not have to be forced upon goodness, rather they are spontaneous and willing (*Philem.* 14).

(h) God has provided the Scriptures so that by the instruction they provide we may be thoroughly equipped for every good work (*II Tim.* 3: 17), for the wisdom they impart from above ensures a harvest of good deeds (*Jas.* 3: 17).

(i) God provides strength and encouragement to persevere in good works (*II Thess.* 2: 17; *Heb.* 13: 20, 21).

(j) Good works honour God: they make the teaching about God our Saviour attractive in the eyes of the world (*Tit.* 2: 10), and they compel men to praise our Father in heaven (*Matt.* 5: 16).

(k) It is not surprising, therefore, that the Christian should be eager to do good (*I Pet.* 3: 13).

39. FAITHFULNESS

Question: What is the faithfulness required of us?

Answer: Faithfulness is our proper response to God's faithfulness, and an outworking of living faith in Jesus Christ. Faithfulness is loyalty, reliability and dependability. It expresses itself in unswerving loyalty to God at any cost. It means fulfilling our duties and responsibilities to others, irrespective of how convenient or easy these obligations may be. Faithfulness is the principal virtue our Lord Jesus Christ chooses to reward.

1. Faithfulness is an outstanding feature of God's character (*Isa.* 49: 7; *I Cor.* 1: 9; 10: 13).

(a) He is the faithful God who keeps covenant and steadfast love with those who love Him and keep His commandments (*Deut.* 7: 9).

(b) He cannot lie (*Num.* 23: 19; *Tit.* 1: 2).

(c) His faithfulness is unfailing (*II Tim.* 2: 13), great (*Lam.* 3: 23) and incomparable (*Ps.* 89: 8).

(d) His faithfulness is determined (*Ps.* 89: 33), immeasurable (*Ps.* 36: 5), certain (*Ps.* 89: 2; *Isa.* 54: 10), and everlasting (*Ps.* 119: 90).

(e) His faithfulness is revealed in nature's order and balance (*Gen.* 8: 22; *Jer.* 33: 20–22).

(f) His faithfulness shows itself in the fulfilment of His

promises to His people (*Josh.* 21: 43; *Ezek.* 37: 11–14; *Isa.* 25: 1).

(g) His faithfulness has been gloriously expressed to us in our Lord Jesus Christ (*John* 1: 14; 13: 1; 14: 6; *Rev.* 19: 11).

2. Faithfulness is an essential aspect of Christian character.

(a) It is part of the fruit of the Spirit, and that fruit is the sum of Christian character (*Gal.* 5: 22, 23).

(b) Character is the test of a man's religion (*Matt.* 7: 15–20; *Luke* 6: 43–45), and is the one thing we cannot borrow, lend or escape for it is the real "us" (*Prov.* 9: 12; cf. 14: 10).

(c) Faithfulness arises from what a man is through and through—it does not occur accidentally (*Luke* 16: 10).

(d) The general principle holds true with regard to faithfulness that as a man thinks in his heart so he is (*Prov.* 23: 7).

(e) Faithfulness needs to be gloried in, and meditated upon in the heart, if it is to show itself in conduct (*Prov.* 3: 3).

(f) Faithfulness should extend to every aspect of life (*I Tim.* 3: 11).

(g) The person who is faithful in very little will be found faithful also in much (*Luke* 16: 10).

(h) Without faithfulness our characters are deficient of an essential quality (*Jas.* 1: 2–4).

(i) Christian character, however, is not produced in a moment (*Rom.* 5: 4): many of the testings which God permits, He overrules so as to develop faithfulness on our part (*Jas.* 1: 2 ff).

3. Faithfulness has relevance to our speech and our general use of words.

(a) Faithful speech is honest, direct, and unambiguous (*Matt.* 5: 37); when we say either "Yes" or "No" we must mean what we say (*II Cor.* 1: 18).

(b) Faithful speech is strictly truthful and avoids exaggeration (*Jas.* 5: 12).

(c) Faithful speech is the opposite of lying, false witness and evasive speech (*Prov.* 14: 5; *Hos.* 4: 1, 2).

(d) Faithful speech rebukes when such is necessary, but

with kindness and love (*Ps.* 141: 5; *Prov.* 27: 6).

(e) It is not enough to protest loyalty with our lips and then to deny it by conduct (*Prov.* 20: 6).

(f) Since it is characteristic of God to be always faithful to His promises, so must we be faithful to the promises we make (*Heb.* 10: 23; *Matt.* 5: 48; *II Cor.* 1: 17–20).

4. Faithfulness is to mark our relationship to God.

(a) Genuine faith in God must always lead to faithfulness to Him (*Hab.* 2: 4).

(b) God requires our total loyalty (*Luke* 16: 13), and our foremost expression of faithfulness must be to Him (*Acts* 11: 23).

(c) Faithfulness itself, even more than the fruits of faithfulness, is that for which God looks (*Matt.* 24: 20–23), and if it is absent He has a controversy with us (*Hos.* 4: 1).

(d) Christians are called of God to show faithfulness to Jesus Christ His Son (*Eph.* 1: 1; *Col.* 1: 2), a faithfulness which must be steadfast and continuing (*Acts* 11: 23).

(e) We are to be faithful in doing the will of God no matter what the obstacles (*Heb.* 10: 36), even in the face of death (*Rev.* 2: 10).

(f) Our faithfulness is precious to God (*I Pet.* 1: 7), and it causes us to find favour and good repute in His sight (*Prov.* 3: 4).

(g) Faithfulness is also a condition of our growing in the knowledge of God (*Hos.* 2: 20).

(h) Our faithfulness to God is very much influenced by our appreciation of His faithfulness to us (*Heb.* 10: 23).

(i) Fortunately, our occasions of faithlessness do not nullify the faithfulness of God (*Rom.* 3: 3; *II Tim.* 2: 13); God is willing to heal our faithlessness when we return to Him in repentance (*Hos.* 14: 4).

5. Faithfulness is to mark all our other relationships.

A. Husbands and wives.

(a) **Husbands** should be completely faithful to their wives (*Prov.* 5: 15–20; *I Tim.* 3: 2, 12), a faithfulness which should extend to their thoughts (*Ex.* 20: 17; *Matt.* 5: 27, 28).

(b) A faithful husband loves his wife as he loves his own body (*Eph.* 5: 28), and finds his satisfaction in her (*Prov.* 5: 15).

(c) A faithful husband treats his wife with consideration, bestowing honour upon her as the weaker vessel (*I Pet.* 3: 7).

(d) A faithful husband strives to love his wife as Christ loves the Church (*Eph.* 5: 25 ff).

(e) **Wives** are to be consistently faithful to their husbands' interests (*Prov.* 31: 12).

(f) A faithful wife helps her husband play his part in the community (*Prov.* 31: 23).

(g) A faithful wife can be completely trusted by her husband (*Prov.* 31: 11), and her affection for him will fill him with delight at all times (*Prov.* 5: 19).

(h) A faithful wife is her husband's pride and joy (*Prov.* 12: 4).

B. Parents and children.

(a) Faithful **parents** recognise that their children must never have precedence over discipleship of the Lord Jesus (*Mark* 10: 29; *Luke* 18: 29; *Matt.* 19: 29; cf. *I Sam.* 2: 20, 29; *Heb.* 11: 17).

(b) Faithful parents are careful in the training of their children, recognising that the course their children adopt in later life depends upon the training they initially receive at home (*Prov.* 22: 6), and so they give their children instruction and good precepts from their earliest age (*Prov.* 4: 1–4).

(c) Faithful parents diligently discipline their children because they love them (*Prov.* 13: 24).

(d) Faithful parents not only teach their children the way of wisdom but they lead them in the paths of uprightness (*Prov.* 4: 11), conferring upon them for life the benefit of godly example (*Prov.* 20: 7).

(e) Faithful parents teach their children about the past dealings of God with His people, appreciating their responsibility for the generations which are to follow (*Ps.* 78: 5, 6).

(f) Faithful **children** obey their parents on the strength of the commandment, "Honour your father and mother" (*Eph.* 6: 2; *Ex.* 20: 12).

(g) Faithful children listen to their father and do not despise their mother when she is old (*Prov.* 23: 22).

(h) Faithful children do not regard the property of their parents lightly, and avoid the snare of imagining that what is wrong outside the family is permissible within it (*Prov.* 28: 24).

(i) Faithful children appreciate that they have duties as well as rights: they are careful, therefore, in their treatment of their parents, and make necessary provision for them (*Prov.* 19: 26).

C. **Employers and employees.**
(a) Faithful **employers** do not withhold proper wages (*Jas.* 5: 4).

(b) Faithful employers are conscientious and responsible towards those who serve them as they expect them to be in turn towards them (*Eph.* 6: 9).

(c) **Employees** are to be faithful to their employers (*Tit.* 2: 10).

(d) A faithful employee does not pilfer (*Tit.* 2: 10); rather,

he should be so reliable, for example, in handling money entrusted to him, that he does not need to be checked up upon (*II Kings* 12: 15).

(e) A faithful employee is never rude or insolent to his employer (*Tit.* 2: 10).

(f) A faithful employee renders to his earthly employer service as if it were to the Lord Jesus Christ Himself (*Eph.* 6: 5–8), and in this way, by his behaviour at work, he commends the gospel to others (*Tit.* 2: 10).

D. **Christian fellowship.**
(a) We are to be faithful brothers and sisters to one another because of our common relationship to the Lord Jesus Christ (*Col.* 1: 2).

(b) We must, for example, be always eager to believe the best of one another (*I Cor.* 13: 7).

(c) Where wrong needs to be put right, we must be faithful in speaking the truth to one another in love (*Prov.* 27: 6; *Eph.* 4: 15, 25).

(d) We must stand by one another, even when trouble may result (*Heb.* 10: 33).

(e) We must be faithful in our

171

exercise of the gift of hospitality (*III John* 5).

(f) We must serve one another all the better because of our relationship in Christ (*I Tim.* 6: 2).

(g) To be faithful to one another we must make time, and seize opportunities, to meet with other Christians so as to encourage and help one another (*Heb.* 10: 25).

(h) We must be faithful to the spiritual leaders God gives us, so that they may fulfil their task joyfully and not sadly (*Heb.* 13: 7; *I Thess.* 5: 12, 13).

6. Faithfulness also finds expression in our service of God, and the use to which we put all He has given us.

(a) Faithfulness is a primary qualification for service and office in the body of Christ, the Church (*I Tim.* 3: 11; *II Tim.* 2: 2).

(b) God is to be served with faithfulness (*Josh.* 24: 14; *Matt.* 24: 45; *Heb.* 3: 1, 2, 5, 6): we cannot serve two masters (*Luke* 16: 13).

(c) God entrusts us with a stewardship and it is required of stewards that they should be found faithful (*I Cor.* 4: 2).

(d) If, for example, our service is the communicating of God's Word in any way, we are to speak that Word faithfully, as in the sight of God (*Jer.* 23: 28; *II Cor.* 2: 17), renouncing all that is underhand or insincere (*II Cor.* 4: 2), and ensuring that we pass God's Word on accurately and faithfully (*Josh.* 11: 15; *Acts* 20: 27).

(e) We are to serve God faithfully by maintaining and upholding the faith (*II Tim.* 4: 7), earnestly contending for the faith which was once for all delivered to God's people (*Jude* 3).

(f) Whatever service we render to others, we are to render it faithfully (*III John* 5).

(g) We serve God faithfully as we use our money and material possessions in the interests of His kingdom (*Luke* 16: 11), recognising that all we own is a gift from Him (*I Chron.* 29: 14).

7. Faithfulness has great importance in respect of the rewards our Lord Jesus Christ wants to give.

(a) The Lord rewards every

man for his faithfulness (*I Sam.* 26: 23).

(b) The true standard of reward is faithfulness to opportunity rather than length, honour or seeming importance of service (*Matt.* 20: 1–16).

(c) The Lord knows the truth about our faithfulness (*Rev.* 2: 13, 19).

(d) A faithful individual will abound with blessings (*Prov.* 28: 20).

(e) The Lord Jesus will reward His faithful servants on His return (*Matt.* 24: 46): equal gifts, if used with unequal faithfulness, will be unequally rewarded (*Luke* 19: 12–27); unequal gifts, used with equal faithfulness, will be equally rewarded (*Matt.* 25: 14–30).

(f) A crown of righteousness awaits the servants of Christ who have kept the faith and been faithful in service (*II Tim.* 4: 7, 8): significantly, those who are described as being in the closest proximity to the Lord Jesus Christ in heaven are described as those who have proved themselves faithful (*Rev.* 17: 14).

(g) We should be watchful concerning our faithfulness, lest we lose our reward (*II John* 8).

8. The Bible provides us with many examples of faithfulness.

(a) Abraham was found faithful in his heart to the Lord (*Neh.* 9: 8; *Gal.* 3: 9).

(b) Moses was faithful to the tasks God committed to him of caring for God's people (*Num.* 12: 7; *Heb.* 3: 2, 5).

(c) Joseph was faithful to his Egyptian master at great cost to himself (*Gen.* 39: 7 ff) and then also to the keeper of the prison (*Gen.* 39: 22, 23).

(d) David was faithful to Saul in spite of all the injustices he suffered at his hands (*I Sam.* 22: 14).

(e) Daniel was faithful both to the Lord and to his earthly employer, the king of Babylon (*Dan.* 6: 4, 10).

(f) Shadrach, Meshach and Abednego were outstanding examples of faithfulness to God as they obeyed His commandment (*Dan.* 3: 28; *Ex.* 20: 5).

(g) Ruth's answer to Naomi is a classic example of faithfulness (*Ruth* 1: 16, 17).

(h) Paul sought to be faithful in not holding back any truth God wanted His people to receive from him (*Acts* 20: 20, 27).

(i) Silvanus, or Silas, was a faithful brother in his service of both Peter (*I Pet.* 5: 12) and the apostle Paul (*Acts* 15: 40; *I Thess*, 1: 1).

(j) Onesimus was a Christian who was faithful in his relationship to his fellow-Christians (*Col.* 4: 9).

(k) Tychicus was faithful in serving others for Christ's sake (*Eph.* 6: 21).

(l) Timothy was faithful to the apostle Paul in the tasks delegated to him (*I Cor.* 4: 17; *Phil.* 2: 19–24).

(m) Antipas was faithful in his witness to the Lord Jesus even though it meant martyrdom (*Rev.* 2: 13).

(n) The recollection of the witnesses of the faith and those who have been faithful in the past inspires us to faithfulness (*Heb.* 11; 12: 1, 2).

(o) We do well to imitate the faith and faithfulness of godly leaders who have both helped us and have been an example to us in the past (*Heb.* 13: 7).

10. Faithfulness may bring its own costly consequences.

(a) Faithfulness may bring reproach and persecution as it did to our Lord Jesus Christ (*Rom.* 15: 3).

(b) There is great blessing, however, in hardship or persecution which comes as a result of faithfulness (*Matt.* 5: 11, 12).

(c) Even our lives may be put in jeopardy by faithfulness (*Dan.* 3: 16–19; *Rev.* 2: 13).

(d) But suffering on account of faithfulness to God, and to others because it is God's will, will bring its own experience of God's help (*II Tim.* 1: 8), and it is, of course, only by God's help that faithfulness can be achieved (*I Cor.* 7: 25).

40. MEEKNESS

Galatians 5: 22, 23: "The fruit of the Spirit is . . . meekness" (A.V.).

Question: What is the meekness required of us?

Answer: The meekness required of us is an inward attitude which enables us to be

174

in a position of submission to the will of God, irrespective of difficulty, and to treat others with gentleness, humility, courtesy, and considerateness. (Meekness is not a commonly appreciated or admired quality, for, in its contemporary use, it carries a suggestion of spinelessness. **Gentleness** is the alternative in many modern translations (e.g. R.S.V., N.I.V.), but it is not completely satisfactory. Aristotle defined meekness as the happy medium between excessive anger and excessive angerlessness. Gentleness, humility, courtesy, considerateness and meekness—put together—best express the Greek word prautēs.)

1. The nature of meekness.

(a) Meekness is part of love's outflow (*I Cor.* 4: 21).

(b) It is frequently linked in the New Testament with patience and forbearance (*II Cor.* 10: 1; *Eph.* 4: 2; *Col.* 3: 12, 13), and also with humility (*Matt.* 11: 29; *Eph.* 4: 2; *Col.* 3: 12).

(c) It is a gift of the Spirit, and a fruit of the wisdom from above which God gives (*Jas.* 3: 13).

(d) It is a duty laid upon us by God as an essential part of the life to which He has called us in Christ (*Eph.* 4: 2; *Col.* 3: 12).

(e) Meekness may be thought of as part of the Christian's essential clothing (*Col.* 3: 12), which he must never be without (*Tit.* 3: 2).

(f) **Submission to the will of God** is the most important aspect of meekness (*Jas.* 4: 10; *I Pet.* 5: 6).

(g) Meekness strives to choose God's will before self-will (*Mark* 14: 36; *Matt.* 26: 39; *Luke* 22: 42).

(h) Even if submission to God means being regarded as the scum of the earth, meekness accepts obedience to God's will, and strives to act in a manner pleasing to God (*I Cor.* 4: 13)—cf. the example of Stephen (*Acts* 7: 60).

(i) Meekness cries to God in prayer, and reverently accepts His answer whatever it may be (*Heb.* 5: 7).

(j) Meekness goes hand in hand with triumphant waiting upon God (*Ps.* 147: 6; 149: 4; *I Pet.* 2: 21–23)—it causes a man to counsel himself, "Be

175

still before the Lord, and wait patiently for Him" (*Ps.* 37: 7).

(k) Meekness discovers the unique peace that comes from submission to God's will (*Ps.* 131: 1, 2).

(l) Mary is an example of meekness before God: "I am the Lord's servant . . . May it be to me as you have said" (*Luke* 1: 38).

(m) Consideration for others is the second most important aspect of meekness—humble before God, we learn to be gentle in our dealings with others (*I Pet.* 5: 5, 6).

(n) Meekness is synonymous with universal courtesy (*Tit.* 3: 2).

(o) Meekness is unassuming (*Zech.* 9: 9; *Matt.* 21: 5) and makes us approachable (*Matt.* 11: 29).

(p) Meekness is a mark of a servant of God (*Isa.* 42: 1 ff; 53: 6 f; *II Tim.* 2: 24, 25), of someone who genuinely strives to walk in the Lord Jesus Christ's footsteps (*I Pet.* 2: 21–24).

(q) Meekness is much more concerned to serve God than to advance personal status (*Num.* 12: 3; *Phil.* 2: 5 ff).

(r) Meekness is an indispensable characteristic of the ideal teacher (*Matt.* 11: 29; *II Tim.* 2: 25).

(s) It is also an indispensable factor in the exercise of discipline (*I Cor.* 4: 21), and in the spirit in which the erring or wayward Christian is to be sought out and brought back into fellowship (*Gal.* 6: 1).

(t) Moses exhibited meekness to a remarkable degree, more than all his contemporaries (*Num.* 12: 3), and, significantly, he was described by God as His true servant (*Num.* 12: 7).

2. The meekness of our Lord Jesus Christ.

(a) Meekness was a promised characteristic of the Messiah in the Old Testament prophecies (*Isa.* 42: 1 ff; *Zech.* 9: 9).

(b) Meekness was, in fact, one of the foremost characteristics which our Lord Jesus Christ exhibited during His earthly life (*II Cor.* 10: 1), and was part of His own self-description (*Matt.* 11: 29).

(c) **Submission to the will of God the Father** was an important aspect of our Lord's meekness (*Heb*. 10: 7).

(d) His food was to do the will of the Father and to finish His work (*John* 4: 34).

(e) His submission was epitomised in the Garden of Gethsemane when He prayed, "Not my will, but yours be done" (*Luke* 22: 42).

(f) It was also displayed in His submission to the wrongs inflicted upon Him as He discharged His ministry as God's suffering Servant: "He was oppressed, and He was afflicted, yet He opened not His mouth" (*Isa*. 53: 7); He did "not shout or cry out, or raise his voice in the streets" (*Isa*. 42: 2).

(g) When insults were hurled at Him, He did not respond with retaliation; His response was simply to entrust Himself to Him who judges justly (*I Pet*. 2: 23).

(h) But the second important aspect of our Lord's meekness was **His consideration for others,** and especially His unassertiveness and His tenderness to the weak and inadequate (*Isa*. 42: 2, 3)—e.g. His dealings with the Samaritan woman (*John* 4), the woman taken in adultery (*John* 8: 1–11), and Zacchaeus (*Luke* 19: 1–10).

(i) He encouraged men and women to come to Him precisely because of His meekness (*Matt*. 11: 29).

(j) His consideration for the disciples was marked: for example, He was concerned for them when they were tired (*Mark* 6: 31), and when they were troubled and needed comfort (*John* 14: 1 ff).

3. **Meekness may be better understood by appreciating some of the opposite features of human behaviour with which it is contrasted.**

(a) Self-assertiveness or arrogance (*I Pet*. 3: 15).

(b) Jealousy and selfish ambition (*Jas*. 3: 13, 14).

(c) Quarrelsomeness (*Isa*. 42: 2; *Matt*. 12: 19; *II Tim*. 2: 24, 25).

(d) Self-justification and self-defence (*Isa*. 42: 2; *Matt*. 12: 19).

(e) Resentment (*II Tim*. 2: 24, 25).

(f) Abrasiveness (*Matt*. 11: 29, 30).

(g) Anger (*Jas.* 1: 20, 21).

(h) Violence and being war-like (*Matt.* 21: 5).

(i) Aggressiveness (*I Cor.* 4: 21).

(j) Unnecessary sternness in the application of discipline (*I Cor.* 4: 4, 21; *II Tim.* 2: 25).

4. The practice and expression of meekness.

(a) Its practice is to be continuous, like the wearing of clothes (*Col.* 3: 12); it is to be actively pursued (*I Tim.* 6: 11).

(b) It expresses itself in believing submission to God's will, even when it cannot understand what God may be doing (*Job.* 1: 21; *Acts* 20: 22–24; 21: 10–14; *I Pet.* 4: 19).

(c) It expresses itself in submissive listening and obedience to the instruction of God's Word, even if that obedience involves the acceptance of rebuke and the need for repentance (*Jas.* 1: 21).

(d) It expresses itself in respect for all people, not for whom or what they are, or what their attitude may be in return (*Tit.* 3: 2; *I Pet.* 3: 15).

(e) It expresses itself in restraint when provoked (*II Tim.* 2: 25).

(f) When authorities or others ask for an account of the Christian's profession of faith, it is to be given with meekness, even though injustice which has been suffered might prompt indignation or hurt (*I Pet.* 3: 16).

(g) It expresses itself in tenderness in dealing with those who need to be corrected (*Isa.* 42: 3; *II Tim.* 2: 25), correcting them without arrogance, impatience or anger, and endeavouring to give no unnecessary offence (*Gal.* 6: 1).

(h) It expresses itself in accepting the example of the Lord Jesus as the only acceptable norm for obedience to God and service of man (*II Cor.* 10: 1; *Phil.* 2: 5 ff).

5. The importance of meekness.

(a) Meekness finds its place among the Beatitudes: "Blessed are the meek, for they will inherit the earth" (*Matt.* 5: 5).

(b) Meekness makes us true helpers of others after the pattern of our Lord Jesus Christ (*Matt.* 11:29), for rather than antagonising people we may win them over to what is right by love's expression through meekness (*II Tim.* 2: 25).

(c) Meekness is a necessary condition for knowing God's guidance (*Ps.* 25: 9).

(d) Meekness is a condition of receiving God's blessing (*Ps.* 37: 11).

(e) The Lord causes meekness to prosper—He adorns the humble with victory (*Ps.* 149: 4).

(f) While it may be a mystery and a paradox to the unbelieving world, meekness is a secret of happiness (*Ps.* 37: 11; *Matt.* 5: 5).

41. SELF-CONTROL

Galatians 5:22, 23: "The fruit of the Spirit is . . . temperance (self-control)."

Question: What is the temperance or self-control required of us?

Answer: Temperance (the Authorised Version transla-tion) gives the wrong impression of self-control. The self-control required of us is self-mastery, so that through the help of the Holy Spirit, we are not under the power or dominion of any sin or habit, but we willingly use our Christian freedom to serve Christ by serving others. It is different from the rest of the fruit of the Spirit because it is neither Godward nor manward in its primary emphasis, but more properly selfward.

1. Areas in which self-control is most obviously relevant.

(a) In fact, self-control is relevant to the whole of human life (*I Thess.* 5: 6, 22).

(b) Eating (*Prov.* 23: 20; 25: 16).

(c) Drinking (*Eccl.* 10: 17; *Rom.* 13: 13)—drunkenness leads to uncontrolled actions and excess (*Eph.* 5: 18).

(d) Sex (*Tit.* 2: 5): the sex instinct is a good gift of God which is built into man but is meant to be exercised in marriage alone (*Mark* 10: 7), and even there it is a precious benefit to be enjoyed in a manner consistent with self-control (*I Cor.* 7: 1–6).

(e) The exercise and satisfaction of human desires (*I Pet.* 2: 11; 4: 4; cf. *Matt.* 14: 4; *Mark* 6: 18), and the enjoyment of human **pleasures** (*Matt.* 14: 6, 7; *Mark* 6: 21, 22).

(f) Occasions of **temptation** (*Mark* 14: 37–40, 66–72): sometimes the self-controlled Christian will know that the wisest course will be to flee from it (*II Tim.* 2: 22; *Jas.* 1: 14).

(g) **The estimate we have of ourselves,** and the exercise of pride (*Rom.* 12: 3, 16; cf. *Phil.* 2: 3).

(h) Weaknesses of temperament —for example, a man's tendency to be cowardly (*Mark* 6: 26; *Matt.* 14: 9; *II Tim.* 1: 7).

(i) **The expression of our feelings:** for example, if insulted it is the fool who shows his irritation straightaway; whereas it is the prudent, self-controlled man, who keeps his feelings out of sight (*Prov.* 12: 16).

(j) **Temper** (*Ps.* 37: 8; *Eph.* 4: 26; *I Thess.* 5: 14).

(k) **The use of the tongue** (*Matt.* 14: 7; *Mark* 6: 22, 23; *I Tim.* 3: 8; *Jas.* 3: 1, 2), and

in the promises we may make (*Ex.* 8: 8, 15; *Eccl.* 5: 2; *Matt.* 14: 7; *Mark* 6: 22, 23).

(l) Resistance to worldly pressures to live with a wholly **materialistic outlook** (*I Tim.* 6: 6–10): it is only by self-control that we can avoid the sin of coveting (*Acts* 20: 33; *Rom.* 7: 7; 13: 9), and ensure that our treasure is in heaven rather than on earth (*Matt.* 6: 19, 20; cf. *John* 6: 27).

(m) The use of **time** (*Eccl.* 3: 1 ff; *Eph.* 5: 15, 16; *Col.* 4: 5).

(n) **Spiritual experience:** our calling to freedom must not mean indulgence of our sinful nature (*Gal.* 5: 13); our spiritual joy and exuberance must not lead to excess (*Eph.* 5: 18–20); and our exercise of spiritual gifts must not be selfish but for the edifying of the whole body of Christ (*I Cor.* 14: 12, 26–33, 40).

2. **Opposites of self-control.**

(a) **Undisciplined living** with all its sad consequences (*Prov.* 21: 25; 26: 14; *Eccl.* 10: 18; *I Pet.* 1: 13, 14; 4: 3, 4).

(b) **Sexual immorality, impurity and licentiousness** (*Gal.* 5: 10)—all illustrations of a lack of control of the body and its sexual appetites.

(c) **Idolatry,** of which covetousness is a form (*Gal.* 5: 20; *Col.* 3: 5)—a lack of control over our eyes and coveting, and a lack of discipline with regard to the acquisitive spirit encouraged by society (*I John* 2: 15, 16).

(d) **Hatred, jealousy, and envy** (*Gal.* 5: 20, 21)—all failures to control the wrongful feelings which our sinful nature prompts.

(e) **Discord, selfish ambition, dissensions and factions** (*Gal.* 5: 20)—these all arise from the failure to control self and its display in forceful and selfish feelings or points of view.

(f) **Fits of temper** (Gal. 5: 20) —failure to control our anger and our tongue.

(g) **Drunkenness and orgies** (*Gal.* 5: 20)—failure to control thirst and the desire for pleasure.

3. What self-control means in practice.

(a) It is essentially self-mastery or dominion over oneself (*Rom.* 6: 13, 14), leading to an orderly life (*Eph.* 5: 15).

(b) It means coming to terms with the truth about ourselves and our flesh: our flesh is weak (*Mark* 14: 38; *Rom.* 6: 19; 8: 1), sinful (*Rom.* 8: 3), and always looking for an opportunity to have its fling (*Rom.* 13: 14; *Gal.* 5: 13).

(c) It means making our body our slave rather than allowing it to be our master (*I Cor.* 9: 27).

(d) It means being sufficiently honest with ourselves to appreciate that self-discipline must begin with our mind and our thoughts (*I Pet.* 1: 3; *Phil.* 4: 8; cf. *Matt.* 5: 28).

(e) It means having before us clear goals, so that we live our lives with purpose and a clear sense of direction (*I Cor.* 9: 24–27).

(f) It means having an eye to the good of others as well as our own: our Christian freedom is not to please ourselves but to choose to please others for their good, following the example of our Lord Jesus (*Rom.* 15: 1–3).

(g) It means recognising the place of watchfulness (*Matt.* 26: 41; *Mk.* 14: 38) and not overestimating our strength (*I Cor.* 10: 12).

(h) It means recognising the place of prayer, and giving time to it (*Matt.* 26: 41; *Mark* 14: 38; *I Pet.* 4: 7).

(i) It means honest and drastic action often with regard to the known sources of temptation (*Matt.* 5: 29; 18: 8, 9; *Mark* 9: 43–47), giving no room for the gratification of the desires of our sinful flesh (*Rom.* 13: 14)—in other words, the readiness to say "No" to ungodliness and worldly passions (*Tit.* 2: 12).

(j) It means being like an athlete in our approach to life (*I Cor.* 9: 25; *II Tim.* 2: 5).

(k) It means perseverance (*II Pet.* 1: 6).

(l) It means being inwardly strong through the resources of Jesus Christ (*Phil.* 4: 13; *II Tim.* 1: 7; 2: 1).

4. The necessity and priority of self-control.

(a) It is an essential part of godliness which, sadly, will be despised in the last days (*II Tim.* 3: 2–4).

(b) It is an essential qualification for holding office in the Church of God (*I Tim.* 3: 2; *Tit.* 1: 8).

(c) It is linked with righteousness (*Acts* 24: 25), one of the principal priorities of Christian living (*I Pet.* 2: 24).

(d) It is part of our present experience of God's salvation (*Tit.* 2: 12, 13).

(e) It is the climax of the fruit of the Spirit (*Gal.* 5: 23), and is relevant to every age-group (*Tit.* 2: 2, 5, 6, 12).

(f) It is part of the freedom to which our Lord Jesus Christ calls us (*John* 8: 36; *Gal.* 5: 1, 13)—a freedom purchased at tremendous cost (*Gal.* 3: 13).

(g) Without self-control we are easy prey for Satan (*I Cor.* 7: 5; *Eph.* 4: 26).

(h) Without self-control we may bring harm to others as well as to ourselves (*Mark* 6: 20, 21–28; cf. *II Sam.* 11: 1–5, 17; 12: 15).

(i) It is essential if we are to maintain and safeguard the value of our Christian testimony and service of the Lord Jesus (*I Cor.* 9: 25–27).

(j) It is part of our conformity to the likeness of our Lord Jesus Christ (*Rom.* 8: 29): His whole life was disciplined so as to fulfil the Father's will (*Luke* 9: 51; *John* 4: 34); He was disciplined in prayer (*Mark* 1: 35; *Luke* 11: 1), before temptation (*John* 6: 15; *Luke* 22: 39–46), and in the face of extreme ill-treatment (*I Pet.* 2: 23).

(k) We shall be judged with regard to our exercise of self-control (*Acts* 24: 25; *I Cor.* 9: 25).

42. CHRISTIAN DISCIPLESHIP

Question: What is Christian discipleship?

Answer: Christian discipleship is our response to the call of Jesus Christ to follow Him. It involves a counting of the cost and a total commitment to Jesus Christ, so that the whole of our life is given to seeking first God's kingdom and His righteousness.

1. The cost and conditions of discipleship.

(a) "Disciple", the Greek word for "apprentice" or "learner", is the word used most often in the New Testament—in fact, some 250 times —to describe members of Christ's kingdom (*Luke* 11: 1; 14: 26 ff).

(b) Disciples of the Lord Jesus were not called "Christians" until the establishment of the church in Antioch (*Acts* 11: 26), and then it was but a nickname.

(c) Discipleship constitutes our answer to the call of Jesus Christ to follow Him (*Matt.* 4: 19; *Mark* 1: 17; 2: 14; 10: 21; *Luke* 9: 59; *John* 1: 43), in the light of His death and resurrection on our behalf (*Matt.* 28: 18–20; *Acts* 9: 1–22; *Rom.* 12: 1, 2; *Phil.* 3: 1–11).

(d) No one, however, should be allowed to embark upon discipleship without first appreciating the cost (*Matt.* 19: 21; *Luke* 18: 22)—our Lord went to great trouble to underline its demands (*Luke* 14: 25–33).

(e) The love we have for people, and the desire we may have that they should become disciples, must not mean that we neglect to make them count the cost (*Mark* 10: 21).

(f) The basic principle is that no man can serve two masters; if he tries to do so, the

183

results are bound to be unfortunate (*Matt.* 6: 24; *Luke* 16: 13).

(g) For some, the cost may relate particularly to wealth, since discipleship involves the abandonment of every idol that would take Christ's place in a person's life (*Matt.* 19: 21; *Mark* 10: 21; *Luke* 18: 22).

(h) The home is not to assume priority over discipleship of Christ (*Luke* 18: 28 ff).

(i) Discipleship begins with a renunciation, and it is not intended that the act of renunciation should be left until later (*Matt.* 19: 21; *Mark* 10: 21; *Luke* 18: 22).

(j) Looking back is no more possible for the disciple than it is for someone who flees persecution (*Luke* 17: 31 f; cf. *Gen.* 19: 17, 26), or for the man who has put his hand to the plough (*Luke* 9: 62; cf. *I Kings* 19: 20 f), or for the athlete who does not look back at the ground he has covered but at the finishing tape ahead (*Phil.* 3: 13 f).

(k) Discipleship means, secondly, a sincere acknowledgement of the Lordship of Christ (*Matt.* 7: 21–23; *Luke* 6: 46; 13: 26–27).

(l) Discipleship means, thirdly, a life of devotion to Christ—the relationship we have to Him supercedes every other relationship (*Matt.* 12: 49, 50; *Mark* 3: 34, 35; *Luke* 8: 21).

(m) Devotion to Christ may bring reproach from men but it is something of tremendous value to Him (*Matt.* 26: 10; *Mark* 14: 6).

(n) Discipleship means, fourthly, the acceptance of the principle of dying to self (*John* 12: 23–26).

(o) Our Lord Jesus Christ set a pattern for all disciples to follow: the man who loves his life will lose it, but the man who is willing to act as if he hates his life, out of allegiance to Christ's cause, will keep it for eternal life (*Matt.* 10: 39; 16: 25; *Mark* 8: 35; *Luke* 9: 24; 17: 33; *John* 12: 25).

(p) Only when this principle of dying to self is genuinely accepted can there be a true readiness for tribulation and persecution (*Matt.* 5: 10–12; *Mark* 9: 49; cf. 8: 34–37).

(q) Only when the disciple is

willing to die daily to himself will he be ready to serve others for Christ's sake without reservation or personal choice (*Matt.* 20: 26, 27; *Mark* 10: 43, 44).

(r) Discipleship means, fifthly, **the discipline of instruction** (*Matt.* 10: 24, 25; *Luke* 6: 40).

(s) Discipleship means doing the will of the Father, and to this end the Word of God must be both listened to and obeyed (*Matt.* 12: 49, 50).

2. The proof of discipleship.

(a) The proof of which our Lord spoke most often is the proof of **obedience** (*Matt.* 7: 21, 24–27; 12: 50; *Mark* 3: 35; *Luke* 6: 46–49; 8: 21; 11: 28).

(b) It is by our obedience to Christ that we show our love for Him, so that disobedience is synonymous with an absence of love (*John* 14: 21, 24).

(c) True obedience to Christ will frequently incur the world's hatred (*John* 15: 17–27).

(d) The proof of discipleship is seen often, therefore, in the correspondence between the world's reaction to the ministry of Christ's disciples and the reaction our Lord Himself received in the course of His own ministry as He obeyed the Father (*John* 15: 20).

(e) **Fruitfulness** is picked out as a proof of discipleship (*John* 15: 8)—there are different levels of fruitfulness (*Matt.* 13: 8, 23; *Mark* 4: 8, 20; *Luke* 8: 8, 15), and it does not happen all at once (*Luke* 8: 14, 15).

(f) When disciples abide in Christ by means of obedience, they become spiritually fruitful (*John* 15: 5), so that fruitfulness becomes a legitimate test of any profession of discipleship (*Matt.* 12: 33; *Luke* 6: 43, 44).

(g) Chastisement—or bearing in mind the picture of fruit, pruning—is a necessary part of the discipleship calculated to make us more profitable to God (*John* 15: 2).

(h) **Love** is a proof of discipleship (*John* 13: 34 f).

(i) Love for God is the substance of the first summary of the commandments, and love for others the substance of the second (*Matt.* 22: 36–39; *Mark* 12: 28, 31; *Luke* 10: 27).

(j) The love disciples exhibit

is to go beyond the limits of ordinary human love (*Matt.* 5: 46, 47; *Luke* 6: 32–35).

(k) **An obvious awareness of privilege** is another proof of discipleship, since we quickly learn that we did not choose Christ but that He chose us (*John* 15: 16).

(l) Over all the work of disciples there stands, in effect, the principle: having paid nothing for what they receive, they charge nothing for what they do (*Matt.* 10: 8; *Acts* 3: 6; 20: 33 ff; cf. *Rom.* 1: 5).

(m) **Humility** is a further proof of discipleship (*Mark* 9: 35; cf. *Matt.* 11: 28 ff; *Phil.* 2: 5–11).

(n) Greatness in the sight of God involves humble service (*Mark* 9: 35): it expresses itself in the willingness to take upon ourselves the function and attitude of a servant (*Matt.* 20: 26; *Mark* 10: 43; *Luke* 22: 26).

(o) Our Lord warned against the desire for status (*Luke* 14: 11; cf. *Mark* 10: 15 f).

(p) Like a child, we should know how lowly we really are (*Matt.* 18: 1–5).

(q) Disciples, desiring to walk in Christ's footsteps, willingly wash one another's feet (*John* 13: 14).

(r) A final proof of discipleship is **faithfulness**—the one who stands firm to the end is the man who shall be saved (*Matt.* 24: 13).

(s) The parables of the talents and pounds emphasise the need for faithful service during this present period of history, prior to the Lord's return (*Matt.* 25: 14–30; *Luke* 19: 12–27).

3. The aims of discipleship.

(a) Perhaps the principal, all-comprehending aim, is simply Christlikeness of character (*Matt.* 10: 24, 25; *Luke* 6: 40), the character outlined in the Beatitudes (*Matt.* 5: 3–10); and summed up in the fruit, of the Spirit (*Gal.* 5: 22, 23).

(b) The aim of discipleship is to share in the work of the Lord Jesus whether in terms of what we **are**—for example, as salt (*Matt.* 5: 13) and light (*Matt.* 5: 14 ff)—or in terms of what we are to **do**—for example in catching men (*Luke* 5: 10), harvesting the spiritual harvest (*Matt.* 9: 37; *John* 4: 35–38), preaching the kingdom of heaven (*Matt.* 10: 5 ff), serving others with the spirit of a servant (*John* 13: 1 ff), and making disciples (*Matt.* 28: 19, 20).

(c) The aim of discipleship is to glorify the Father on earth by finishing the work He has given us to do (*Matt.* 5: 16; *John* 17: 4).

(d) The aim of discipleship is to express such unity among disciples that the world knows that the Father sent the Son into the world to show His love (*John* 10: 16; 17: 20–23).

(e) In essence, the aim of discipleship is to bear witness to our Lord Jesus Christ (*Luke* 24: 48; *Acts* 1: 8), and to His total pre-eminence in God's purposes, both in creation or redemption (*Acts* 3: 20, 21; *Col.* 1: 15–20).

4. The benefits of discipleship.

(a) First, a spiritual relationship to God through His Son Jesus Christ (*Mark* 3: 32–35) —eternal life is to know God the Father and Jesus Christ whom He sent (*John* 17: 3).

(b) Secondly, a personal attachment to Christ which shapes the whole of life (*Mark* 2: 18 ff; *John* 21: 19, 22)—we are one with Him in His death, resurrection and ascension (*Rom.* 6: 1–4; *Eph.* 2: 6, 7).

(c) Thirdly, a discovery of God's purpose for life (*Rom.* 12: 1, 2; *II Cor.* 5: 9, 15).

(d) Fourthly, a sharing of a wonderful fellowship (*Mark* 3: 13, 14; *Luke* 12: 32; *Acts* 1: 14; 2: 42; *I Pet.* 5: 9, 13).

(e) Fifthly, a learning of the way to joy—the Beatitudes, for example, emphasise that the disciple possesses the secret of true happiness or joy (*Matt.* 5: 3–10).

(f) Joy is the result of discovering the kingdom of heaven (*Matt.* 13: 44).

(g) The disciple's joy is not in what he has achieved himself, but in what God has done for him through His Son (*Luke* 10: 20).

(h) Our Lord Jesus desires that His own joy should be in His disciples, and that their joy should be full (*John* 15: 11; 17: 13).

(i) Sixthly, a freedom from the besetting worries of human existence: as we seek first God's kingdom and His righteousness, food, clothing, housing and all we need besides will be given us in addition, without our needing to be anxious about them (*Matt.* 6: 33–34).

(j) Seventhly, a joyful anticipation of heaven (*John* 14: 1 ff; 17: 24), and the recompense the Lord Jesus will give His faithful disciples (*Matt.* 16: 27).

(k) As our Lord Jesus was not of this world, so too disciples are no longer of this world; as He was exalted because of His faithful obedience, so His faithful disciples shall be exalted (*II Tim.* 2: 12)—none can measure the joy of the disciples' spiritual inheritance (*I Pet.* 1: 4; cf. *Ps.* 16: 11).

43. OBEDIENCE

Question: What does the Bible teach concerning obedience?

Answer: Obedience is doing everything God commands, of which our Lord Jesus Christ is the perfect example. The Christian life begins with obedience and continues by means of it. It is the proof both of new birth and discipleship, and it constitutes the secret of the happiness the Christian enjoys, no matter how costly that obedience may be.

1. The Bible defines obedience.

(a) Obedience is doing everything God commands (*Ex.* 19: 5; *Deut.* 5: 10; *Josh.* 22: 2; *Jer.* 7: 23).

(b) The Scriptures, God's Word, are to be the rule of our whole life (*II Tim.* 3: 16, 17).

(c) Obedience is our practical response to the Word of God (*Matt.* 13: 23; *Gal.* 5: 7; *Jas.* 1: 22–25).

(d) Christian obedience is our coming to Christ, hearing His words, and putting them into practice (*Luke* 6: 47; *John* 8: 51).

(e) Obedience is closely associated with a sensitive conscience, which is constantly educated and informed by the Holy Spirit by means of the Scriptures, and is consistently obeyed (*Acts* 23: 1; 24: 16; *II Cor.* 1: 12; *II Tim.* 1: 3).

(f) Obedience is synonymous with walking with God (*Gen.* 6: 9) and loving God (*I John* 5: 2).

2. Our Lord Jesus Christ is the perfect example of obedience.

(a) Obedience was the foremost characteristic of His earthly life (*Heb.* 10: 7).

(b) He obeyed the Father's commands and remained in His love (*John* 15: 10).

(c) His perfect obedience in accepting even death (*Phil.* 2: 8) made possible our acceptance with God and our fellowship with Him as we believe in Him as the Son of God and Saviour (*Rom.* 5: 15–19).

(d) His obedience to the Father should be the pattern of ours (*John* 15: 10).

3. Obedience has an important place both in the beginnings of the Christian life and in its continuance.

(a) Under the New Covenant obedience is God's gift to enable His people to enjoy His favour, rather than a necessary condition to be achieved before His favour may be enjoyed (*Jer.* 31: 33; 32: 40).

(b) The Christian life begins with obedience (*John* 6: 29; *Acts* 26: 19; *I Pet.* 1: 22), having as its first object the form of teaching presented in the gospel (*Rom.* 6: 17), summarised in the words, "Repent and believe the gospel" (*Mark* 1: 15; *Acts* 2: 38).

(c) Discipleship begins with an act of obedience (*Matt.* 9: 9; *Mark* 2: 14).

(d) We are chosen, redeemed and sanctified with our obedience to Jesus Christ in view (*I Pet.* 1: 2).

(e) It is as a result of our new relationship to God by new birth that we are called upon to obey Him (*I Pet.* 1: 14).

(f) Obedience is God's work in us, as a consequence of the new birth, for God works in us to will and to act according to His good purpose (*Phil.* 2: 13, 14).

4. The priority of obedience.

(a) Obedience has from the beginning of creation been an indispensable obligation, since God has every right to command His creatures, and has made known His requirements (*Gen.* 2: 15–17).

(b) The results of Adam's failure to obey indicate its priority: by his failure to obey the whole of mankind was involved in guilt, condemnation and death (*Rom.* 5: 19; *I Cor.* 15: 22).

(c) The Old Covenant required obedience as a condition of God's favour (*Ex.* 19: 5; *I Kings* 3: 14; *II Kings* 21: 8; *Neh.* 1: 5).

(d) Obedience sums up our whole duty to God (*Deut.* 10: 12, 13; *Eccl.* 12: 13) and is commanded (*Deut.* 13: 4; *Ps.* 119: 4).

(e) Obedience is more important than isolated acts of service to God, religious observances and externals (*I Sam.* 15: 22; *I Cor.* 7: 19).

(f) Obedience is the mode of practice by which we please God (*I John* 3: 22).

(g) Where obedience to God clashes with obedience to man, God is to be obeyed rather than man (*Acts* 5: 29).

(h) Obedience is the condition of our dwelling in our Lord Jesus Christ's love (*John* 15: 10), and enjoying a personal relationship to Him (*Matt.* 12: 50).

(i) Obedience is a prerequisite of unbroken fellowship with the Father and the Son (*John* 14: 23–24; *I John* 1: 3, 7).

(j) Obedience is the means of our growing in holiness (*Luke* 1: 6).

(k) Obedience is the perfecting of our love for God (*I John* 2: 5).

5. Practical implications of obedience.

(a) Obedience involves devoting ourselves to the study and observance of God's Law (*Ezra* 7: 10).

(b) Obedience demands a change in the pattern of our life compared with what it was before our conversion (*I Pet.* 1: 14): obedience to God is opposite to the service of sin (*Rom.* 6: 17).

(c) Obedience includes loving God's children (*I John* 5: 2).

(d) Obedience requires holiness in all we do (*I Pet.* 1: 15, 16).

(e) Obedience results in practising the humility our Lord Jesus exemplified (*John* 13: 12–17; *Phil.* 2: 5–8).

(f) No matter how difficult or complicated a problem or a decision, the first course of action to be followed is that of obedience to God (*Phil.* 2: 12, 13).

(g) Obedience to God demands obedience within family relationships: subjection to one another out of reverence for Christ (*Eph.* 5: 21); the subjection of a wife to her husband (*Eph.* 5: 22); and the obedience of children to their parents (*Eph.* 6: 1–3).

(h) Obedience to God expresses itself in obedience within the fellowship of the local church, as we follow the direction of our spiritual teachers (*Phil.* 2: 12), and as we obey our spiritual leaders (*Heb.* 13: 17).

(i) Obedience to God includes rendering the obedience He commands to the governing authorities (*Matt.* 22: 21; *Rom.* 13: 1 f, 6, 7; *I Pet.* 3: 13, 14; *Tit.* 3: 1).

6. Characteristics of obedience.

(a) Obedience recognises God's supreme authority to command (*I Sam.* 3: 10; *Acts* 9: 6).

(b) Obedience springs from a delight in the law of the Lord and meditation on it (*Ps.* 1: 2; 119: 104, 105, 129).

(c) Obedience is diligent (*Heb.* 6: 11) and persevering (*Heb.* 10: 36).

(d) Obedience is rendered even when apprehension concerning the results of that obedience exist (*Acts* 9: 10–19).

(e) Obedience is precise and wholehearted (*Matt.* 6: 24; *John* 15: 14).

(f) Obedience, once practised, is taught and communicated to others (*Matt.* 5: 19).

7. The significance of obedience when found in the life of an individual.

(a) Obedience is the proof of discipleship (*John* 10: 27), and is never burdensome to the true believer (*I John* 5: 3).

(b) Obedience results from spiritual birth (*Eph.* 2: 10).

(c) Obedience proves the reality of our knowledge of God (*I John* 2: 3).

(d) Obedience demonstrates our love for God (*Dan.* 9: 4; *John* 14: 15, 23, 24; *II John* 6).

(e) Obedience indicates that we dwell in Christ and that He dwells in us (*I John* 2: 6; 3: 24).

(f) Obedience provides a measure of our fruitfulness as Christians (*Matt.* 13: 23;

Mark 4: 20; Luke 8: 15; John 15: 10, 14, 16).

(g) Obedience marks us out as faithful (Rev. 12: 17).

7. Obedience's incentives.

(a) Faith prompts and sustains obedience (Heb. 11: 8), with right views of Christ constituting our secret of faith (Heb. 12: 2).

(b) Meditation upon the value of our Lord's friendship encourages obedience (John 15: 14).

(c) The consideration of God's goodness stimulates obedience (I Sam. 12: 24; Ps. 26:3; Rom. 12: 1).

(d) The knowledge of the certain rewards of obedience serves to energize obedience: happiness (Luke 11: 28; Jas. 1: 25); joy (John 15: 1–11); God's blessing (Mal. 3: 10–12); confidence before God in prayer (I John 3: 21, 22); spiritual stability (Luke 6: 46–49); everlasting life (John 8: 51; Rev. 2: 10) and a graciously generous reward (Matt. 6: 24; John 12: 26).

44. CHRISTIAN WITNESS

Question: What is Christian witness?

Answer: Christian witness is the privilege and duty which arises from the experience of God's salvation in Jesus Christ. Commanded by God, and worldwide in its scope and intention, its purpose is to set forth God's saving acts in the death and resurrection of our Lord Jesus Christ, in accordance with the Scriptures, and in dependence upon the Holy Spirit.

1. Witness is both a privilege and a duty arising from the experience of God's salvation.

(a) Witness is the spontaneous and natural consequence of an experience of our Lord Jesus Christ's power (Mark 5: 20; Luke 8: 39; John 4: 29, 30).

(b) Those who love God's salvation delight to say "The Lord be exalted" (Ps. 40: 16).

(c) A sense of compulsion lies behind Christian witness —we cannot help speaking about what we believe and know about Jesus Christ (Acts 4: 20; II Cor. 4: 13).

(d) Christ's love compels us to witness (*II Cor.* 5: 14).

(e) Reconciled to God, through the atoning work of Christ, we find ourselves entrusted with the message of reconciliation (*II Cor.* 5: 18, 19).

(f) Christian witness finds its impetus in the personal experience of salvation (*Isa.* 12: 2–4; *II Tim.* 1: 11, 12).

2. Witness is expected, and commanded by God.

(a) All who know, believe and understand that the Lord is both God and Saviour are commissioned to be His witnesses (*Isa.* 43: 10, 11).

(b) Testimony to the Lord Jesus Christ is to be given without shame (*Luke* 12: 8, 9; *II Tim.* 1: 8).

(c) The Word of life is to be held out by all Christians (*Phil.* 2: 16).

(d) Witness is to be given courageously and fearlessly (*Phil.* 1: 14).

(e) This witness, however, is to be given with gentleness and with respect for the individuals to whom it is addressed (*I Pet.* 3: 15).

(f) At any time, as opportunity provides, we are to be ready to witness (*I Pet.* 3: 15); if we do not aim at witnessing at every proper opportunity, as commanded (*Col.* 4: 5), we shall probably not witness at all (*Eccl.* 11: 3, 4).

(g) Our witness should be consistent and continuous, for the success which may attend it can never be predicted (*Eccl.* 11: 6; *Heb.* 10: 23).

(h) Our witness should be clear—like a city on a hill (*Matt.* 5: 14)—and effective— like salt (*Matt.* 5: 13).

(i) Restraint should be removed from our lips when there is opportunity for witness (*Ps.* 40: 9).

(j) To conceal our testimony to God's faithfulness and salvation is sinful (*Ps.* 40: 10).

3. Witness is to be world-wide in its scope and concern.

(a) Witness should begin with our family and our immediate acquaintances (*Mark* 5: 19; *Acts* 16: 31).

(b) Ideally, corporate Christian witness should have a repercussive and spreading effect throughout a whole neighbourhood and area (*I Thess.* 1: 8).

(c) In fact, the scope of Christian witness is to be the world (*Isa.* 12: 2–4; *Acts* 1: 8), and it is God's ordained means of spreading the gospel to all creation (*Matt.* 28: 19, 20).

4. Witness cannot be separated from the life and conduct of the individual Christian and the local church.

(a) Witness of life and speech go together but there is a sense in which the witness of life must come first (*Phil.* 2: 15, 16; *I Pet.* 3: 1, 2).

(b) Witness must be confirmed by the evidence of a cleansed life (*Ps.* 26: 6, 7; 51: 1–19).

(c) The truth of Christian witness is substantiated by the good effects it has upon men's lives (*I Cor.* 1: 6) in distinctive Christian character and conduct (*Matt.* 5: 13).

(d) Good conduct, in spite of provocation and opposition, constitutes essential Christian witness (*I Pet.* 2: 12).

(e) The witness of the life must support the witness of the lips (*I Thess.* 1: 7, 8; *I Pet.* 3: 1).

(f) The corporate life of God's people—especially in their display of Christian love—is fundamental to their witness (*Phil.* 2: 14–16; *I Pet.* 1: 22; 2: 9).

5. Witness is, nevertheless, primarily that of word or speech.

(a) Christian witness requires the witness of words (*I Pet.* 3: 15).

(b) With the great end of redemption as the confession "Jesus Christ is Lord", it is clearly our duty to bear testimony to this truth now (*Phil.* 2: 11).

(c) Witness involves this confession of the mouth that "Jesus is Lord" (*Rom.* 10: 9), a confession we are to make before the world (*Matt.* 10: 32; *Luke* 12: 8).

(d) In giving witness we speak of the glory of God's kingdom and we tell of His might (*Ps.* 145: 11), and how both are made known to us so wonderfully in Jesus Christ (*Acts* 8: 12).

(e) The witness of words cannot help but often find expression in song (*I Chron.* 16: 8, 9; *Ps.* 9: 11; 18: 49; 40: 3; *Isa.* 12: 4, 5; *Eph.* 5: 19).

6. Witness requires the power of the Holy Spirit to be effective.

(a) Power for witness is given by God (*Acts* 1:8; *Rev.* 4:8, 31).

(b) Witness needs not only words, but the power of the Holy Spirit to give those words strong conviction (*I Thess.* 1: 5).

(c) Effective witness depends completely on the enduement and power of the Holy Spirit (*Luke* 24: 48, 49; *I Cor.* 12: 3).

7. The central subject of witness is what God has achieved through the work of His Son, the Lord Jesus Christ.

(a) Witness is the making known of God's deeds among the people (*I Chron.* 16: 8; *Ps.* 9: 11; *Isa.* 12: 4; *Jer.* 51: 10; *Mark* 5: 19; *I Pet.* 2: 9–10).

(b) At its simplest, witness is proclaiming how much Jesus has done for sinners (*Mark* 5: 19, 20; *Luke* 8: 39).

(c) It is the proclaiming of the good news of Jesus Christ (*I Cor.* 1: 6; 15: 15; *I John* 1: 1–4).

(d) It centres around the death of Christ, His resurrection from the dead, and the mess-age of light and life which springs from these saving events (*Acts* 26: 23; *I Cor.* 15: 1–4).

(e) Central to all that is stated is the message of Jesus Christ and Him crucified (*I Cor.* 2: 2; *Gal.* 6: 14).

8. What God has achieved through the work of His Son, Jesus Christ, is described in the Bible as "the Word of God".

(a) The good news of Christ is identical with the Word of the Lord which abides for ever (*I Pet.* 1: 25); the gospel of salvation through Christ is the Word of truth (*Eph.* 1: 13).

(b) All Scripture is inspired by God and is able to make men wise for salvation through faith in Jesus Christ (*II Tim.* 3: 15, 16).

(c) The principal theme of the whole of the Word of God is that Christ, the Messiah, had to suffer and then to rise again on the third day, and that through what He accomplished repentance and forgiveness may be preached to men (*Luke* 24: 45–47).

(d) This fact explains the early Church's concern to preach

the Word of God with boldness (*Acts* 4: 4, 29, 31).

(e) Preaching the Word was the priority of the early Church (*Acts* 6: 2, 4), in that the whole evangelistic programme of the early Church is summed up in expressions relating to the preaching of the Word of God (*Acts* 13: 5, 7, 44, 46, 48, 49; 14: 25; 15: 7; 15: 35, 36; 16: 6, 32; 17: 11, 13; 18: 11; 19: 10).

(f) The progress of the early Church in witness is described in terms of the spread of the Word of God (*Acts* 6: 7; 12: 24; 19: 20).

(g) Witness and evangelism go forward as the Word of the Lord spreads on and is honoured (*II Thess.* 3: 1).

(h) To preach the Word of God is to preach Christ, for He is the Incarnate Word of God (*John* 1: 1; *Rev.* 19: 13)— by Him God has spoken to men (*Heb.* 1: 2), and all the Scriptures speak of Him (*Luke* 24: 27).

(i) It was for the Word of God and the testimony they maintained that the martyrs were slain (*Rev.* 6: 9).

9. Christian witness, therefore, is according to the Word of God and from the Word of God.

(a) Christian witness is the declaration of God's attested truth (*Luke* 24: 44–45; *I Cor.* 2: 1).

(b) It begins with the great proclamation that God has spoken (*Heb.* 1: 1), first, in the Old Testament (*Heb.* 1: 1), and secondly, in a unique and final manner by His Son Jesus Christ (*Heb.* 1: 2).

(c) Christian witness to the Lord Jesus Christ is according to the pattern of sound teaching given us in God's Word (*II Tim.* 1: 8, 13).

(d) Christian witness emphasises that everything that happened in the life of the Lord Jesus Christ was in accord with the Old Testament Scriptures (*Acts* 26: 22, 23; *I Cor.* 15: 3, 4; *Heb.* 1: 1–4, 5–13).

(e) Christian witness bears testimony to what the Scriptures declare concerning the death and resurrection of Jesus, and the repentance and forgiveness to be preached in consequence (*Luke* 24: 46, 47).

(f) Christian witness consists of teaching and preaching (*Acts* 5: 42; 15: 35) so that the Word of God is presented in its fullness (*Col.* 1: 25). The facts having been taught (*II Cor.* 5: 17, 18, 19), the appeal by preaching can be made to men's will, "Be reconciled to God" (*II Cor.* 5: 20).

(g) Christian witness, therefore, is not a matter of fine words or human cleverness, but rather the simple declaration of God's Word (*I Cor.* 2: 1), so that the hearers may confirm the truth of what has been said by their private examination of the Scriptures (*Acts* 17: 11).

(h) Christian witness may be summed up as bearing witness to the Word of God and the testimony of Jesus Christ (*Rev.* 1: 2).

10. Christian witness requires a recognition of the carefulness with which the Word of God should be handled and used.

(a) We must handle the Word of God honestly, always refusing to use deception, or to distort it (*II Cor.* 4: 2).

(b) As we witness by setting forth the truth plainly, we commend ourselves to every man's conscience in the sight of God (*II Cor.* 4: 2).

(c) The Word of God is the Spirit's sword (*Eph.* 6: 17).

(d) It is the instrument God uses to bring spiritual life to men and women (*Jas.* 1: 18; *I Pet.* 1: 23).

11. Our witness is inevitably and vitally linked with our knowledge of, and obedience to, God's Word.

(a) We are to be instructed in the Word (*Acts* 2: 42; *Gal.* 6: 6).

(b) By constant use of the Scriptures, we should be skilful in our use of them (*Eph.* 6: 17; *Heb.* 5: 13, 14).

(c) We should do our best to present ourselves to God as those who are approved, workmen who do not need to be ashamed, and who correctly handle the Word of truth (*II Tim.* 2: 15).

(d) We are to let the Word of God dwell in us richly (*Col.* 3: 16).

(e) When the Word of God is at work in our lives we impart it to others (*I Thess.* 2: 13; cf. 1: 7, 8).

12. The Holy Spirit adds His power to the Word of God when it is proclaimed faithfully.

(a) The secret of witnessing to the Word of God with boldness and effectiveness lies in being filled with the Spirit (*Acts* 4: 31).

(b) Desiring above everything else to witness to our Lord Jesus Christ, the Holy Spirit delights to bear witness to the Word of God's grace in Christ when it is faithfully declared (*John* 15: 26; *Acts* 14: 3).

(c) As genuine witness to Christ is given, according to the Word of God, the Holy Spirit adds His own spiritual power to it (*I Cor.* 2: 4).

(d) When the Holy Spirit does this, faith is awakened by the message which comes through the Word of God (*Rom.* 10: 17), and as the Word of God is received, those who receive it are brought to living faith in Christ and membership of His Church (*Acts* 2: 41; cf. 2: 22–36).

(e) The confidence of Christian witness, therefore, is not in plausible words or subtle argument but in the power of the Word of God and the Holy Spirit (*I Cor.* 2: 1–5).

45. PERSONAL EVANGELISM

Question: How are we to fulfil our responsibilities in personal evangelism?

Answer: We are to see ourselves as workers together with God, understanding what is His work in bringing a person to saving faith in Jesus Christ, and what is our part. As we present the gospel to all to whom God gives us the opportunity, we are to look expectantly for such evidence of the Holy Spirit's activity in their lives as the Bible leads us to expect.

1. Essential truths should influence all our thinking and acting when endeavouring to lead others to faith in our Lord Jesus Christ.

(a) Such activity is pleasing to God: there is more joy in heaven over one sinner that repents than over ninety-nine who need no repentance (*Luke* 15: 7).

(b) It is by means of this activity that the Christian Church grows and multiplies (*Acts* 2: 47; 6: 7; 9: 31; 12: 24).

(c) The New Testament assumes that all Christians will be ready to engage in making the gospel known to others (*Matt.* 28: 19; *Phil.* 2: 15, 16; *Col.* 4: 5; *I Pet.* 3: 15).

(d) To endeavour to lead others to Christ is part of loving our neighbour as ourself (*Luke* 10: 27; *II Cor.* 5: 14; *John* 1: 40 ff).

(e) We know that it is not God's will for any to perish but for all to come to repentance (*II Pet.* 3: 9).

(f) We are in conflict all the time with the devil while we endeavour to do this task (*Eph.* 6: 12): he has blinded the minds of unbelievers, to keep them from seeing the light of the gospel of the glory of Christ (*II Cor.* 4: 4). We do not despair, however, for we know that the work is God's (*I Pet.* 1: 2; *Acts* 16: 14; *Gal.* 1: 15, 16).

(g) We are workers together with God in this task (*II Cor.* 6: 1; *I Cor.* 3: 5–9).

(h) We work not for time but for eternity (*Dan.* 12: 3).

(i) Our supreme motive is the glory of God (*I Cor.* 1: 30, 31).

2. **We must be clear as to what God alone can do, and what we, therefore, cannot do.**

(a) Conviction of sin is the work of God the Holy Spirit (*John* 16: 8).

(b) God alone can give repentance to men (*Acts* 5: 31; 11: 18)—it is His gift.

(c) Only God can draw men and women to Christ (*John* 6: 44).

(d) God alone can reveal Jesus (*Acts* 9: 3, 4; *II Cor.* 4: 6).

(e) It is God's unique prerogative to bring about new birth (*John* 1: 13; 3: 3, 5).

3. **We must be clear as to what God requires of us by way of preparation for this work.**

(a) We need an awareness of our own dependence upon the Lord Jesus for salvation (*Gal.* 2: 20b; *I Tim.* 1: 15).

(b) We must know the Scriptures.

(i) They alone equip us effectively (*II Tim.* 3: 17).

(ii) Only the Scriptures contain the truth men need in order to be saved (*II Tim.* 3: 15).

(iii) The Scriptures bring about conviction of sin (*Acts* 2: 37).

(iv) By the Spirit's power, the Scriptures bring regeneration (*I Pet.* 1: 23).

(v) The Scriptures are the means the Spirit uses to give saving faith (*Rom.* 10: 17).

(vi) To help people by means of the Scriptures requires diligent study and growth in understanding on our part (*II Tim.* 2: 15).

(c) We need an understanding of the desperately urgent plight of men without Christ (*Matt.* 9: 36).

(i) They are lost (*Luke* 19: 10).

(ii) Their need should touch our emotions (*Acts* 20: 31).

(d) We must be in earnest when we engage in this work.

(i) We should know great sorrow and unceasing anguish in our hearts for men without Christ (*Rom.* 9: 1, 2).

(ii) We should long in our hearts for the salvation of others (*Rom.* 10: 1).

(e) The whole of our life needs to be open before God, and cleansing should be sought for all known sin (*II Tim.* 2: 20, 21; *Ps.* 51: 10, 12, 13).

(f) We must be filled with the Holy Spirit (*Eph.* 5: 18; *Acts* 6: 5; cf. 8: 12, 29, 39, 40; *I Cor.* 2: 4).

4. **We must be clear as to what God requires of us by way of co-operation in this work.**

(a) Although the work of conversion is essentially God the Holy Spirit's work, He calls us to work with Him in achieving it (*Acts* 26: 18).

(b) God has given us all that is necessary for performing the task: the authority of Jesus, His commission to preach, the message of salvation (symbolised in baptism), the commandments of Jesus; and His presence by the Spirit (*Matt.* 28: 18–20).

(c) Our responsibility is to make known the Word of God (*Acts* 16: 14; *Rom.* 10: 14–17).

(d) We should endeavour to make it known to all men without being influenced by any kind of prejudice (*Gal.* 6: 10; cf. *Luke* 14: 21–23; *I Cor.* 1: 26–29).

(e) We should urge men to seek God (*Luke* 13: 24, 25; *Isa.* 55: 6, 7), to repent (*Matt.* 4: 17; *Acts* 17: 30), to be converted (*Matt.* 18: 3), and to believe on the Lord Jesus Christ (*Acts* 16: 31).

(f) In doing these things we must be willing to show them real and genuine friendship, which will often be costly in time, energy and many other things (*Luke* 10: 29, 33–35; *II Tim.* 2: 10).

(g) We are to be ready to do this work at any time and anywhere.

(i) This work begins where we are and extends to wherever God may call us (*Acts* 1: 8).

(ii) Whether in our homes (*Acts* 18: 26) or in public places (*John* 4: 7–26; *Acts* 17: 17), on board ship (*Acts* 27: 24, 25) or in prison (*Acts* 16: 30, 31; *Phil.* 1: 12, 13; 4: 22), in the open air (*Acts* 16: 13, 14) or from house to house (*Acts* 20: 20), we are to be ready to make Christ known.

(h) We co-operate with God by means of prayer.

(i) James tells us that we have not because we ask not (*Jas.* 4: 2).

(ii) The reality of our concern will be seen in our prayers for the salvation of others (*Rom.* 10: 1).

(iii) We may ask God to do the things which He alone can do (*Acts* 4: 29, 30).

5. We need to be clear as to the essential facts of the gospel which must be made known before any response should be anticipated.

(1) The gospel which has to be understood.

(a) The appointed time, concerning which the prophets in the Old Testament had spoken and to which the people of God had looked forward, has come. Through Christ God has visited and redeemed His people (*Acts* 2: 16–21).

(b) This act of God, intervening in human history, is to be seen in the life of Jesus Christ, the Messiah, sent by God, rejected, put to death by men, and raised up by God on the third day (*Acts* 2: 32, 36).

(c) By His death and resurrection Jesus Christ has conquered sin and death and opened the kingdom of heaven to all believers. In no one else is salvation to be found (*Acts* 4: 12).

(d) The proofs of God's present power in the world are to be found in the fact of the resurrection and the evidences of the Holy Spirit's working in the Church (*Rom.* 1: 4; *Eph.* 1: 19, 20; *Acts* 4: 33).

(e) This is but the beginning of God's kingdom. Christ will come again as Judge, and God's kingdom will be finally established (*Acts* 3: 20, 21; 17: 30, 31; *II Thess.* 1: 7–10).

(f) Therefore all men everywhere should repent and be baptised in the name of Jesus the Messiah for the forgiveness of their sins, and thus receive the gift of the Holy Spirit (*Acts* 2: 38).

(2) **Fundamental to a person's understanding of the gospel is appreciation, therefore, of at least the following truths:**

(a) Christ's coming and death were part of God's eternal plan and were no accident (*Acts* 2: 23; *I Pet.* 1: 20).

(b) Jesus is the Christ, the Son of God (*John* 20: 31; *Acts* 8: 37).

(c) Christ's purpose in coming into the world and in dying upon the cross was to save sinners (*Gal.* 2: 20; *I Tim.* 1: 15).

(d) Christ's resurrection was God the Father's declaration of Christ as His Son and evidence of His satisfaction with His work (*Rom.* 1: 4).

(e) To enter into the benefits of Christ's work—to know forgiveness, the gift of God's Spirit and a place in His kingdom—repentance and open confession of Christ are required (*Acts* 2: 38).

(f) A Christian recognises his personal sinfulness (*Rom.* 7: 24; *I Tim.* 1: 15).

(g) A Christian knows his personal indebtedness to Christ in that He gave His life a ransom for him (*Mark* 10: 45; *Gal.* 2: 20; *I Pet.* 2: 24).

(3) **The benefits promised by the gospel.**

(a) Reconciliation with God (*II Cor.* 5: 18–21).

(b) Justification (*I Cor.* 1: 30; 6: 11).

(c) Deliverance from condemnation (*John* 3: 18; *Rom.* 8: 1; *I Cor.* 11: 32).

(d) Belonging to the people of God (*Acts* 2: 41, 47; *I Cor.*

1: 2; 6: 1, 2; 16: 1, 15; *I Pet.* 2: 4–10).

(e) Membership of the kingdom of God (*I Cor.* 6: 10; *Col.* 1: 13).

(f) The gift of the Holy Spirit (*Acts* 2: 38; *I Cor.* 2: 12; 6: 19).

(g) Eternal life (*John* 3: 16; 11: 25, 26).

(h) The resurrection of the body (*I Cor.* 6: 14; 15: 53, 57).

6. We need to adhere to the principles which are always to govern our presentation of the gospel.

(a) We act towards people in the light of what the Bible says about the unconverted and unregenerate.

(i) They are dead in trespasses and sins (*Eph.* 2: 1).

(ii) Their unbelieving minds are blinded by Satan (*II Cor.* 4: 4).

(iii) They are lost (*Luke* 19: 10).

(iv) They are slaves of sin (*John* 8: 34).

(b) We are always to think of the other person's good rather than of our own (*I Cor.* 10: 33).

(c) We are to be direct and straightforward in our presentation of the gospel and its demands, never allowing our presentation of the truth to be influenced by people's reactions (*II Cor.* 4: 2).

(d) We are to be direct and forthright in speaking of sin (*Acts* 24: 25; *Mark* 7: 20–23).

(e) We are to aim at speaking clearly to people, i.e. in terms which they can understand (*Col.* 4: 4).

(f) Gentleness and respect are to characterise our words (*I Pet.* 3: 15; *Col.* 4: 6).

(g) Love, in all its aspects, is to be dominant in our approach (*I Cor.* 13).

(h) We are to deal with people from the Scriptures (*II Tim.* 3: 15; *Acts* 8: 30–35), our confidence being not in our skill of presentation but in the power of God's truth (*I Cor.* 2: 1, 2, 4), knowing that the word of the Cross will be the power of God to those who are to be saved (*I Cor.* 1: 18).

(i) We are to act in the assurance that if a person really seeks God, he will find Him (*Matt.* 7: 7, 8; *Acts* 10: 1–8, 30–33, 44–48).

(j) We are not to hesitate to give our personal testimony

(*I Pet.* 3: 15; *Acts* 22: 6–11; 26: 12–18; *I Tim.* 1: 15).

(k) We are to depend all the time upon God the Holy Spirit.

(i) We need to be sensitive to His promptings (*Acts* 16: 6, 7), and there may be occasions when He urges us to be very direct in our approach (*Acts* 8: 30).

(ii) The work we do is valuable only as it is done in the demonstration and power of the Holy Spirit (*I Cor.* 2: 4).

(iii) If the Holy Spirit is at work, we know that He will complete His work (*Phil.* 1: 6).

7. There are certain things we are to look for in dealing with people whom we would lead to Christ.

(a) Conviction of sin (*Acts* 2: 37).

(b) An awareness of God's holiness (*Isa.* 6: 5; *Luke* 5: 8).

(c) The deflation of pride (*Jas.* 4: 6).

(d) A submission to what God says (*Jas.* 4: 7).

(e) A resistance to those considerations which would turn aside a person from having dealings with God (*Jas.* 4: 7).

(f) Readiness to use the means God has given us of drawing close to Him (*Jas.* 4: 8).

(g) Eagerness to hear the Word of God (*Acts* 16: 14).

(h) Prayer (*Acts* 9: 11; 10: 2; *Jas.* 4: 8).

(i) Changing attitudes, habits and actions (*Jas.* 4: 8).

(j) Sorrow for sin (*Jas.* 4: 9).

(k) A humility before God (*Jas.* 4: 10).

(l) When these things are present we may be sure that God is at work in people's lives and we may encourage them to call upon the name of the Lord Jesus for salvation (*Rom.* 10: 13), knowing that He will lift them up (*Jas.* 4: 10).

46. THE MISSIONARY TASK AND MISSIONARY MOTIVES

Question: What is the missionary task, and what are the considerations and motives which demand our involvement in missionary enterprise?

Answer: The missionary task is to make disciples of all nations.

The Bible presents many motives for supporting and engaging in missionary work, prominent among which are concern for God's glory, obedience to our Lord's commission, the desperate need of men without Christ, the adequacy and purpose of the atonement, and the coming again of our Lord Jesus Christ.

The Missionary Task

1. **Our Saviour's commission to us is to make disciples of all nations (Matt. 28: 19, 20).**

(a) As the ministry of reconciliation is exercised (*II Cor.* 5: 18–20), and the fragrance of the knowledge of Christ is spread everywhere (*II Cor.* 2: 14), men and women will receive the gospel, take their stand upon it, hold it fast, and be saved by it (*I Cor.* 15: 1–11); they are then to be made into true disciples (*Matt.* 28: 19).

(b) The most common description of Christians in the Acts of the Apostles is "disciples" (*Acts* 6: 2, 7).

(c) The task of missions is to make disciples (*Acts* 14: 21), that is to say, to secure the obedience of men and women in word and deed to Christ (*Acts* 6: 7; *Rom.* 15: 18; cf. (*Acts* 8: 36–39; 9: 18).

2. **The whole world, therefore, is our concern.**

(a) Starting from home to the ends of the earth is our sphere of operation (*Acts* 1: 8).

(b) The scope of our endeavours is to take in "all who are far off" (*Acts* 2: 39).

(c) The world is to be thought of as a plentiful harvest field (*Luke* 10: 2).

(d) Pentecost was an illustration of the scope of missions: everyone—no matter what his nationality—heard the good news of Christ in his own tongue (*Acts* 2: 6–11).

(e) Our commission is to preach the gospel to every creature, no matter what human barriers and prejudices have to be overcome in the process (*Acts* 10: 1–48, and especially 10: 28, 34).

(f) The obligation that is upon us is to preach the gospel to all (*Rom.* 1: 14, 15; *Luke* 10: 5, 6).

3. **Priorities have to be determined and recognised in the**

furtherance of the missionary task.

(a) Our Lord's primary attention, for example, was directed towards the Jews (*Matt.* 10: 5, 6), although this in no way implied that the gospel was not to go to the Gentiles: it was merely a question of priorities in the early days.

(b) Those among the Jews who had not heard His message were a priority to our Lord (*Mark* 1: 37, 38; *Luke* 4: 42, 43).

(c) The aim of missions must always be to preach the gospel where the name of Christ is as yet unknown (*Rom.* 15: 20).

4. The conversion of whole families is to be a priority in missionary work.

(a) The household is to be the objective (*Luke* 10: 5): if we aim only at the children, we delay the founding of the church for a generation.

(b) The conversion of whole households is to be looked for and expected (*Acts* 10: 24, 33, 44; 16: 15, 31–34; 18: 8).

(c) The first church in a place may well be a house-church (*Acts* 16: 14, 15; *Philem.* 2).

Missionary Motives

5. The glory of God.

(a) Our desire is to be that God should be glorified in all things (*I Pet.* 4: 11).

(b) Our concern for God's glory should be a consuming passion (*John* 2: 17).

(c) Our chief purpose in life is to glorify God (*I Cor.* 10: 31).

(d) The great end of the plan of redemption is the glory of the Father (*Phil.* 2: 11; *Eph.* 1: 6, 14).

(e) God is glorified when men are caused to praise Him (*Ps.* 50: 23)—for no reason do men praise Him more than for His salvation (*Luke* 2: 10–14, 20).

(f) God is glorified when redeemed men and women bring glory to God for His mercy to them (*Rom.* 15: 8–12).

(g) Our Lord Jesus glorified the Father on earth, having accomplished the work which the Father gave Him to do (*John* 17: 4)—we should have the same objective.

6. The command of our Lord Jesus Christ.

(a) We are to go into all the world and preach the gospel

to every creature (*Mark* 16: 15).

(b) We are to go and make disciples of all nations (*Matt.* 28: 19).

(c) This was the final command of our Lord Jesus which He gave with impressive authority (*Matt.* 28: 18).

7. The trust which the gospel is in itself.

(a) The gospel is a trust (*I Thess.* 2: 4).

(b) Its value cannot be overestimated (*Gal.* 1: 8, 9).

(c) It is a ground of universal joy, and it demands to be proclaimed (*Luke* 2: 10, 11, 17).

(d) The message of God's love is so great (*John* 3: 16) that it must not be kept secret.

8. The experience we ourselves have of salvation.

(a) Knowing the joy of God's salvation, we feel compelled to teach transgressors God's ways, and to cause sinners to return to the Lord (*Ps.* 51: 12, 13).

(b) Our experience of God's salvation puts us under an obligation to declare it to others (*Rom.* 1: 14–16).

9. The constraint of Christ's love.

(a) Knowing Christ's love for us, we find ourselves motivated by His love for others to reach them with the gospel (*II Cor.* 5: 14).

10. The need of those who are without Christ.

(a) Men and women without Christ are without hope and without God in the world (*Eph.* 2: 12).

(b) They do not know God, and their lives are governed by their passions (*I Thess.* 4: 5).

(c) Their main concerns are what to eat, drink and wear, not knowing the love of a heavenly Father (*Matt.* 6: 32; *Luke* 12: 30).

(d) They are often led astray to dumb idols (*I Cor.* 12: 2).

(e) The sorrows of those without Christ are multiplied because of the false gods they follow (*Ps.* 16: 4).

(f) They are spiritually blind and imprisoned (*Isa.* 42: 7).

(g) Compassion for the harassed souls of men is a great missionary motive (*Matt.* 9: 36).

(h) It is part and parcel of loving our neighbour as ourself (*Luke* 10: 27).

11. The adequacy of the atonement.

(a) Christ is the propitiation for our sins, and not for ours only but also for the sins of the whole world (*I John* 2: 2).

(b) The death of Christ was not for the Jewish nation only, but to gather into one the children of God who are scattered abroad (*John* 11: 52).

(c) By His blood Christ ransomed men for God from every tribe and tongue and people and nation, and He has made them a kingdom and priests to God (*Rev.* 5: 9, 10).

12. The revealed and declared purposes of God concerning the Church.

(a) God's purpose from the beginning has been to bless all the nations of the earth through the obedience of Abraham (*Gen.* 22: 17, 18).

(b) His purpose is that all nations shall flow to Zion (*Isa.* 2: 2).

(c) Throughout the Scriptures God has given assurance of His purpose to call the heathen to faith in Himself (*Mal.* 1: 11).

(d) His purpose is to take out of all peoples a people for His name (*Amos* 9: 11, 12; *Jer.* 12: 15 f; *Isa.* 45: 22; *Acts* 15: 14–18).

(e) The Father has promised the nations as His Son's inheritance (*Ps.* 2: 8).

(f) The knowledge that God is going to call men and women to Himself is a powerful motive (*Acts* 2: 38, 39; 18: 9, 10).

13. The desire to please Christ, and to receive His commendation.

(a) It is right for us to want Christ to see of the travail of His soul and to be satisfied (*Isa.* 53: 11).

(b) In communicating the gospel our desire is to please God who tests our hearts (*I Thess.* 2: 4).

(c) The parables of the pounds and the talents encourage us to work for the commendation of our Master, in fulfilling the great task He has assigned to us (*Luke* 19: 11–

27; *Matt.* 25: 14–30; cf. *II Cor.* 10: 18).

(d) Knowing what it means to fear the Lord, and to want to please Him, we try to persuade men (*II Cor.* 5: 11).

14. **The judgment which is to come.**

(a) The fact that Christians must stand before the judgment seat of Christ too is not to promote fear but the desire to please Him now, so that they may be pleasing to Him then (*II Cor.* 5: 9, 10).

(b) The certainty of judgment is a great incentive to urgent preaching (*II Tim.* 4: 1, 2; *II Cor.* 5: 11).

(c) The judgment will be a time of misery for those who have rejected the Lord Jesus Christ (*Rev.* 1: 7; *II Thess.* 1: 8, 9).

(d) Those who have disobeyed the truth and obeyed wickedness will experience the wrath of God and eternal punishment (*Rom.* 2: 8; *Jude* 15; *Rev.* 20: 15).

15. **The return of the Lord Jesus Christ.**

(a) The coming of the Lord is a missionary motive because the gospel is to be preached to all nations and throughout the whole world as a testimony to all nations, before the end (*Mark* 13: 10; *Matt.* 24: 14).

47. MISSIONARY WORK

Question: What governing concept should we have of missionary work?

Answer: Missionary work is essentially God's work, by which our Lord Jesus Christ's ministry and work are continued, and in which He requires our active co-operation and hard work.

1. **Missionary work is the Lord's work.**

(a) God assigns the workers (*I Cor.* 3: 5).

(b) God gives the spiritual increase (*I Cor.* 3: 7).

(c) God makes the appeal through His ambassadors (*II Cor.* 5: 20).

(d) God shines into the hearts of men and women with the light of the gospel (*II Cor.* 4: 6, 7).

(e) God calls men and women to faith in His Son (*Acts* 2: 39).

(f) God opens the hearts of individuals so that they give heed to the message of the gospel (*Acts* 16: 14).

(g) God gives to men and women the gift of repentance unto life (*Acts* 11: 18).

(h) God opens the door of faith to individuals (*Acts* 14: 27; cf. 15: 4, 12).

(i) The Lord adds day by day those who are being saved (*Acts* 2: 47).

(j) The task of missions is to work together with God (*II Cor.* 6: 1).

2. Missionary work is the continuation of Christ's ministry and work.

(a) The Church is to continue what the Lord Jesus began to do and teach (*Acts* 1: 1–3; *Luke* 10: 16).

(b) While the whole emphasis is to be upon teaching and preaching, a concern for the whole man is to be shown by missions (*Luke* 10: 9).

(c) This fact implies that there is a place for the healing ministry in missions, but such a ministry must be clearly administered in the name of Jesus Christ (*Acts* 4: 9, 10).

3. The example and principles established by our Lord Jesus should be followed carefully.

(a) Certain fundamental principles were laid down in the sending out of the twelve (*Mark* 6: 8–13; *Matt.* 10: 1, 5–14; *Luke* 9: 1–6), as too in the sending out of the seventy (*Luke* 10: 1–12).

(b) There are occasions in the Acts of the Apostles where we can see Paul following the pattern set by our Lord (*Acts* 13: 51; 18: 6).

4. Missionaries are God-appointed.

(a) The Lord appoints His messengers (*Luke* 10: 1).

(b) The Lord assigns the tasks to which they are called (*I Cor.* 3: 5).

(c) The Lord chooses His particular instruments for His particular tasks (*Acts* 9: 15, 16).

(d) The Lord tells the churches the individuals to be set apart for the work to which He has called them (*Acts* 13: 2).

210

5. God gives specific commissions to individuals to fulfil.

(a) Peter was entrusted, for example, with the gospel to the circumcised, and Paul with the gospel to the Gentiles (*Gal.* 2: 7–9; *Acts* 22: 17–21).

(b) Some may be assigned to planting, others to watering; some to laying foundations, others to building upon foundations already laid (*I Cor.* 3: 5–10).

6. Missionary work is a matter of partnership.

(a) First, it is to be undertaken in partnership with God (*I Cor.* 3: 7, 9; *II Cor.* 6: 1).

(b) Secondly, it is to be undertaken in partnership with other missionaries, and other missions (*Gal.* 2: 9; *I Cor.* 3: 7–10; *Luke* 10: 1; *Acts* 20: 4; *Rom.* 16: 1–4).

(c) Thirdly, it is to be undertaken in partnership with the local church or churches (*Phil.* 1: 5).

(i) The church is to be regarded as the sending or directing agency under the guidance of the Holy Spirit (*Acts* 13: 2, 3);

(ii) Missionaries are to be commended to the grace of God by the church which confirms the missionaries' call (*Acts* 14: 26);

(iii) The whole church is to be concerned in the missionary enterprise of its members (*Acts* 15: 22, 25), with all its members involved and interested in all that God does with and through them (*Acts* 14: 27);

(iv) Missionaries are to work in close partnership with the church or churches which, under God, send them forth (*Acts* 14: 26);

(v) Missionaries have a responsibility to report to the churches what God has done with them and through them (*Acts* 15: 4, 12; cf. *Acts* 14: 27).

7. Different contributions are necessary in missionary endeavour.

(a) There are varieties of gifts, service and working, but it is the same God who inspires them all in every one (*I Cor.* 12: 4–6).

(b) Some missionary work is foundation laying, while other is building upon a foundation already laid (*I Cor.* 3: 10).

(c) Some missionary work is

planting, while other is watering that which another has planted (*I Cor.* 3: 8).

8. Missionary work requires hard work and often suffering.

(a) A harvest field requires labourers (*Luke* 10: 2).

(b) "Labour" is a term frequently used by Paul to describe missionary enterprise (*Phil.* 1: 22; *II Cor.* 11: 23; *Phil.* 2: 30; cf. *Acts* 15: 38).

(c) Missionary work involves identification and accommodation to other people and their ways (*Luke* 10: 8; *I Cor.* 9: 19–23).

(d) Missionary work means sacrifice, hardship and suffering (*II Cor.* 4: 7–18; 11: 23–29; 6: 3–10; cf. *Acts* 9:16).

(e) Missionary work often meets with great opposition, sometimes because it conflicts with vested interests: the gospel is to be proclaimed nevertheless (*Acts* 16: 19–24; *I Thess.* 2: 2).

(f) Opposition is to provide no hindrance to our fulfilment of the task (*Luke* 10: 3).

(g) We should be willing to endure anything for the sake of winning the elect (*II Tim.* 2: 10).

48. MISSIONARY STRATEGY

Question: What are the first principles of missionary strategy?

Answer: The first principles of missionary strategy are the divine wisdom in choosing the foolishness of preaching, and the priority, therefore, of the teaching and preaching of the Word of God for the birth and consolidation of witnessing churches.

1. The divine wisdom in choosing the foolishness of preaching.

(a) While to us who are being saved the cross is the power of God, to those who are perishing the preaching of the cross is utter foolishness (*I Cor.* 1: 18).

(b) It pleases God through the folly—in the world's eyes—of what is preached through the gospel, to save those who believe (*I Cor.* 1: 21).

(c) Human ways of thinking may be quite contrary to God's strategy (*I Cor.* 1: 26–31).

(d) We are reminded that missionary work is carried

on, not according to earthly, material considerations but according to eternal considerations (*II Cor*. 4: 16–18).

2. The concept of progress which should be uppermost is the growth and multiplication of the Word.

(a) The main task of missions is to proclaim the Word (*Acts* 17: 10–13), to deliver the essential truths (*I Cor*. 15: 3), so that hearing the preaching of Christ, men and women may come to faith (*Rom*. 10: 14–17).

(b) Missionary progress is to be thought of in terms of the growth and increase of the Word of God (*Acts* 6: 7; 12: 24; 19: 10, 20).

(c) In seeking prayer for himself and his fellow-missionaries, Paul significantly urged his friends, "Pray for us, that the Word of the Lord may speed on and triumph, as it did among you" (*II Thess*. 3: 1, R.S.V.).

3. Missionary endeavour must concentrate on teaching the Word.

(a) Our task is to teach disciples all that the Lord Jesus has commanded disciples to observe (*Matt*. 28: 19, 20).

(b) Fulfilling the task of teaching disciples all that the Lord Jesus Christ has commanded disciples to observe involves, of necessity, providing disciples with the Scriptures in their own tongue (*Matt*. 28: 19, 20).

(c) The emphasis of the apostles was clearly upon teaching:

(i) The Jewish authorities directed their opposition at the apostles' speaking and *teaching* in the name of Jesus (Acts 4: 18);

(ii) Miraculously released from prison, Peter and John were found in the temple again *teaching* the people (*Acts* 5: 25);

(iii) The apostles taught in Jesus' name so effectively that the opposing authorities said that they had filled Jerusalem with their *teaching* (*Acts* 5: 28);

(iv) Every day in the temple and at home the apostles did not cease *teaching* and preaching Jesus as Christ (*Acts* 5: 42);

(v) Following the Conference at Jerusalem, Paul and

Barnabas returned to Antioch and stayed there, "where they and many others *taught* and preached the word of the Lord" (*Acts* 15: 35);

(vi) Having received the assurance from the Lord that He was calling out many people, Paul continued in Corinth for eighteen months, "*teaching* them the Word of God" (*Acts* 18: 11);

(vii) At the end of the Acts of the Apostles we find Paul confined to his lodgings, but he "preached the kingdom of God and *taught* about the Lord Jesus Christ" (*Acts* 28: 31).

(d) A right balance is clearly necessary between teaching and preaching (*Acts* 8: 5, 25, 35, 40; 15: 35; 28: 31).

(e) The apostolic pattern was to deliberately entrust Christian teaching to faithful men who, in turn, would be able to teach others also (*II Tim.* 2: 2).

4. Witness should be established in key centres.

(a) In the Mediterranean, Paul operated from Antioch, the third city of the Roman empire (*Acts* 11: 25–30; 12: 25; 13: 1–3; 14: 24–28).

(b) Paul spent three years in Corinth, which was one of the largest commercial centres of the Roman Empire (*Acts* 18: 1–18).

(c) He had a long stay in Ephesus, the capital of the province of Asia and the centre of trade for Asia Minor (*Acts* 19: 1–41).

(d) Missionary work is clearly to take in the villages and the rural areas with the cities and towns (*Luke* 10: 1; *Mark* 1: 35–39; *Acts* 8: 5, 25, 40).

(e) Key cities and centres, however, are the obvious starting point in any new area: when, for example, the gospel came to Europe, the first preaching point was "Philippi, a Roman colony and the leading city of that district of Macedonia" (*Acts* 16: 12).

5. A simple course of strategy should be followed.

(a) Work should begin with those who are most disposed to listen, with the intention of working out into the community from such:

(i) Thus, in a Jewish situation, the apostles preached first of all in the temple (*Acts* 5: 20, 25), and Paul's first approach where there were any Jews in the community was to seek to preach the gospel in the synagogue (*Acts* 9: 20; 13: 5; 17: 1, 2, 10, 17; 18: 4, 5).

(ii) Where there was no synagogue, Paul's first approach was to seek to preach to any who sought to follow the Jewish religion, although perhaps not Jews, and any who were at all religious, and thus used to thinking of God and His claims (*Acts* 16: 13; 17: 22–34).

(b) A clear order of priorities so far as spheres of witness in a community were concerned seems to have been followed:

(i) First, religious meeting places were a prime approach, and these were Jewish synagogues in the early years of gospel preaching (*Acts* 18: 4, 5; 19: 8);

(ii) Secondly, meeting halls were used when religious meeting places were not available (*Acts* 19: 9);

(iii) Thirdly, public places, such as markets, where people congregate, were resorted to where the opportunity presented itself (*Acts* 17: 17);

(iv) At the same time, and sometimes as an only possible means, the homes of believers and interested unbelievers were used (*Acts* 5: 42; 18: 7; 20: 20).

6. **Missionary work couples church-planting with disciple-making.**

(a) As men and women are brought to faith and discipleship, they are to be gathered together regularly for instruction in the Word, fellowship and the breaking of bread (*Acts* 2: 42), and also for common action, where necessary (*Acts* 6: 2).

(b) Believers are to be taught to gather together on the Lord's day for the breaking of bread, and the ministry of the Word (*Acts* 20: 7–12).

(c) Believers are so to be gathered and integrated together that they know themselves to belong together (*Acts* 9: 2, 19, 26); they are to be instructed in brotherhood (*Acts* 9: 17; *I John* 3: 17, 18).

(d) Believers are to be taught the priority of prayer and the

215

ministry of the Word (*Acts* 6: 4).

(e) Believers are to be taught concerning the type of men they are to call to serve as elders and deacons (*Acts* 6: 1–6; *I Tim.* 3: 1–13; *Tit.* 1: 5–9).

7. The key to world-evangelisation is witnessing churches.

(a) Believers are to be taught that whatever circumstances effect their lives, and wherever they may have to go, they are to preach the Word (*Acts* 8: 4).

(b) Once established, a church is to become a sending-church: for example, the church at Antioch (*Acts* 11: 20–30; 13: 1–3; 14: 26–28).

(c) The testimony of lip and the transformation of life of those who have newly experienced God's delivering power are two of the most powerful means of drawing attention to the gospel and of bringing people to faith (*Acts* 3: 9–16; 4: 4, 14; 9: 20, 21).

(d) Young churches are to be taught to shine in their communities, by the quality of their corporate life, like stars lighting up the sky, thus enabling them to offer effectively the message of life (*Phil.* 2: 15, 16).

(e) The transformation of lives through the gospel is a most powerful means of spreading the message of the gospel through the whole of an area, and beyond (*I Thess.* 1: 7–10).

8. Spiritual leaders are to be looked for and encouraged within the newly-emerging churches.

(a) It is to be expected that the Spirit will give gifts to a young church as to a more established church (*Acts* 13: 1–4).

(b) The lack of education men may have and their very ordinariness must not influence our assessment of what the Spirit can do through them—for example, Peter and John (*Acts* 4: 13).

(c) It is to be expected that the Holy Spirit will raise up in the young churches men and women of equal spiritual gifts to those who have brought the gospel to them (*Acts* 13: 1–4; 15: 35).

(d) The appointing authority of spiritual leaders—or better, the recognising body, for the Holy Spirit raises up spiritual leaders—is the church, not the missionaries (*II Cor.* 8: 19, 23).

9. Missionary advance must go hand in hand with church-consolidation.

(a) Sustained periods of teaching and preaching are to be the pattern of missionary work (*Acts* 18: 11; 19: 8–10).

(b) The aim of missions is to fully preach the gospel (*Rom.* 15: 19), to declare to new converts all that is profitable (*Acts* 20: 20), and to deliver to them the whole counsel of God (*Acts* 20: 27); this means their being instructed in the moral demands of the gospel (*I Thess.* 4: 1–8), and appreciating the tribulations which may well be before them as a consequence of faith in Christ and obedience to Him (*Acts* 14: 22).

(c) The work of missions is to build up babes in Christ to make them spiritual men (*I Cor.* 3: 1–3).

(d) The strengthening of young churches, therefore, is as necessary as starting work in new areas, and it may have a greater priority at times (*Acts* 18: 18–23; 14: 21–23).

(e) Believers are to be firmly established, and they are not to be left in an untaught state (*Acts* 8: 14–17); no effort is to be spared to this end (*I Thess.* 3: 1–3, 10).

(f) The task of missions is to see newly-founded churches governed by elders from among their own number (*Acts* 14: 23), and such spiritual leaders obviously profit from being called together and exhorted concerning their duties and warned of the dangers to which they may be prone (*Acts* 20: 17–35).

(g) Young churches need to be encouraged by visits for the purpose of edification (*Acts* 15: 36; 20: 2): they need to be stirred up by way of remembrance concerning truths they already know (*Rom.* 15: 15), and guided on important issues where more experienced Christians and churches have discovered the will of God (*Acts* 16: 4, 5).

10. The proper relationship of missionary to local converts must be appreciated.

(a) The relationship of missionaries to converts must be that of brethren (*Acts* 15: 36).

217

(b) Missionaries are to be in partnership with the Christians they see established as a fruit of their labours (*Acts* 13: 1–3; cf. 11: 25).

(c) Missionaries are directed by the Spirit through the united conviction of the church—whether the sending church or the receiving church (*Acts* 13: 1–4).

(d) Missionaries should be subject to the teaching, ministry and discipline of the local church, even if it is a newly-established church (*Acts* 13: 1–4).

(e) Missionaries should teach converts, by example, to live according to the Scriptures (*I Cor.* 4: 6).

(f) Missionaries should reproduce themselves in the people among whom they serve so that they themselves can move on, knowing that the church will continue with a spiritual ministry (*Acts* 13: 1–4).

(g) The work of missions is not to make converts or churches dependent upon missionaries (*I Cor.* 3: 4, 5).

(h) Converts and churches should be taught to appreciate that the missionary's objective is not to bind them in allegiance to him but to Christ (*II Cor.* 11: 2).

11. Literature has an important place in church consolidation.

(a) Paul's letters in the New Testament bear witness to the place and importance of literature dealing with doctrine and conduct.

(b) Young Christians, particularly from heathen backgrounds, need literature to guide them (*Acts* 15: 20, 23–29).

49. HIDDEN FACTORS IN MISSIONARY ENTERPRISE

Question: What are the hidden factors we must take account of in missionary enterprise?

Answer: First, the Holy Spirit is the agent of God's new creation in Christ—the Church —and His power is essential. Secondly, we engage in a spiritual work when we engage in missionary work and our dependence upon God, expressed in prayer and the activity of faith, must be real.

1. The Holy Spirit is the Agent of God's new creation in Christ —the Church.

(a) The Holy Spirit's activity in God's new creation is all-important:

(i) He puts the redeemed in possession of the results of the Father's love and the mediation of Christ (*II Cor.* 3: 9; *John* 7: 38, 39);

(ii) Justification takes place through the name of the Lord Jesus and the Spirit of God (*I Cor.* 6: 11; *I Pet.* 1: 2);

(iii) Through the Spirit the redeemed are brought into the one body, the Church, this act being described as a baptism (*I Cor.* 12: 13);

(iv) The Spirit is the Author of the new birth (*John* 3: 5, 6).

(b) The Holy Spirit is directly associated with the extension of God's new creation—the Church (*Matt.* 28: 19; cf. *Acts* 1: 4, 8).

(i) He ensures that messengers are raised up and men sent forth to proclaim the gospel (*Matt.* 9: 38; cf. *Acts* 13: 2, 4; 16: 6, 7, 10; 20: 28);

(ii) He accompanies the preaching of the gospel with His power (*I Pet.* 1: 12);

(iii) He shows men their need of salvation by convincing them of sin (*John* 16: 8–11);

(iv) He bears witness to Christ (*John* 15: 26), and by His influence men are enabled to say "Jesus is Lord" (*I Cor.* 12: 3);

(v) For the care of the Church the Spirit raises up guardians or pastors (*Acts* 20: 28);

(vi) He allots varying gifts to Christians (*Rom.* 12: 6–8);

(vii) In each Christian the Spirit desires to manifest Himself in some particular way, for some useful purpose (*I Cor.* 12: 4–11);

(viii) The Spirit's purpose is to equip God's people for work in Christ's service, to the building up of the body of Christ (*Eph.* 4: 11–13).

(c) Not surprisingly the Lord Jesus, therefore, taught the apostles that they were dependent upon the Holy Spirit for the fulfilment of their commission (*Acts* 1: 4, 5).

(d) Missionary work should be marked by power (*Luke* 10: 17–19), and we need at every stage to acknowledge our dependence upon the Holy Spirit.

2. When we engage in the work of missions, we engage in a great spiritual battle.

(a) The work of missions is part of a great spiritual battle (*II Cor.* 10: 3, 4).

(b) Missionary work is in open conflict with the god of this world who has blinded the minds of unbelievers to keep them from seeing the light of the gospel of the glory of Christ (*II Cor.* 4: 4).

(c) Opposition and indifference, therefore, are not to take us by surprise (*Luke* 10: 10, 11; *II Cor.* 4: 3, 4).

3. Dependence upon God is to characterise missionary enterprise.

(a) It is to be clear to all that missions and missionaries depend upon God (*Luke* 10: 4).

(b) This fact is not to be interpreted, however, to the detriment of the responsibility of Christians to support missionary work: those who give themselves completely to the work of the gospel may live by the gospel (*I Cor.* 9: 1–18; *Luke* 10: 7).

(c) Furthermore, dependence upon God does not rule out the missionary being self-supporting where that would seem to be the more honourable thing to do (*Acts* 18: 3; 20: 34).

4. Our confidence in missionary work is in the Lord, not in the converts.

(a) God begins the good work in people's lives, and He will bring it to completion at the day of Jesus Christ (*Phil.* 1: 6).

(b) Missionaries may have confidence in God about their converts (*II Thess.* 3: 4).

5. The priority of prayer.

(a) Missionary endeavour is to be born in prayer, and carried through by prayer (*Acts* 4: 23–31).

(b) Paul's prayers for the churches indicate the priority he himself gave to it in his endeavours (*Eph.* 1: 16–23; 3: 14–21; *Phil.* 1: 3–11; *Col.* 1: 9–12).

6. Missionary work involves acting according to faith.

(a) We are called to work, believing that the Lord Himself will work with us (*Luke* 10: 1; *Matt.* 28: 20; *Mark* 16: 20).

(b) The assurance we have, by faith, that God's purposes shall be fulfilled gives us the necessary grace to persevere (*Acts* 18: 9–11).

7. Missionary work is momentous.

(a) The kingdom of God comes near men and women by means of missionary endeavour (*Luke* 10: 9–11).

(b) The response men and women give to the missionary representatives of Christ is the response they give to Christ himself (*Luke* 10: 16).

50. SUPPORTING MISSIONS

Question: How are we to support missionary work?

Answer: We are to support missionary work wholeheartedly and generously, by finance and prayer, as part of our worship of God.

1. Some preliminary considerations.

(a) Giving people the gospel means giving them our very selves in service—there is no room for half-heartedness (*I Thess.* 2: 8).

(b) Christians in churches which have been brought into being and blessed through the gospel should provide the wherewithal for others to labour in new and emerging churches (*II Cor.* 11: 8).

(c) Those who come to faith are to be taught to have a sense of responsibility for one another in every way, both spiritually and materially (*Acts* 4: 32–37).

(d) Missionary service should not be a burden to those who are served (*I Thess.* 2: 9; *II Thess.* 3: 7–9).

(e) Missionaries have a right to be supported (*I Cor.* 9: 4–14): those who proclaim the gospel should get their living by the gospel, according to the Lord's command (*I Cor.* 9: 14).

(f) A basic principle of missions is that it is more blessed to give than to receive (*Acts* 20: 35).

(g) The whole of the local church is involved in the sending forth of a missionary, under the direction of the Holy Spirit (*Acts* 13: 1–4).

(h) God's people should be encouraged to have a sense of responsibility and of partnership in missionary enterprise (*Phil.* 1: 3–5; 4: 15).

(i) A truly worshipping church is a missionary-minded church (*Acts* 13: 2).

(j) A missionary-minded church happily sees its most gifted members sent forth as missionaries (*Acts* 13: 1–4).

2. Supporting missions by finance.

(a) The tribes, in the Old Testament period, were required to give from their inheritance a certain portion for the use of those who were set apart for God's service (*Josh.* 21; cf. *I Cor.* 9: 13, 14; *Gal.* 6: 6).

(b) Giving is part of our honouring God and fearing His name (*Mal.* 1: 6–8).

(c) Our giving proves the reality of our faith (*II Cor.* 9: 13).

(d) Giving is part and parcel of our confession of the gospel of Christ (*II Cor.* 9: 13).

(e) Giving is to be by all (*I Cor.* 16: 2), by tithes and by offerings (*Mal.* 3: 10).

(f) To share what we have is a spiritual sacrifice pleasing to God (*Heb.* 13: 16); there is a fellowship of giving and receiving (*Phil.* 4: 15).

(g) We should so give that there is an abundance in God's house (*Mal.* 3: 10).

(h) When it comes to giving, it is best to say little, and do much (*Mal.* 1: 14).

(i) Giving is part of our missionary partnership (*Phil.* 4: 15), and properly used it brings thanksgiving to God (*II Cor.* 9: 12).

(j) Giving should be regular and systematic (*I Cor.* 16: 2), according to how we have decided for ourselves (*II Cor.* 9: 7) and promised (*II Cor.* 9: 5); our giving is to be cheerful (*II Cor.* 9: 7), loving (*I Cor.* 13: 3), according to our ability (*Acts* 11: 29), and in proportion to our prosperity (*I Cor.* 16: 2).

(k) Our giving should be in the light of God's inexpressible gift to us (*II Cor.* 9: 15).

(l) The more God enriches us, the more scope we should find for generous giving (*II Cor.* 9: 11); our gifts should not be exactions but a bounty (*II Cor.* 9: 5).

(m) The Lord watches the giving of His people, and He does not despise any gift: the value of the gift is in proportion to what a person has left, and what it has cost them to give (*Mark* 12: 41–44; *Luke* 21: 1–4).

(n) Giving is not to be influenced by the difficulties of the times: the difficulties serve to provide an even greater opportunity of proving God (*Mal.* 3: 10).

(o) We are foolish if we say we cannot afford to give and to be generous (*Prov.* 22: 9; cf. *Deut.* 15: 9, 10; *II Cor.* 9: 7, 8; *Prov.* 19: 17; 28: 27).

(p) When we fail to give, we work hard with little profit; we eat, but never have enough; we drink, but we are always thirsty; we clothe ourselves, but we are never warm; we earn a wage but it goes nowhere (*Hag.* 1: 6).

(q) Generous giving to meet the needs of others brings blessing from God (*Prov.* 22: 9; *Hag.* 1: 5, 7, 9–11).

(r) As we meet the needs of others God will meet ours (*Mal.* 3: 11; *II Cor.* 9: 8, 9, 10; *Phil.* 4: 19).

(s) Sparse sowing means sparse reaping, and bountiful sowing means bountiful reaping in the sphere of giving, both for the work at home and the work abroad (*II Cor.* 9: 6).

(t) In distributing our money set apart for others, we need to recognise that we do not always know who needs help most, but others do: we should happily leave the distribution to such as know the needs (*Acts* 4: 34–37; cf. *Acts* 5: 1–11; *I Cor.* 16: 1–4).

3. **Supporting missions by prayer.**

(a) Missionary concern is seen in prayer to God (*Rom.* 10: 1).

(b) We should begin by praying for governments and world leaders, that they may be enabled to maintain peace and order so that the preaching of the gospel may go forward, according to God's pattern and will (*I Tim.* 2: 1–4).

(c) Paul's requests for prayer guide us in the kind of petitions we should bring to God on behalf of missionaries:

(i) Deliverance from malicious unbelievers (*Rom.* 15: 30, 31);

(ii) Acceptance with God's people (*II Cor.* 1: 11; *Rom.* 15: 31).

(iii) Health of mind and body (*Rom.* 15: 32; *II Cor.* 1: 8–11).

(iv) The ability to speak the right words boldly at the moment of opportunity (*Eph.* 6: 19);

(v) The turning of untoward circumstances to good (*Phil.* 1: 19);

(vi) God-given opportunities for preaching Christ (*Col.* 4: 3);

(vii) Progress in the establishment of the church through the Word (*II Thess.* 3: 1).

(d) Paul's prayers for the young churches guide us in the kind of petitions we should bring to God on behalf of our Christian brethren among whom and alongside whom our missionaries work (*Eph.* 1: 16–23; 3: 14–21; *Phil.* 1: 3–11; *Col.* 1: 9–12).

(e) Our support by prayer should be unceasing (*Eph.* 1: 16).